# A FATHER'S LOVE

# A FATHER'S LOVE

*Van Rushton*

VAN RUSHTON

*Proverbs 2:1·5*

ELITE

Xulon Press Elite
2301 Lucien Way #415
Maitland, FL 32751
407.339.4217
www.xulonpress.com

Printed in the United States of America.

ISBN-13: 9781545629376

# INTRODUCTION

O NE OF MY GRANDKIDS WAS LED DOWN THE WRONG
trail as most of us are at one time or the other. At least
there was a time in my life where I was. As I was praying for
my grandkid and asking God to shield them from Satan's fiery
darts, I heard it as if He was talking to me audibly,

"What are you doing about it"?

It certainly stopped me in my tracks, and then I asked myself,
*Well, what are you doing?* Was I leaving the all-important
learning years up to the world to teach my grandchildren?

I know, I hear you, mine go to church also, but that is not
enough. What was I personally doing to further their Christian
education, to help them grow in the Lord? In Psalm 78, Asaph
says we must teach the children so that they can teach their
children and so on and so on. So, about this time, I walked
through the living room, and there they were all six of my grandkids laying around on the couch, texting and playing with their
phones. Two of them were texting each other. How do you communicate with kids who only communicate with a phone?

Simple answer: with a phone! So, I started texting my kids
and grandkids a morning devotional every day with a teaching,
a somewhat evangelical text message. I wanted them not only
to grow, but to learn how to witness to others. I knew they had
all been saved, but I wanted them to grow.

About this same time, I met an older lady who really had not grown in the Lord very much. She had fifty years of being a Christian, but only one year of Christian knowledge and just repeated the same year of knowledge year after year, sort of like spinning her wheels, living off of milk instead of meat and potatoes. Paul spoke of Christians living as children and not growing up.

They should have been teaching but did not have the knowledge. I do not want my kids and grandkids to wake up twenty years from now and still be sucking a bottle as far as Bible knowledge is concerned. I want them to be advancing the kingdom! And so here we are today, hoping many children (of all ages) of the Lord will grow in their Christian knowledge. Somewhere along the way my middle daughter decided to post my little devotionals on a Facebook page so that her friends could read them. Then one thing led to another, and now we have over six hundred followers reading daily devotions on Facebook. Someone said why not put it in book form, so here we are.

I began this journey being led every day by the Holy Spirit. Without Him, this would never have happened. Thanks also to my family for the loving support.

# ABOUT THE AUTHOR

H E IS THE HOLY SPIRIT.
These daily devotions are about love—God's love for us and my love for my children and grandchildren!

The hands He used are those of a Christian and Bible school teacher in Southern Baptist churches for thirty-plus years, who has been married fifty-two years with three children and six-plus grandkids.

Van Rushton
John 3:16

# PRELUDE: HOW GREAT IS "THE FATHER'S LOVE"?

WE DO NOT HAVE ENOUGH LANGUAGE TO DESCRIBE His love for us. We do not know the magnitude of His love. His love is far superior to our love. Think about this: we are called children of the living God. Think about it for a moment; if you are a born-again Christian, you are an adopted child of God through Jesus Christ our Lord. *You are a child of God.*

There is a place set at His table for you, and there will be a great banquet in His honor. He is preparing a place for us for all eternity. He told us that in,

> John 14:2"In my Father's house are many rooms;
> if it were not so, I would have told you. I am
> going there to prepare a place for you."

Why wouldn't every living soul be excited about this?

You want to know why the world does not want to know us; it is because the world did not and does not know Jesus as the one and only Son of God. Christians are being persecuted all over the world, and many are being killed as I write this message. The world hates Christianity. Why?

It is because we proclaim that Jesus is the only way to the Father in heaven and not just *a way*, but the only way! There is no other way to the Father accept through Jesus the Christ.

There are only two roads; one leads to hell, and one leads to heaven.

Do you believe the world or the very word of God, the Bible? One is wrong. The world is wrong!

Our loving Father gave us eternal life with Him in heaven for all eternity if we only believe in His Only Son.

What love He has for us; it is indescribable.

Thank you, Jesus for your love and all you did for all of us.

Have a great day in our Father's love, and keep looking up. He could come back for us any day.

Remember, God loves you.

# HAPPY NEW YEAR IN CHRIST January 1

Are you ready for something different this year, rather than the same old thing? Guess who can make it happen? You can!

How many times have you set a New Year's resolution to read through the Bible? Now compare that to how many times you actually have read through the Bible in one year. Now compare that to how many years you have been a Christian. I would venture to guess that not many have completely read through the Bible even once. Listen, folks, what on this earth today could be more important than knowing what God has to say to you? You are right; there is not anything more important. So, this year, make the resolution to read through the Bible and then make a game plan to make it happen.

Something has to change for you to complete your resolution. Find something you enjoy that would make a good trade. Trade something you enjoy for something you will enjoy much more. Get an accountability partner, and they will help you keep your commitment.

I promise, if you make this the year that you actually read through the complete Bible, you will treasure this year as one of your best! I have a friend that is on his seventh year of reading the Bible in a year. He tells me every year it is a new experience, God is so good!

Just do it!

God loves you!

# WILL YOU READ? January 2

We are writing this to make our joy complete. This is in 1 JOHN 1:4. Writing the books he wrote gave John joy to share what he saw and what he heard from the Lord Jesus, and more, he knew it would give anyone who read it joy. John wrote four books of the Bible, and he wrote of God's love for us. Anytime I need a word of knowledge, most of the time I go to one of John's books where I can always find how much God loves me.

I was thinking, I am writing but I don't know if anyone is reading. When John sent his letters, people were eager for the words from God on paper so that they could know about His love and know how to live a life of trials and know how to get through them. Life was not easy back then; is it easy today?

No, I don't think so. If you don't work, you don't eat. So, you will have to work your whole life just so you can eat. Then you will need clothes and transportation, and none of it comes easy. You will have to work hard for it.

I wonder if John ever thought whether anyone was reading his letters.

My purpose for writing is to try to teach my folks as much as I can while I have the ability. I failed to do that when I was younger; sorry, kids, all I did was work, so there was not much time for teaching.

But in today's world with everyone with their heads down, looking at their phones, all I need from you is a minute or two to read and a little while to think about a few words. If I don't write, it is on me; if you don't read, it is on you. I know you have time; that is easy enough to see. At least when you look at your phone, or these writings you will have something to help your day go better because you will know when you read my message, that your Pop loves you and wants the best for you, and more than anything, he wants you to walk in the light.

God loves you.

# ARE YOU DRESSED PROPERLY? January 3

10 Finally, be strong in the Lord and in his mighty power. 11 Put on the full armor of God, so that you can take your stand against the devil's schemes. 12 For our struggle is not against flesh and blood, but against the rulers, against the authorities, against the powers of this dark world and against the spiritual forces of evil in the heavenly realms. 13 Therefore put on the full armor of God, so that when the day of evil comes, you may be able to stand your ground, and after you have done everything, to stand. 14 Stand firm then, with the belt of truth buckled around your waist, with the breastplate of righteousness in place, 15 and with your feet fitted with the readiness that comes from the gospel of peace. 16 In addition to all this, take up the shield of faith, with which you can extinguish all the flaming arrows of the evil one. 17 Take the helmet of salvation and the sword of the Spirit, which is the word of God. (Ephesians 6:10–17)

Put on your armor this morning so that you may be able to stand against the ploys of the evil one. Put on your helmet, and don't go out there without your sword. There is more wickedness than you realize. Be ready for all that is thrown at you. Be aware of your surroundings!

If you are ignorant of it, it can overtake you. Allow your filter, our great God the Spirit, to take control of your day, and have a great day!

God loves you.

# PICTURE THIS IN YOUR MIND January 4

> Therefore, put on the full armor of God, so that
> when the day of evil comes, you may be able
> to stand your ground, and after you have done
> everything, to stand. 15and with your feet fitted
> with the readiness that comes from the gospel of
> peace. (Ephesians 6:13).

Picture a football dummy in your mind; this is the guy that doesn't get to play much, and he has to hold the pad for all the rest of the team to come and hit him as if they were blocking. He has to have good cleats on his feet so that he can stand his ground, and as they come at him, he has to keep on standing. He has to take a lot of pounding, but don't worry; he has his pad to protect him. He has to stand and keep on standing, or he will get run over.

Satan will send his best at you. Make sure you have your cleats on today (the gospel of peace), and stand firm in your faith.

Have a good day today.

God loves you.

# YOUR SWORD, THE BIBLE. January 5

13 Therefore put on the full armor of God, so that when the day of evil comes, you may be able to stand your ground, and after you have done everything, to stand. . ..

17 Take the helmet of salvation and the sword of the Spirit, which is the word of God. (Ephesians 6:13, 17)

I said to put on your helmet and get your sword. Now you might say I don't have a sword, and even if I did I might get locked up if I took it out with me to work or play. But God knows this, and He gave us a different kind of sword; it is called His word, the Bible.

Now the question is, do you know it well enough to protect yourself with it? Hmmm the silence is deafening! It is a good question!

So, what do you have as a passion that you love more than God? Of course, you will say *nothing*!

But I wonder what God would say about it? How much dust is on your Bible? He left it for our protection as our sword to fight the evil one with. Have a good day and blow the dust off your sword. Put it beside your bed, and open it every night and learn how to protect yourself.

God loves you.

# WE ARE NOT THERE YET January 6

"And pray in the Spirit on all occasions with all
kinds of prayers and requests. With this in mind,
be alert and always keep on praying for all the
Lord's people" (Ephesians 6:18).

Okay, we have our helmet of salvation on; our sword, or
word; and our cleats; and our breastplates; but you might as well
be naked if you are not praying earnestly.

The helmet is your salvation if you are saved and you have
the sword, but without praying and asking God to help you
empty yourself and fill you up with Himself, it is all for naught.

You should pray always, and here is a good prayer: Lord
Jesus, help me to decrease in my life, and Lord, you increase
in my life.

John the Baptist said it in John 3:30: He must increase but
I must decrease!

Easier said than done, I know, but that is how you grow as
a Christian, He must be in charge of your life. You don't need a
copilot; you need *a pilot*.

Have a great day in the Lord today.

God loves you.

# CAN YOU QUOTE? January 7

Read John 3:16. Think about it for a moment. I am sure most of you can quote it without reading it, and if you can't, you should be able to. "For God so loved the world, that He gave His only begotten Son, that who so ever believes in Him shall not perish but have ever lasting life."

But, can you quote 1 Corinthians 3:16? Maybe not, so let me quote it for you: "Don't you know that you yourselves are God's temple and that God's Spirit dwells in your midst?"

Your body is the temple of the living God. So, wouldn't you then think that we should keep ourselves as holy as we can, and doesn't that tie into what we looked at yesterday morning? With God as our pilot and living inside us, then our day will go much better than we deserve.

Remember you are the temple of the living God; live your life accordingly. I love you all!

And God loves you.

# CAN YOU BE UNBORN? January 8

Read John, chapter three. Jesus said to Nicodemus, unless you are born again you cannot enter the Kingdom of heaven, (my paraphrase). And Nick said how is that possible, I cannot enter the same place I left to be born again.

He was absolutely right; that is not possible. But Jesus was speaking of salvation—spiritual things, not physical things. We all must be born again to experience God's grace. We know that, right? Right. So back to the question, can you be unborn in a spiritual way, or can you lose your salvation?

> Let's see what John says. John 3:18 there is *no* condemnation against anyone who believes in the Lord Jesus Christ!

How many times have you heard *no* means *no*. Well, guess what? *No* means *no*, and He said *no* condemnation, if you believe!

Jesus died for *all* sins, not some, not a few, not half, and not just past sins but *all*.

You can't be unborn, it is a physical impossibility! And *no* means *no*, so it is a spiritual impossibility also!

Think about it and thank God for his grace.

God loves you.

# WHAT IS YOUR FAVORITE DRINK? January 9

John 4,

7 When a Samaritan woman came to draw water, Jesus said to her, "Will you give me a drink?" 8(His disciples had gone into the town to buy food.)9 The Samaritan woman said to him, "You are a Jew and I am a Samaritan woman. How can you ask me for a drink?" (For Jews do not associate with Samaritans.)

10 Jesus answered her, "If you knew the gift of God and who it is that asks you for a drink, you would have asked him and he would have given you living water."

11 "Sir," the woman said, "you have nothing to draw with and the well is deep. Where can you get this living water? 12 Are you greater than our father Jacob, who gave us the well and drank from it himself, as did also his sons and his livestock?"

13 Jesus answered, "Everyone who drinks this water will be thirsty again, 14 but whoever drinks the water I give them will never thirst. Indeed, the water I give them will become in them a spring of water welling up to eternal life."

What is your favorite drink? I hope it is the living water that Jesus gives us to drink, Jesus said to the woman at the well, if you drink of this water you will thirst again, but if you drink of the water I give you, you will never thirst again, (for all eternity). It becomes a fresh bubbling spring within you, giving you eternal life. So, you might ask, like the woman at the well, how do I get this water? Guess what? You have it; when you became a believer, you have the fresh water that gives you eternal life.

*A Father's Love* | 9

But the question is, is it bubbling out of you? Are you sharing your fresh water with those who do not have living water? We are only on this planet for a moment or two to work, and an eternity to enjoy the fruits of our labor. Is there someone in your life that you see regularly, who does not have the fresh water to drink? *Do you need to share some of yours?*

Of course, you do; it is a matter of life and death, eternal life or eternal death!

Go and share!

God loves you.

## YOU ARE LIKE MUD. January 10

The Potter and the Clay, Jeremiah 18,
1 The LORD gave another message to Jeremiah.
He said, 2 "Go down to the potter's shop, and I
will speak to you there." 3 So I did as he told me
and found the potter working at his wheel. 4 But
the jar he was making did not turn out as he had
hoped, so he crushed it into a lump of clay again
and started over.

That's right, we are nothing but mud on a wheel — a potter's
wheel. As Jeremiah 18 says, the potter molds and makes a clump
of clay into something beautiful, just as God has molded you
into something beautiful.

But what happens if you, as all of us do, decides to do things
your way instead of His way? Think of the potter with the wheel
spinning. He is working and molding it to something very good,
but then he notices a flaw, so what does He do? He wads up the
clay and starts over again with the same clay and remakes us
into, yep, you guessed it, something beautiful again. He can do
this again and again.

Why would we make Him have to keep on remolding us,
when all we have to do is let Him be in charge of our lives and
follow His plan not ours? Our plan has flaws; His does not!

Now as a new pot, don't fill it up with yourself; let Him fill
you up — more of Him and less of you! Have a great day today!

God loves you.

# WHAT IS TRUTH? January 11

In John 3:24, Jesus is speaking, and He says,

> "I tell you the TRUTH, those who listen to MY message and believe in God who sent me have ETERNAL life. They will NEVER be condemned for their sins, but they have already passed from death into life."

What is truth, the stuff you absolutely know without a shadow of doubt to be true? If Jesus said it you can believe it! There is so much tolerance and the bending of the truth that it is very hard to know what truth is and what it is not. Some folks say something a certain amount of times, and then they think that it is truth. But it is only a lie wrapped like the truth.

Be careful because the world looks at truth as something that is anti-tolerant. The world does not agree with God's truth because the way to heaven is too narrow, and they just can't believe that there aren't many ways to get to heaven.

Jesus said in John 14:6,

"I am the way and the truth and the life, no one will see the Father except through Me."

That is truth! Have a good day today, please, and don't listen to the world's lies.

God loves you.

# WE ARE LIKE SHEEP. January 12

Jesus said, "Behold, I send you out as sheep in the midst of wolves; so be shrewd as serpents and innocent as doves" (Matthew 10:16).

Here are a few facts about sheep, since Jesus likened us to them and He said He is our Shepherd.

Did you know that sheep are the only living animals that cannot live in the wild? They are the only animal that needs man to guide and protect them because they have no defense system. Just as we need our Lord to guide and protect us. Sheep are best known for their following instinct. But they know their shepherds voice, and they will not follow any other voice *unless* they are sick; much like us, when they are sick, they will follow the wrong person.

They stay in groups, *kids*, because there is safety in numbers. It is much harder for a predator to pick out one in a group than it is for them to lead off a straggler or a loner. The thing you have to be careful of is when one sheep moves, they all move, even if it is not a good idea. Therefore, beware of your surroundings. Sheep are very timid animals; they are easily spooked because they have good instincts. Kids, you need to have good instincts and know where the group is going.

Class, we need to be followers of our Lord every day. Psalm 23 says it all. Can you quote it by heart? The Lord is my Shepherd . . .. How many can quote it?

Jesus does not need spies, this is not a covert operation. He wants us to follow Him and His ways.

He knows everything; He is never surprised! He is the Great I AM.

God loves you.

# HEAVEN IS FOR REAL. January 13

Revelation 21,
3 I heard a loud shout from the throne, saying, "Look, God's home is now among his people! He will live with them, and they will be his people. God himself will be with them. 4 He will wipe every tear from their eyes, and there will be no more death or sorrow or crying or pain. All these things are gone forever.

We are living in a world of tears, but one day there will be no more tears, no more sorrow, no more deaths, and no more funerals.

In the beginning, we were created for eternity but because of sin in the garden, we have justice; now we deserve to die for our sin. How could anyone expect to be with an entirely pure, perfect God while toting a bag of sins with them? Frankly, it is not possible. God will not look at us, and He can't!

God knew this and because He created us and loves us so, He gave us a blood sacrifice to pay the penalty for all of our sins. God wants us with Him, but the only way that could happen is for His Son to take our place in the judgment that had to be paid.

Because of Jesus, we can look forward to a wonderful home in heaven with our Savior. We have hope! We have something to live for! We have an eternity to be in heaven with our friends and family, where there will be no more corruption and no more temptation.

Everything you need to find satisfaction, will be in heaven. We will rest in heaven—not a physical rest but a mental rest—with no worries, no pain, and living in a glorious new perfect body.

Please live each day with the view of eternity in your minds' eyes.

Nothing evil will be allowed to enter, nor anyone who practices shameful idolatry and dishonesty—but only those whose names are written in the Lamb's Book of Life. Rev. 21:27

*A Father's Love* | 14

Is your name in God's Book of Life? If you have been saved and you are living for Christ and are following Him on the narrow road, there is good news. Your name is there, and when the roll is called, you will hear your name called. Keep looking up; He could come get us any day now!

God loves you.

# DO YOU LISTEN TO GOD? January 14

Matthew 7,
The Narrow Gate

13 "You can enter God's Kingdom only through
the narrow gate. The highway to hell is broad,
and its gate is wide for the many who choose
that way. 14 But the gateway to life is very
narrow and the road is difficult, and only a few
ever find it.

Do you listen to God, or do you listen to what man says?
God would have you walking in the middle of the narrow road,
but man, or the ruler of this world, Satan, would keep you in
the ditch. We, as followers of Christ, experience a bad case of
stupid from time to time; we don't want to but we listen to the
wrong person or thing, and well, we just get stupid, and stupid
likes it in the ditch. Remember God wants us on the road; Satan
wants us in the ditch.

So, when you find yourself in the ditch, you got it, you got
stupid for a time. One thing to learn when you find yourself in
a ditch is to throw away the shovel. Grab a ladder and get out as
fast as you can. Some do; some don't. Only the smart ones do.

I want all of mine to be smart enough to fight off the stupid's and stay out of the ditch. But when you get in it, and you
will until you are smart enough to listen only to the Shepherd's
voice, get out fast. Walk in the road with our Lord; it is so much
smoother. You don't even need a seat belt with Him driving!

God loves you.

# SHOULD I FEAR GOD? January 15

Psalms 112:1 says, "1 Praise the Lord. Blessed are those who fear the Lord, who find great delight in his commands."

Do you think Moses feared God when he saw a bush burning but not burning up? Do you think Moses feared God when he saw Him writing on the side of a mountain? Or how about when the waters of the sea parted—was there a fear of the Lord then? But on the other hand, do you think the little children feared Jesus when they walked up to Him? Or did they hug Him? When Samuel called down rain in a time of the year when it never rained, the people were afraid for their lives! Was Noah afraid when it did not stop raining until all he could see was water?

God, our Creator, will be the same God who sends people to hell; should we fear Him? But the same God who will do that is the same God who made a beautiful rose for us to admire or a puppy to play with.

Could you remain standing in the presence of our *Creator*? I know I couldn't. I would try to *be the dirt*, I was face down on. We are to have a healthy fear of God; how could we not fear Him? We are to be totally respectful to Him and never use His name in vain.

We do not have to be terrified of God, but we should have a strong sense of reverence and *awe*, of the God of our creation and the God of our salvation! He is the King of our Kingdom! He has all power over us! He is in charge!

Thank You, Jesus, for loving us.

# HEY, KIDS, WHO ARE YOU? January16

If you are like most normal folks, you are not who you think you are, and you are not who others think you are, but *you are* who you think, *others* think you are. Did you get that? We worry so much about what others think that we are not so concerned about what Jesus thinks and who He wants us to be!

Did you know that if you are not on your guard, you can let other people with worldly thoughts and motives define who you are? That can only happen, though, if you worry too much about what everybody thinks of you. Don't be a product of peer pressure.

Who would say, "I am self-made, I am who I am, and I define who I am"? Well, guess what, that is not good, either! We need to let Jesus define who He wants us to be. Remember we said *more of Him and less of me*! That is very important. Jesus can shape and mold you into exactly who or what He wants you to be or do—if you let Him!

He will let you have it your way, if you are determined to do it that way, but His way is the correct way! Open your mind to His suggestions and His word, and let Jesus Christ define who you are!

Have a great day!
God loves you.

# I DO NOT WRITE. January 17

1 John 2:21–22
To you because you do not know the truth, but because you do know it and because no lie comes from the truth. Who is the liar? It is the one who denies that Jesus is the Christ. Such a man is the antichrist, he denies the Father and the Son.

There are antichrists all around us. You have to understand there will be an antichrist in the end days who will lead many people through the doors of hell. But there are antichrists all around us now, too, and as we get closer to the end times, there will be more and more. These people will try to lead you down a dark road.

Anyone who denies Jesus is the Son of God is an antichrist. The world is full of them.

Like John, I am not writing the messages because I think you do not know Him. I know that you know Him. But with antichrists all around us, we have to stay in His word.

Kids, listen to what John says, "Do not believe every spirit, but test them to see if they are of God." There is a very easy test: do they believe that Jesus came in the flesh and that He is our Lord and Savior, or not? If they do not, then they are of the world.

How can you keep from being led astray if you don't think about the Lord daily? Every day and every hour of the day you need to be aware of His presence. He is with you all the time. John says the one who is in you is greater than the one who is in the world. It is not like he needs to take a break from you for a while and come back later. Nope, He is here all the time as He promised. In His last few words in Matthew, Jesus said, "and surely, I am with you *always*, to the very end of the age." He is with us always, or until we are with Him.

God loves you.

# WHERE DO YOU FIND BIG FISH? January 18

I heard Rick Warren speak about this;

Obviously, if you want to catch big fish you have to fish in the deep water.

Jesus told Peter and Andrew, follow Me and I will make you fishers of men.

What do you think He meant by that—fishers of men?

Jesus wanted him to catch men for the Kingdom of God. Jesus taught him how to walk the good walk so that men would see Jesus in him, and then they would want what Peter had, such as joy and peace and love for their neighbors. He started witnessing to folks and telling them what Jesus did for him. That's right, Peter told people his story. He told them that a lowly fisherman was being used by God to catch big fish, human beings.

He began fishing in the deep water. God used Peter, and he became the cornerstone of the Church. Peter was the rock.

If God is with you do you think you will catch big fish? Yes? Then what are you doing in the shallow water? You have to step out in the deep water. It is a step of faith.

Jesus told the apostles, "When you go, don't worry about what you will say because He will speak through you."

Get out in the deep water, and let Jesus fish through you.

Have a great day fishing!

God loves you.

# WHO WAS ENOCH? January 19

We have been talking a lot about our walk with God. There was a man named Enoch who was the son of Jared; he had an interesting walk with God. The Bible tells us that Enoch walked with God for three hundred years. Now that is a walk with God! Do you think Enoch was God's friend? I do. If two are walking together for a long period of time, I think you could say that they were in agreement. I think it is obvious that God loved Enoch, and Enoch loved God.

For 300 years, they walked and talked, and then one day Enoch was no more. God walked Him to His house. They just kept walking one day until they were in heaven. Enoch did not die as far as we know.

> Genesis 5,
> 22 After he became the father of Methuselah, Enoch walked faithfully with God 300 years and had other sons and daughters. 23 Altogether, Enoch lived a total of 365 years. 24 Enoch walked faithfully with God; then he was no more, because God took him away.

How would you describe your walk with God? Would you say that you were in agreement with God? Do you keep the light on?

Elijah was another man, who had a good relationship and a good walk with God. One day, a chariot of fire with horses of fire came down and gave him a ride to heaven. He did not die, either!

One day soon we hope Jesus will come back for us. Those who are believers in Christ and are still alive will not die, either; they will be lifted up in the resurrection to be with Him forever. I hope He comes back today, what about you? If you have your eyes on Him and you are walking with Him, like Enoch, you will be one of those who take a long walk and wind up in heaven.

God loves you.

# DANIEL January 20

Did you know you and your kids have everything you need in this world to make a difference for God? Look at Daniel; he was transported from his homeland to Babylon, like the modern-day Las Vegas. The people there worshipped idols; they were not much better than Sodom and Gomorrah as far as their lifestyle was concerned.

But God was with Daniel because he stood strong in his faith. He would not bow down to idols, and he would not eat food that was unclean, according to his religion.

These were young men about fifteen or sixteen years old who got transported. And by that time, they were strong in their faith. Listen, at fifteen or sixteen, they had a strong faith. Teenagers, you know what? They knew all the Bible stories.

Moms and Dads, what are you allowing your kids to look at or listen to? Are you working on developing their souls as much as developing their talents in sports or music or whatever? What will last the longest?

How about it, kids, what are you looking at on your phones?

Kids, are you as strong in your faith as Daniel was when he was your age? You are a product of your thought life; you are what you think and you are what you eat.

> Listen to Daniel 1:17, how God repays a strong faith in Daniel and his three friends: "17God gave these four young men an unusual aptitude for understanding every aspect of literature and wisdom. And God gave Daniel the special ability to interpret the meanings of visions and dreams."

Listen, kids, moms and dads, too,
to Proverbs 22:6 that says, "Train up a child in the way he should go: and when he gets old, he will not depart from it."
God loves you.

# SHADRACK, MESHACK, AND ABEDNEGO.
## January 21

This story can be found in Daniel 3. These three young men were good friends of Daniel. All of them were strong in their faith, and as I said yesterday, they were about fifteen or sixteen years old, when they were deported. These three defied the king by not falling down to worship a golden statue of the king. The king gave them one more chance to worship the statue before he threw them into a very hot burning furnace. But they stood strong in their faith.

When the king asked, "Are you not afraid of the furnace," they said, "No, if we are thrown into the fiery furnace our God will deliver us, and He will deliver us out of your hand, oh King."

People, I don't know about you, but I can tell you that I know these kids had a firm foundation in the Lord.

Well, the king threw them in the fire fully clothed and bound up tight. The fire was so hot that the fire leaped out and killed the soldiers who put them in the fire.

Then the king in amazement said, "Didn't we throw three men in the fire?" They said yes. The king said, "Then how could I see four men walking around in the fire unharmed?"

I personally think it was Jesus in there with them; they were now unbound and smiling and talking to the Lord.

The king told them to come out, and when they did, there wasn't as much as a hair singed on their head.

Kids, God protected them because their faith was strong.

Do you know there are children getting their heads cut off because they won't deny their faith in Jesus? They were children that are very strong in their faith, who chose death over rejecting Jesus Christ. And now, they are with their Lord Jesus in heaven.

This is real, folks; we are living in evil times and don't think it is not coming our way. The United States is not immune to these kinds of evil ways.

All we know as far as the future is concerned is that God loves you kids!

# THE FIFTY-TWENTY PRINCIPLE. January 22

The fifty-twenty principle is found in

> Genesis 50:20. "You intended to harm me, but
> God intended it for good."

Joseph's brothers sold him to people in a caravan as a slave to be sold in Egypt. They intended to kill him, but Reuben, the oldest brother, did not want to kill him. The brothers did not like Joseph because he was his father's favorite son. He had dreams about his brothers bowing down to him, and he told his brothers about the dreams, which made them hate him even more, so they sold him.

But God blessed Joseph, and he became the Pharaoh's right-hand man. You see, God blessed Joseph with many gifts; he could read dreams, and he was a great planner and organizer. Joseph and God had a great relationship, and God used Joseph to save his people in a time of famine. His brothers came to Egypt to find food, but instead they found their brother in charge. So, they bowed down to him and asked for food for their family.

His dream from God came true.

Joseph let God take control of his life and God used him in a mighty way. He waited on God to work things out in His timing.

Please, Kids, let God have control of your lives also, and when someone means harm to you, God will make something good out of it in a completely different way than you could ever imagine. Joseph never dreamed he would be in charge of a country, but he let God have the control panel.

It is simply the fifty-twenty rule. "You intended to harm me, *but God* intended it for good!"

God is so good to us!

Have a great day today.

He loves you.

# YOUR MOUTH HAS GREAT POWER.
## January 23

So, keep it shut, but when you open it, speak thoughtfully, honestly, and softly.

"We can make a large horse go wherever we want by means of a small bit in its mouth. And a small rudder makes a huge ship turn wherever the pilot chooses to go, even though the winds are strong. In the same way, the tongue is a small thing that makes grand speeches. But a tiny spark can set a great forest on fire. And the tongue is a flame of fire. It is a whole world of wickedness, corrupting your entire body. It can set your whole life on fire, for it is set on fire by hell itself.

People can tame all kinds of animals, birds, reptiles, and fish, but no one can tame the tongue. It is restless and evil, full of deadly poison. Sometimes it praises our Lord and Father, and sometimes it curses those who have been made in the image of God. And so, blessing and cursing come pouring out of the same mouth. Surely, my brothers and sisters, this is not right! Does a spring of water bubble out with both fresh water and bitter water? Does a fig tree produce olives, or a grapevine produce figs? No, and you can't draw fresh water from a salty spring".

James 3:3-11
"Wise words are like deep waters; wisdom flows from the wise like a bubbling brook.

Fools' words get them into constant quarrels; they are asking for a beating.

The mouths of fools are their ruin; they trap themselves with their lips.

Rumors are dainty morsels that sink deep into one's heart". Proverbs 4, 6-8

"Fire goes out without wood, and quarrels disappear when gossip stops.

A quarrelsome person starts fights as easily as hot embers light charcoal or fire lights wood". Proverbs 26:20-21

Children, just a few words of wisdom from James, and Solomon about your tongue.

Keep these in mind today and speak less and smile more, and when you speak let it flow like living waters.

God loves you.

# ALL OR NOTHING? January 24

I listen to sermons on the radio all the time, probably too much. I have been since the early 1980s when I was traveling around I-285 in Atlanta. You have to be careful what programs you listen to because in a lot of cases, all you get is the watered-down version of the truth. On one occasion, I was listening, and my mind kept telling me *it is all or nothing*. I know it was a watered-down sermon because I quit listening to the speaker and kept saying over and over, all or nothing! I began to wonder what that means or whether it means anything at all. When you read in Corinthians, Paul is all about, "all or nothing." But I kept thinking *what does this mean*? Is it for me; is there something meaningful here? I obviously do not give 100 percent of my time to Christianity. So maybe it is to me—all or nothing! It is clear to me I can do more. What about you?

Are we full-time Christians or part-time? What would it take to become a full-time Christian? Are there times we go on vacation from Christianity? Do we take off days and holidays? Are we really all in?

Are we giving a watered-down message to the people around us, folks who are watching to learn from us? What do I mean watered down? It means half-truth, which really means no truth! Are we allowing the culture and the modern times to convince us that we should be more tolerant and we should relax our values?

> Ephesians 5:15, 16; 15 Be very careful, then, how you live—not as unwise but as wise, 16making the most of every opportunity, because the days are evil. 17Therefore do not be foolish, but understand what the Lord's will is.

It really is "all or nothing." If Christianity is worth anything, it is worth everything! There is no neutral, you are either moving forward or backing up. We should not be part-time Christians, we should not take vacations from Christianity, and we should not take days off.

We have changed our lifestyle; there is no turning back! How would you take a day off from who you are? You cannot, so stop it, and ask God for forgiveness and move on. As soon as you ask, He forgives.

We should live every day for Jesus! We must be *"all in"*!

God loves you.

# WHAT MUST I DO? January 25

Read Matthew 19.

What are you willing to give up to be a Jesus follower?

A man walked up to Jesus and asked Him, "What good thing must I do to have eternal life?"

Jesus told him there is only one that is good. (We know that to be Jesus Himself). Jesus told Him to keep the commandments.

He said, "Oh, I have done that." Then Jesus said, "Well, sell all you have, then, and follow me." The man went away sad because he was very wealthy, and he knew he could not give up the way he lived to follow Jesus.

In this day of technology and very busy life style, we can get wrapped up doing all the things that Satan would have us do in order to keep us from following Jesus.

Being good and then going about your life is not following Jesus. That is what was sad about the story; the man wanted to go to heaven, but he did not want to give up the very things that were keeping him from going.

The question is, what are you willing to give up? What is keeping you from being a follower of Jesus?

This is a sad story because the man wanted to go to heaven for the eternity, but he didn't want to give up his life of sin to get there. Make sure there is absolutely nothing in your life that you would put before Jesus! If you do, you are worshiping idols, which is loving things instead of your Savior.

Eternity is a very long time, compared to this moment or two we are here on this earth.

God loves you.

The story can be found in Luke 18.

# DO YOU LOVE THE WORLD? January 26

> John said in 1 John 2:15, "Dear children, do not
> love the world or anything in the world."

Wait a minute; there is a lot of things in this world that I like to see and do. Why can't I love where I live?

> John says everything in the world, the cravings
> of sinful man, the lust of the eyes, and the pride
> of life, or boasting of what he has and does, do
> not come from the Father but the world. Verse 16.

Remember now, God created all good things in this world, like the air we breathe, the food we eat, and all the beautiful things we have to admire. We can love these things; it is okay and not what John was talking about.

But the world belongs to Satan for a little while longer, and he has made it an awful place to live. There is so much corruption and satanic things we have to live around that we have to be on guard all the time. There are many people out there in this world, who will try to lead you astray.

I know a very godly man that every time he feels someone tugging on him and trying to lead him in the wrong direction, he starts humming hymns to himself; he has a good plan, and it helps him stay in the light. It would be okay to steal his idea; he wouldn't care.

We have to stay in the light. Don't forget your armor today!

Today pray that God will guide you through all the corruption and help you stay on His road.

God loves you kids!

# ARE YOU DRIFTING? January 27

You know how when you are on vacation and you go to the beach; you get in the water, maybe with a float or just catching waves. You play for a while and then you notice, saying, "Wow I am not where I was. I have drifted down the beach, and now I have to get back where I was."

This happens to us in our relationship with our Lord also. Maybe we don't stay in the word or we skip a few Sundays; we drift away, and then the fellowship is broken! Because we forget who we are and what we believe and say and do things we would not normally do, it is really easy to drift, and most times you don't even realize you are drifting.

So how do you get back to where you were on the beach? You get out of the water and head back in the right direction.

You have to make a decision to get out of the water and face the direction you want to go. It is the same thing if you are off track: face it, confess your wrongdoing, and get back to where you were.

Get back on the right road. God loves you and wants unbroken fellowship with you. So, do it; ask Him to forgive you this morning and go to His house and worship Him, and the day will go much better for you.

I promise this will put a smile on your face.

God loves you.

# HOW MANY DEGREES? January 28

How many degrees can you be off and still be on the road? Let's see. If you take off on a plane in Atlanta and set the correct course to LA, and a little wind comes up and blows you five degrees off, what city do you think you would land in? I can pretty much guarantee it would not be LA' it might even be in Oregon.

Okay, Pop, what does this have to do with anything?

We have talked about staying on the narrow road and how Satan loves to keep you in the ditch on the side of the road. I need all of you to understand just how narrow the road really is. If you are off just a degree or two, you will not stay on the road. That is one of Satan's tactics.

The devil speaks really good religion stuff. He knows the Bible much better than most of us, so it is easy for him to twist the words around to where it sounds really good and religious.

But you got it, he is just a few degrees off center.

Here is an example: Jesus is a God, one of many. Hmm, sounds like good religion, who wouldn't want to be a god? But it is off several degrees. There are people going house to house trying to sell this nonsense.

There is only *one* God! He is one in three persons: The Father, Son, and Holy Spirit.

There are many more examples, so always test what you hear by His word. His word, the Bible, will keep you on the narrow road.

Walking in the Light everyday will also help you see the road ahead. Stay on course, don't vary even one degree! Even being off one degree will not get you there; more to come on this, too.

God loves you.

# WALK IN THE LIGHT January 29

Are you walking in the light or in the darkness? It should be easy enough to answer that question. Can you see where you are going or are you stumbling along, banging in to stuff?

> John said in 1 John 1:5–6, "God is light; in Him there is no darkness. 6 If we claim to have fellowship with Him yet walk in the darkness, we lie and do not live by the truth."

To walk in the light is to live in fellowship with the Father and the Son. Sin interrupts fellowship but cannot change a relationship. Confession restores fellowship, and immediate confession keeps fellowship unbroken.

Think about that, kids. What could be better than an unbroken relationship with our Lord Jesus? You cannot have a good relationship without fellowship. So how do we walk in the light, or walk with God? Work on your relationship with Him, and stay away from things of darkness.

God is good! Satan is bad! God is Light! Satan is darkness. Keep the light on.

Keep Satan hidden under the rug like a bug, and step on it. When you turn a light on in a dark room, bad things run and hide because they hate the light. It exposes them and their evil.

I said it to be cute, but if you are walking in darkness, you are stumbling along and that way is the evil way—not the right road!

Walking with Jesus, the light, will make your day go much better.

Have a bright day walking in the Light!

God loves you.

1st John 2:3–4 says, "We can know that we have come to know Him if we *obey* His commands. 4 The one who says, I know Him, but does not do what He commands, is a liar, and the truth is not in him."

You might say, "What does He command me to do? I don't want to be a liar."

He also says in verse 9, "Anyone who claims to be in the light, but hates his brother is still in the darkness."

So what command do I follow"?

All the commandments are in these two: Love the Lord your God with all your heart, and with all your soul and with all your strength and with all your mind and love your neighbor as yourself! Luke 10-27.

You cannot walk in the light with hatred in your heart.

Remember, we said work on your relationship with God. He might tell you to repair any others that need repairing before you worry about Him.

Who is my neighbor? Anyone who is not God.

He has given us only two commands: Love God and love your neighbor.

God is love. How much does He love us? Enough to go to the cross and die a miserable death for us. You mean all I have to do is love folks?

Yes, but just think of all that means. Think of all the things you would not do when you love someone! It just can't be that easy, you might say.

Well look it up in Matthew 22:37–40.

Have a great day loving folks.

# A DEFINING MOMENT January 31

Has there been a defining moment in your life, a moment that changed the direction you were going? It could be a moment in time when you made a decision when you needed a major change in your life. If you say, "Oh yes, I accepted Jesus into my life on such and such date," that is wonderful, a very good eternal life insurance decision.

But did it define a change in the way you live? Did you do a 180 on the road you were on and start moving in the opposite direction, the Christ-like direction, the road Jesus would have you walk down?

You know what some people do? Instead of a 180 they do a 360! They make a change, and in the process of getting to the 180, they can't slow down. They keep moving until they get right back where they were, and you got it; there is no change, no real defining moment, that people can see!

If people can't see a change, how will other people see something in you that they want in their life? We are ambassadors for Christ; are we representing Him?

If you have gone too far in your 180 journey, it is not hard to back up, ask God to forgive you, and head back in the right direction. Only this time, use your brakes and keep it on 180. And stay on the narrow road.

God loves you.

# DO YOU KEEP GOD IN A BOX? February 1

Some people keep God in a box accept on Christian holidays. We get busy with day-to-day work or house- work or playing, or whatever it is you do, but where is God in your everyday life? Is He in a box on the shelf, along with your Bible?

What does it mean to keep God in a box?

How often do you talk to God? How often do you need Him? How good is your relationship with Jesus? Some people go day after day and do not need God. Kids go to school, men go to work, and housewives go about their busy lives, cleaning and washing clothes.

So where does God fit in, in all of this life-living? Nice and neatly on a shelf in a box, to open only when you need him? When a crisis comes up? Many of us are very good crisis managers, or firemen putting out little fires as they crop up. All we have to do is open the box and say a little prayer and then close it back and put it back where it was on the shelf. Is this what a personal relationship looks like?

*If He is in you, why can't He be with you*, walking with you, talking to you, and giving you wisdom and guidance? He does not want to be on the shelf. He wants to be an active part of your daily lives!

Does your Bible look shopworn, are there marks in it, have you underlined favorite passages, was it picked up last week after you set it down on Sunday? How important is the Bible in your day to day life? You do know that God speaks to you through His word? Right?

My God can do anything and everything. He will not fit in a box!

He loves you.

# THE NARROW GATE AND THE NARROW ROAD February 2

Have you ever been asked; how could a righteous God send good people to hell?

Answer them this, "There are none good but Jesus!"

I guess it depends on your standard of what good means. If Jesus is unbelievably great and Satan is extremely evil, and if this is how you define good as being closer to Jesus on the scale than Satan, then your thought process is flawed.

As we have recently said one little blemish or white lie can send you to hell without Jesus. God is perfect, and He cannot look at any sin. So, remember that is why we need a mediator!

So, if that is the case, now redefine good. Good is the same as great. There is none good but the Son of God, and He is great, so where do the "good people" fit in now? There are none good but Jesus.

> Matthew 7:13–14
> You can enter God's Kingdom only through the narrow gate. The highway to hell is broad, and its gate is wide for the many who choose that way. 14But the gateway to life is very narrow and the road is difficult, and only a few ever find it.

One of the reasons Jesus says the road is narrow and only few find it is that many people think they are good enough to get to heaven. They have never done anything terrible, and in their eyes, they are better than the next guy. So, they think they are okay! But that thought process gets you on the broad road with a wide gate, the wrong road and the wrong gate.

Think of it: God is not only the judge who condemns us, but He is the Savior who redeems us. We could never be good enough to get to heaven because we are born sinners; we can't help ourselves. We need God, we need our Savior Jesus, and we need our Holy Spirit to keep us in check.

We are lost without them helping us and guiding us on the narrow road! Besides, God does not send people to hell, they decide to go! Pray about it.

God loves you.

# ARE YOU A CHRISTIAN SOLDIER? February 3

Matthew 5:11–12
Jesus said, blessed are you when people insult you, persecute you and falsely say all kinds of evil against you because of me.

Rejoice and be glad, because great is your reward in heaven, for in the same way they persecuted the prophets who were before you.

More about your armor: there are four different responses to the armor. According to Perry Stone's book, *There's a Crack in Your Armor*, first there are those who know nothing about the Armor of God. They live from one spiritual battle to the next, and they want to be a good Christian but they seem to be defeated all the time.

Second are those who know something about the armor but think it is not for them because we all have to learn to deal with our own problems. Not smart!

Third are those who pick and choose their protection, wearing some but not all of the armor, and they wind up getting slammed from an exposed area from the darts of the enemy. They experience a setback when this happens.

Fourth are the Christian soldiers fully equipped every day to withstand all that Satan has to throw at them. They have their protection on, and they know what it represents and how to use it. These folks have battles like everyone else, but they are survivors even through major battles.

Kids, I know all of you are smart enough to figure out which one of the four is best. I will be speaking more about how important your armor is every day. When you step out your front door in the mornings, be prepared to do battle. The battle will come if you are ready or not, so it makes sense to be ready, don't you think?

If you are like your Pop, you will want to win all battles.

Go back and read Ephesians 6 again!

God loves you.

# DO YOU HAVE A TREASURE? February 4

Jesus said, "Do not store up treasures for yourself on earth. But store up for yourself treasures in heaven."

A man named Bob once said, "I have been going to church for a long time, and many preachers have preached on storing up treasures in heaven, so I thought about it a lot over the years. But you know what, no one ever told me how to store treasures in heaven. So, I asked several preachers just how do you store up treasures in heaven? I got answers like you know you got to be good and do the right thing and all that stuff. But when I finished talking to them, I did not know any more than I did before I started."

How do you store up treasures in heaven? It is a good question. Well let me ask you a question: what can you take with you when you go to heaven? And by the way what we think are treasures, gold and silver, will be pavement in heaven. That's right, nada, zip, zero! Just you and, hopefully, a white robe will be going up. So, what can you do with the treasures you have here?

Bob said, "I finally figured it out, if you want to store up treasures in heaven they will need a ride up there, so you have to put them in something going to heaven!" Did you follow that? He said, "If you want your treasures up there, you better put it in folks who are going up there." Okay then, what is a treasure? Let's see, short time here, hmmm long time there, common denominator is time. You mean I need to put *time* into folks that are going up there? Yep, that is one way, spend your valuable time here on earth helping folks get to heaven. Send your "time treasure" with them. Got it! What else can I do? What else is valuable?

Okay, what about your money? If you give your portion to the folks who are trying to win more folks to go to heaven, is it a good investment? Yep, that works! Anything else? Yep, what about your prayers? Will that help folks who are going up there? You bet it will. I know I am going, and I need all the prayer help you can give me, and so do a lot of other Christians.

A treasure to Jesus is a lost soul that has been saved.

He said, "Store your treasures in heaven, where moths and rust cannot destroy, and thieves do not break in and steal. Wherever your treasure is, there the desires of your heart will also be." Matthew 6:20-21

What do you think about more—money or lost souls? Think about it today.

God loves you.

# WHAT IS IN YOUR FUTURE? February 5

Billy Graham was saved at sixteen. Do you think at sixteen he had any idea whatsoever of what God had in mind for his life? How could he know? But Billy turned his whole life over to the Lord Jesus, and Jesus used him in a mighty way. Untold thousands of people came to know our Lord through Billy's preaching all over the world.

Kids, what does Jesus have planned out for you? You can't possibly know. But I will bet you this: I bet it is much more than you can imagine. God will do all that you can do, and then He will do more through you if you allow Him to.

Moms and dads, what do you think God has in store for your lives? Again, it is much more than you can imagine. Do you think what you are doing is God's plan for your life?

You may very well be. But you have to give Him the control panel if you truly want to find out. You see, God does not think like we do, He is all knowing; He doesn't guess.

How many can say if they were the one choosing a new king for Israel, they would choose David, a young shepherd boy?

The difference in what we see and what God sees is that, we see the outside and how they look. He can see inside the heart and soul of a person, He knew what David would be like, and He knew what Billy Graham could accomplish in his life, but we can only guess.

He sees your heart also, and He knows all that you can do.

The happiest you can possibly be, is when you know you are in God's will. And on the flip side, you got it, you can be very miserable if you are not in God's will. And what's worse, you will know it!

Guess how easy it is to get it right? Yep, just talk to *Him* about it. He understands; He will cry with you, He will laugh with you, and He will forgive you. God is what love is all about!

Have a super day today!

God loves you.

# HOW DO YOU SEE YOURSELF? February 6

Do you see yourself as a sinner or as a saint? You might say what is the difference? Your attitude about it is the difference.

If you think, "Well, I am just a sinner saved by grace," you are, but if that is how you see yourself, then that is what you will continue to do. "I am just a sinner, and that is why I keep sinning."

Charles Stanley asks how many letters written by the writers of the Bible start out: To the sinners of Rome or to the sinners of Corinth? Not a one. They are written to the saints. You might think, yes, but they were real saints back then. No, they were real human sinners saved by the grace of God, just like you and me. As new Christians, they had to learn how to be a Christian also. Like a baby learning to walk, they fell on their tails just like we do. If you don't think so, then tell me why Paul had to write the letters. Because they had issues, that's why. And they did not have the complete love letter, the Bible like you do.

But let's suppose you see yourself as a saint, sanctified by the shed blood of Our Savior, with a seat at His table, a child of God. Do you think it might help how you see yourself and your attitude about how you should live? Absolutely, it will.

You were, without a doubt, a sinner that has been saved by the wonderful grace of God. But that was then and this is now! The more you see yourself as a new person, a different person, a living walking ambassador for Christ, your security and freedom in Christ will open your eyes to what He has for you to do!

Put away the old self and live and walk in the light; you are a child of God, so *act like one*!

Get on your knees and ask Him what He wants you to do; open yourself to His will for you, and your day will be so much better than you could imagine, I promise!

Love you kids!

# HOW CAN WE DO IT? February 7

I knew a man one time, who told me I cannot live the way I would need to live to be a Christian. I shared the gospel with Him a lot of times and he would listen intently to all that I had to say, and when I asked him if he would like to ask Jesus into his heart, he would tell me, "No, I can't live that way; I have too much in my past." He said he didn't think he could be forgiven for all that he had done, and he was not good enough of a man to live as a Christian.

He was wrong on a couple of things. Well, he was right about one thing, we can't live a Christian life on our own. It takes the Holy Spirit living within us to help us along the way, and even then, we will slip up from time to time, as much as we don't want to.

Paul wrote about this very thing in Romans chapter 7, beginning at verse 14; it is a good read, but to somewhat sum it up; we cannot let the person we were before we were saved control our minds. We have to let Christ within us take control of our minds, and then we can live a Christ-like life.

We cannot do it without Him; we are too evil minded. But thank God for Jesus Christ who can, if we let Him. Any sin that is in your past can be erased by the shed blood of our Savior, if you will only ask Him to forgive you and ask him into your heart.

I know all of you have done this, but you need to know how to share with others. Don't ever give up on someone; it is a matter of eternal life or eternal death.

Plant seeds for the harvest. This is what really matters!

Love you guys.

# ARE YOU DOING WHAT MATTERS? February 8

Ephesians 5:15–17
"Don't participate in the fruitless works of darkness, but instead expose them. Everything exposed by the light is made clear. Pay careful attention, then, to how you walk—not as unwise people but as wise, making the most of the time, because the days are evil. So, don't be foolish, but understand what the Lord's will is."

The question is, the things that we do, are they things that *matter*? Are you making the most of your time? What could be more important than doing what *matters* to the Lord?

In John 15:5, Jesus said, "Without me you can do nothing."

Literally, you can do nothing that matters without Him in Your life. So, we know what the first step is. Exactly how much time do you have left? Nobody but God knows the answer to that. Okay, so why do we live like we were born yesterday and think we have our whole life ahead of us? And if we live like that, who cares today about what *matters?* Worry about that tomorrow.

We may not say that out loud, but it is what happens unless you *care* about what matters! In other words, you live life on the run, stopping only to sleep a few hours.

So, what does matter? God's will for your life *matters*. Having a healthy relationship with your Savior *matters*, loving folks *matters*, and advancing His kingdom *matters*. Does anyone know where to find God's will for your life? God sure knows what He has for you! Do you want to know?

Well, you could start by asking Him! Wow, Pop, what a concept—you mean talk to God?

Yep! And then read His love letter to you. Look at Matthew 7:7 that says, "Ask and it will be given to you, seek and you will find, knock and the door will be opened to you."

Examine yourself and determine in your day-to-day routine whether there is anything in your life that you are doing that *matters*. If not, why not? There is no time like the present to get on the road to what *matters*.

I wonder how much of our day we could delete because it has no eternal worth that matters. Busy work! A waste of time! Short time here, long time in heaven.

Think about it! Are you doing what matters?

God loves you

# WHAT LIE HAS SATAN SOLD TO YOU?
## February 9

If you have been saved, he can't get you back! You belong to the Lord Jesus, but he can harass the fire out of you and try to keep you from being all God wants you to be. He will try his best to render you ineffective in your walk with Jesus. What is it that Satan has told you that you can't do?

Can't you just hear him say, "Well, look at you; who do you think you are? What makes you think you are good enough to be a so-called Christian? Why would you think God would want you? You can't do that, everyone knows you! You are rotten to the core!" On and on and on he speaks; he is a broken record!

*Listen, folks, and listen well:* How could you be inferior when no one else is like you and you are one of a kind! God made you that way! That is the way He wanted you to be, so you can accomplish what He has for you to do. How could you be inadequate when God is with you? Remember he said, "I am with you always"! So, you can do anything He wants you to do!

You have to claim Philippians 4:13. Who can quote it? "I can do everything through Him who gives me strength."

Turn down Satan's volume, by quoting Jesus. We know who wins!

Have a great day listening to the Savior, not the loser.

God loves you.

# THE THREE TEMPTATIONS February 10

When Satan tempted Eve in the Garden of Eden, he used three basic temptation that he still uses on men and woman today. He used them on Jesus when He was tempted in the wilderness. He probably has used them on all of us as well. I know he has on me.

Let's look at the three basic sins we are tempted with. But before we do, let's see who this Satan that tempts us really is. The story is in Isaiah 14:12–17. Satan was the morning star. He was beautiful, maybe even the most beautiful angel God created, but he decided he was better than God. He wanted to sit on God's throne. Satan was a created being who had so much pride that he thought he could overcome God, his Creator, and take His place. So, God kicked him out. Now he is trying to get back at God by leading God's creation, *man*, to hell with him.

In the beginning in the Garden of Eden, he asked Eve, "Did God really say you must not eat from any tree?" He twisted the words so that they were just a little bit different than what God really said. He made them a few degrees off center, so it sounded good but not the same.

So, the first temptation he used was the fruit was good for food. It would feel good.

The second was that it was pleasing to the eye. It was beautiful fruit. It looked good.

And the third was pride of life; when they ate it, it would give them wisdom, and they would be like God. Satan has always wanted to be like God, but he never will be.

Of course, there are many more ways Satan can tempt you, but these are the basic three.

Kids, this will have to be in a part one, part two, and part three over the next couple of days. But hear this, Satan will tempt you with what looks good, what feels good, and the pride of life over and over as long as he has the ability to do it.

But you have the Holy Spirit who will help you to say *no*.

To be continued,

God loves you.

# THEN HE TEMPTED JESUS February 11

Satan tempted Jesus by telling him the stones would be good to eat if He just turned them into bread, and it would be pleasing to Him. It would feel good.

> Jesus said "It is written, man does not live on bread alone, but on every word that comes from the mouth of God." Matthew 4:4

> Then he said to Jesus, "Throw yourself off the top of the temple, and the angels will save you. It would look good to the people who saw it." He could prove to them that He was who He said He was. Jesus said to him, "It is also written, do not put the Lord your God to the test." Matthew 4:7

And third, he told Jesus, "If you worship me, I will give you all of the kingdoms on the earth; you will be king over all of this." That is called the pride of life.

To me, this was the dumbest thing he could offer the son of God, the Creator of the earth, the very things He created. He owned them already, but Satan was appealing to the human side of Jesus.

> "Jesus said to him, 'Get away from me Satan, for it is written, Worship the Lord your God and serve Him only!" Matthew 4:10

Jesus defeated Satan with His sword, the written word of God, His Bible, His word.

Will you be able to quote scripture when Satan tempts you? He will tempt you; there is no doubt in my mind he will tempt you, so get your sword out and sharpen it up so that you can do battle with him.

God loves you

P.S. Kids, to sharpen your sword means to sharpen your mind by reading the Bible and learn how to win.

To be continued.

So, whoever thinks he stands must be careful not to fall.

No temptation has overtaken you accept what is common to humanity. God is faithful, and He will not allow you to be tempted beyond what you are able, but with the temptation He will also provide a way of escape so that you are able to bear it. (1 Corinthians 10:12–13)

Jesus did battle with Satan by quoting scripture; Satan shies away from truth.

The best way to fight against temptation, when you know you are being tempted is to say, "In Jesus' name, get away from me, Satan!" And then repeat it several times. If you know a scripture that fits the situation, then quote it several times, and the temptation will leave.

The verse above plainly says God will not allow you to be tempted beyond what you are able to withstand, and He will give you a backdoor to escape through. There will always be an out. All you have to do is look for it. It will be like a neon sign blinking on and off, saying, "Go this way." You will literally have to say, "Get away from me, Jesus" to avoid the out He has provided for you.

But sometimes we will be stupid and give in to the temptation. I wish I could tell you why we do it, but I can't, other than we get stupid. But the good news is, we can be forgiven for the stupid's.

Now the worst thing you could ever do is to say to yourself, "Well, I can do this or that, and God will forgive me anyway after I do it!" Remember, I just told you what Jesus said to Satan, "Do not put the Lord your God to the test." Do not ever think you know what God would do in this situation; only He knows that! That is not a good idea! Like playing with fire, you very well might get burnt.

To sum up the last three days: you will be tempted. You will have a backdoor to exit out of the temptation, so look for it! And always quote scripture or repeat several times, "In Jesus' name get away from me, Satan."

Have a safe day today, please.

God loves you!

# GOD MADE US SEEKERS. February 13

In Ecclesiastes, chapter 3, Solomon says that God has set eternity in the human heart. Men and women know that there is more to life than this short time on this earth, and if they have sense, they would like to be in a heavenly place where their Creator is when they pass on from this life to the next.

God made every man and woman to be always seeking Him, and until they find Him, they will not have a happy soul. They will always be seeking God, and they may not know what it is they are looking for.

They can never be happy and content no matter how much they accumulate or what they accomplish. They will keep looking for something to fill the emptiness in their soul. What they are looking for is a relationship with their Father in heaven, and until they have that, they will never be satisfied.

Satan taps in on their search for happiness by leading them down a worldly path of sin. Solomon searched and searched for happiness, and in the end, he said it was nothing but vanity. He found out that the only thing that will satisfy your soul is a relationship with the Father, and the only way to have that now is through Jesus Christ, His son. He is our Savior! He is the door to heaven.

We are called to be separate from the world but not detached; we have to evangelize the world, and it is our mission. We have to live among the folks who are worldly, and whether they know it or not, they need the Lord. And we are the vessels that the Holy Spirit uses to bring them to Jesus.

So, we are to live in the world and be attractive to the lost people seeking inner peace. We have to share what we know about our Lord. We have to be in the world, but not of the world.

God loves you.

To be continued.

# WHAT IS "THE WORLD?" February 14

Is there any difference in you and the world? So, what do I mean when I say "the world"? According to John Phillips, the world, in this context, represents human life and society with God left out!

You might say it is Satan's domain. The place where people are more interested in satanic things, which is the exact opposite of things that God would approve of. Take ISIS for instance; they are killing Christians because their God is Satan, and Satan hates Christians. He might go by a different name, but it is Satan. Billions of people are worshiping a god that in reality is none other than Satan.

In times gone by there were many gods that men worshiped, but their true name was Satan. Every other god you hear about, other than Yahweh, Jehovah, our Creator, has the real name of Satan. All the Greek gods, yep, were Satan. He has always wanted to be a god. So, he dressed himself up as whatever the people wanted to worship. By doing that, men were able to dictate what was blessed by their God. They had a god for every filthy thing they wanted to do. Did you know that there was a god that the people made up that they had to sacrifice their children to, so they made them walk through fire until they burned up? Look it up, Leviticus 18:21. Satan is alive and doing the same kind of things today that he has done throughout history—fighting against our God.

When you think of all the things that we do every day, the worldly things, some of which we do for survival's sake I understand, because we live in the world. But some of the things we do are because the world taught us to do them. We have to be wise; we have to always be aware of our surroundings so that we are living in the world, but there is a unique difference in how we live and how the world lives.

When people look at how we live, they must see something in us that they would like to have in their lives—the peace, joy, gentleness, love, mercy and excitement of being a follower of Jesus Christ.

God loves you.

# HANGING OUT WITH RATTLESNAKES!
## February 15

There is an old legend about a man that wanted to climb a Mountain but did not know where the path was. A rattlesnake slithered out of the bushes and told the man, he knew the way to the top of the mountain. Coincidentally, said the snake, he wanted to go to the top also, and he would show the man the way, if he would only pick him up and carry him up when he went. The man protested, "If I pick you up, you will bite me and I will die". The rattlesnake assured him he had no intentions of biting him, he only wanted to get the top of the mountain. The man said ok and picked up the snake and followed his directions to the top of the mountain. At the end of the journey he thanked the snake for his help, and as he was putting him down, the snake bit him. "You promised you would not bite me", the man said, "and now I am going to die". The rattlesnake replied, "You have no right to complain. You knew what I was when you picked me up".

Why are we surprised when we suffer when we sin? Sin could say to us, "you knew what I was, when you picked me up"!

People have been suffering from sin since Adam and Eve committed the first sin.

Listen again to what David said about his suffering after he sinned;

> Psalm 32,
> 3"When I refused to confess my sin, my body wasted away, and I groaned all day long.
>
> 4Day and night your hand of discipline was heavy on me. My strength evaporated like water in the summer heat".

Why are we so dumb? We play with rattlesnakes and expect not to get bit, we play with fire and expect not to get burned! David said;

5Finally, I confessed all my sins to you and stopped trying to hide my guilt.

I said to myself, "I will confess my rebellion to the LORD." And you forgave me! All my guilt is gone.

Hallelujah! Amen!
God loves you

# YOU ARE THE SALT OF THE EARTH.
## February 16

> You are the salt of the earth but if the salt loses its flavor, how shall it be seasoned? It is then good for nothing but to be thrown out and trampled underfoot by men.
>
> 14 "You are the light of the world. A city that is set on a hill cannot be hidden.
>
> 15 "Nor do they light a lamp and put it under a basket, but on a lampstand, and it gives light to all who are in the house.
>
> 16 "Let your light so shine before men, that they may see your good works and glorify your Father in heaven.
>
> Matthew 5:13–16

What did Jesus mean "You are the salt of the earth"? The world is wasting away through their ignorance of God the Father. Jesus came to shed light on that ignorance. He provided a pathway to the Father through the blood He shed for us. He then sent out the disciples to season the folks with knowledge of the Father's Son, Jesus. Then the disciples set in motion the making of the church, which by the way, is us now, some two thousand years later. And boy, does the world still need salt. You would think that after that long everyone would know, but that is not how it works.

We are to let our light shine so that the Father will be glorified. Jesus said when the salt loses it flavor, it is worthless. It is up to each one of us to provide the flavor. We have to be the vessels that the Holy Spirit uses to spread the knowledge of what Jesus has done for every soul on this Earth. Is your light

# TOLERANCE, PART TWO. February 18

If you are a friend of the world you are an enemy of God. Okay, in today's language, if you think it is cool, then you accept it, and that makes it okay, but God still hates it, even if you don't.

In other words, if the world hates God and you love the world, then does that mean you hate God? Let that sink in for a moment! I know you don't hate God, but see how it works.

In Revelation, chapter 2, when Jesus is speaking to the churches, He warns them not to be tolerant of wickedness, and He tells them He knows their deeds. He tells them that they are lukewarm, neither cold nor hot (That's part Christian and part world, you can't be both).

They tolerated sin until they were doing exactly what they were doing before they were saved. Remember we talked about the 180 repentance turn and how some had passed 180 and went back to 360 where they were before. That is what happens when you become tolerant. There is, then, no distinction between you and the world.

Your witness is everything. How could you possibly witness to someone who knows that you tolerate sin? There has to be a difference in you as a Christian in the world.

Our mission is to be a reflection of Christ so that the lost can see Christ in us. When you look in the mirror do you see a reflection of Jesus or the world?

It is important to guard your witness. I tried to witness to a guy once and invited him to church, but he said those places are full of hypocrites. They go to the bar on Saturday night and to church on Sunday. Now I know that was his excuse not to go to church, but maybe a Christian in his past was tolerant around him and accepted his bad behavior. We have to love the person, but we are not to love the behavior or tolerate it.

That is a lot to think about today, I know.

I think we will talk some more about what tolerance has done to our country later.

God loves you.

# THE OLD YOU, February 19

I heard this on the radio this morning:

There was a Christian counselor who had a lady that he thought was completely delusional because she said she had weekly personal conversations with Jesus. Every week she would come to his office and tell him about their conversation. He was getting tired of her delusions and decided he would put an end to it. He said to her, "I tell you what, the next time you talk to Jesus, ask Him what sin did your counselor, me, commit when he was in college, and you come back and tell me what He says."

The next week she came in, and after they talked for a few minutes, he asked her, "Did you talk to Jesus this week?" She said yes. "Well, did you ask Him about what we talked about?" She said yes. He said, "Well what did He say?" She said, "He doesn't remember! *

Folks, did you here that? He does not remember! The counselor's sins were covered by Jesus' blood, wiped out, and gone!

He was obviously a Christian! Second Corinthians 5:17 says, "Therefore, if anyone is in Christ, the new creation has come: The old has gone, the new is here."

When you accept Jesus, He removes all traces of the person you were, and you are a new creation! The old you is gone in Jesus' mind. The only way the old you gets back in the door is, yep, *you* have to invite him back in.

Don't do that! Listen, folks, the battle has been won. The victory is yours because you are the child of the Victor, the King!

Tell Satan to get lost because you are a brand-new person and your old self has been washed out of your life! What a great story to start the day.

Thank your Lord and Savior this morning for making you a new person and forgetting about the old you!

God loves the new you!

*unknown

# HOW IS YOUR FAITH? February 20

Therefore, I say to you, do not worry about your life, what you will eat or what you will drink; nor about your body, what you will put on. Is not life more than food and the body more than clothing?

26 "Look at the birds of the air, for they neither sow nor reap nor gather into barns; yet your heavenly Father feeds them. Are you not of more value than they?

27 "Which of you by worrying can add one cubit to his stature?

28 "So why do you worry about clothing? Consider the lilies of the field, how they grow: they neither toil nor spin;

29 "and yet I say to you that even Solomon in all his glory was not arrayed like one of these.

30 "Now if God so clothes the grass of the field, which today is, and tomorrow is thrown into the oven, will He not much more clothe you, O you of little faith?

31 "Therefore do not worry, saying, 'What shall we eat?' or 'What shall we drink?' or 'What shall we wear?'

32 "For after all these things the Gentiles seek. For your heavenly Father knows that you need all these things.

33 "But seek first the kingdom of God and His righteousness, and all these things shall be given to you as well.

Matthew 6:25–33

Someone once said that worrying is like a rocking chair; it gives you something to do, but it doesn't get you anywhere. Folks, we worry too much about this or that.

Put your life in God's more than capable hands, and He will provide, not only what you need, but much more than you could dream of! He works things out in our lives in ways we can't even imagine. When you look back on it later, you will see God's hand all in it. Because we are not smart enough to work it out, we should have faith and turn it over to Him.

Then, forget about it.

God loves you.

# ARE YOU REPEATING YOUR FIRST YEAR OF SALVATION? February 21

How many of us find ourselves repeating the same prayers over and over, like, now I lay me down to sleep, or God is great God is good? There is nothing wrong with these prayers, but Charles Stanley asks: could it be your prayers haven't changed because your knowledge of our Lord and Savior hasn't changed?

The big question is, are you seeking the mind of Christ every day? Are you in His word daily?

When we are saved, we start out as babes in Christ and then we learn to walk. Later, we start running. How many of us have been saved for, say, five or more years and yet really, we don't have five or more years of knowledge of our Lord? In reality all we have done is repeat the same year over and over, and we really don't have more than *one year of Christian knowledge* because we just don't take the time to learn about Him.

That is like taking one step forward and one step back— no progress!

What happens to all of our time? We get up early in the morning and go to work or school, and then we come home to stuff that needs doing, like home work or grass that needs mowing or supper or clothes that need washing. And don't forget we have a TV that needs to be watched, a phone that needs to be played with, and people to text or call. But where is the time for us to learn about God and quit repeating that same year of Christian knowledge? It is a real problem. I knew a very nice lady that has been a Christian for over fifty years but had been caught up in life, raising kids and helping with grandkids and whatever, but she did not know her way around the Bible at all. She had been repeating her Christian knowledge year after year until one day she realized how eager she was to learn more about her Savior. So, at that point, she made a concentrated effort to take the time to read her Bible and study the word in a small group. Now she is teaching kids in a Sunday school. It became important to her, and she took action!

What about you? How long have you been a Christian, and how many years of Christian knowledge do you have?

More on this tomorrow.

God loves you.

# GROWING IN THE LORD. February 22

As we grow in knowledge of Him, our relationship will grow also. At some point, you will be able to talk to Him about whatever is on your mind, and your relationship will be growing daily. You will then realize that prayer is not only what you want God to do for you, but it is also asking what you can do for him.

Sometimes we give God a work list: Father, I need this and that and the other, and I need it now, please. If He knows everything, and He does, then He knows what you need, and He is able to decipher what is best for us and what we really need versus what we want and don't really need. We don't have the ability to see down our life's road, but He does.

> Jesus said in Matthew 21:22, "And all things, whatsoever ye shall ask in prayer, *believing,* ye shall receive."

He wants us to pray and ask Him for the things on our hearts, and like a loving Father, He will give His children what they ask for—especially if it is in His will to do it!

Only in asking are you showing your dependence on Him. We should depend on God for everything. We can do nothing that matters without Him, remember, so we have to depend on Him. He is our Father, and we are His children; we need to keep that in perspective.

He taught us how to pray in Matthew 6:9–13. Prayer is a very important part of your Christian walk. Prayer is communicating with your Father, in the name of Jesus, through the power of the Holy Spirit.

Have a great day; pray about it!

God loves you.

# FALSE TEACHERS. February 23

2 Peter 2

But there were also false prophets in Israel, just as there will be false teachers among you. They will cleverly teach destructive heresies and even deny the Master who bought them. In this way, they will bring sudden destruction on themselves. 2Many will follow their evil teaching and shameful immorality. And because of these teachers, the way of truth will be slandered. 3In their greed they will make up clever lies to get hold of your money. But God condemned them long ago, and their destruction will not be delayed.17These people are as useless as dried-up springs or as mist blown away by the wind. They are doomed to blackest darkness. 18They brag about themselves with empty, foolish boasting. With an appeal to twisted sexual desires, they lure back into sin those who have barely escaped from a lifestyle of deception.

We talked about the new and the old self and that false teachers will try to lure you back to the old self. The world is full of them. Most have a central theme; you may have to look hard to find it, but it is there. They will deny that Jesus is the true one and only Son of God.

The truth is, He came to earth as a man and lived and was tempted by all the same things you are tempted by, except He did not give in to any temptation, He was totally sinless! He was the only Man that ever lived or ever will live who could live and not sin because He was both God and Man.

Some will try to tell you that Jesus and Satan were brothers; it is nothing but nonsense. Jesus was Satan's Creator, not his brother. They may try to tell you that you, too, can become a God—yep, more nonsense. There is one God in three persons, which is all there was and all there ever will be!

Always test the nonsense by the word, and the word will put it where it belongs: in hell!

Put your armor on; there is craziness out there today!

God loves you.

# HELL IS REAL! February 24

2 Peter 2:4–10

For God did not spare even the angels who sinned. He threw them into hell, in gloomy pits of darkness where they are being held until the Day of Judgment. 5 And God did not spare the ancient world—accept for Noah and the seven others in his family. Noah warned the world of God's righteous judgment. So, God protected Noah when he destroyed the world of ungodly people with a vast flood. 6 Later, God condemned the cities of Sodom and Gomorrah and turned them into heaps of ashes. He made them an example of what will happen to ungodly people. 7 But God also rescued Lot out of Sodom because he was a righteous man who was sick of the shameful immorality of the wicked people around him. 8 Yes, Lot was a righteous man who was tormented in his soul by the wickedness he saw and heard day after day. 9 So you see, the Lord knows how to rescue godly people from their trials, even while keeping the wicked under punishment until the day of final judgment. 10 He is especially hard on those who follow their own twisted sexual desire, and who despise authority.

Don't you know that when the light (Jesus) shines on you, your sin will be exposed?

The train is going to heaven; are you going to stand on the platform or board the train? When and if you board the train, the conductor will ask you a question: Why should I let you on this train? (Why should I let you into heaven?) If you know the answer, he will say have a seat; if you don't know the answer, you will be escorted off of the train and on to another going in the opposite direction.

Do you know the answer?

Eternity is a long time to be wrong. There is a reason they say there is eternal life and there is eternal death. Kids, you have to know this in order to tell others.

Don't miss tomorrow's note!

God loves you.

# SIN IS LIKE A DEBT. February 25

Like a charge on a charge card, eventually you will have to pay the bill. But, how can you? No one knows how to pay off a sin debt! Do you? Well, if you knew the answer to that, then I suppose you know the answer to the question posed yesterday that the conductor will ask: Why should I let you on the train going to heaven?

"For all have sinned and fall short of the glory of God. Romans 3:23

"And the wages of sin is death. But the gift of God is eternal life in Christ Jesus our Lord." Romans 6:23

That means we have to pay off our sin debt.

Oh, but "God, demonstrated His own love for us, in that while we were still sinners, Christ died for us. Romans 5:8

For it is with your heart that you believe and are justified, and it is with your mouth that you confess and are saved. Romans 10:10

For everyone who calls on the name of the Lord will be saved." Romans 10:13

You see, God made you alive, with Christ. He forgave us all our sins, having canceled the debt, which was against us, (on our charge card), He took it away and nailed it to the cross. And Jesus' blood washed you white as snow. Your bill was paid, and the card cut up. There will be no more charging of sins.

Jesus paid them *all* off. Past, present and future sins—all of them are covered by His blood.

And that is your ticket for the train ride, when the conductor asks you why he should let you on this train to heaven. You just tell him, "I am covered by the blood of Christ! I accepted Jesus in to my life and was baptized in to the new life as a Christian." Aren't you glad you did?

Kids, you just walked down the Romans road; commit it to memory! This is a way to lead someone to Christ.

Do you know why Satan hates Christians? Because he envies your ticket on the train. He gave his away, and he will be escorted to the other train headed in the opposite direction.

> Revelation21:8
> Along with the cowardly, the unbelieving, the vile, the murders, the sexually immoral, those who practice magic arts, the idolaters and all liars-their place will be in the fiery lake of burning sulfur. The second death, the eternal death.

Tomorrow, we will talk about Judgment Day.
Love you.

# THE SHOCK AT JUDGMENT DAY! February 26

(Notes from Chuck Swindoll)

Some will say Lord, Lord, and the King will say, "Go away from me I never knew you!"

Many Buddhists and Hindus and followers of some New Age religions anticipate repeated reincarnation into other life forms. It's sort of like spinning their wheels, don't you think?

Some, like the Taoists, believe that death is ultimate oblivion, and some Muslims believe in a heavenly paradise that promises various carnal pleasures, like Las Vegas, maybe, yeah right!

Mormons believe that they eventually become gods and goddesses of their own world, populating them with their own spirit babies. Sounds like work to me! Think of all the diapers.

The Jehovah's Witnesses believe that only the 144,000 live as spirits in heaven, and the rest have to live perfect lives on earth for a thousand years or get annihilated. By the way, they already have the 144,000, so for the rest, good luck on living a perfect life.

First of all, let me say I did not make this up.

Now before you jump all over these false views of the afterlife, it would surprise you to know that some Christians are just as misled in their ideas of heaven. Some think you will float around on clouds or receive an oversized set of wings. But we need to think of heaven in more biblical terms. Imagine an eternity with a face-to-face relationship with the One who got you there, Jesus Christ, where there is no darkness, no disease, no threat of death, everything open and transparent, flooded with light and filled with the presence of God. We will be with our loved ones that passed away to a better place; they will meet you at the station in heaven when the train comes to a stop. Seriously the train thing is figuratively speaking, of course, but you get the point.

Our loved ones will greet us when we get there. What a great reunion. There won't be a clock because eternity is timeless. Here is a neat way to think about forever: suppose a dove flew to a beach, got a mouth full of sand, and flew it to the moon, and he repeated that until all the sand on all the beaches in the world were empty. When he got the last mouthful and dumped it on the moon, eternity would have just begun.

Listen, kids, all these other religions that are without a ticket (Jesus Christ) will be on the wrong train going in the wrong direction. They need you to witness to them, so keep praying and reading your Bibles. The Holy Spirit will use you, and you may be able to help save someone from everlasting hell.

Pray about it! Love you.

Tomorrow More on Judgment day.

# JUDGMENT DAY. February 27

Matthew 25
But when the Son of Man comes in his glory, and all the angels with him, then he will sit upon his glorious throne. 32 All the nations will be gathered in his presence, and he will separate the people as a shepherd separates the sheep from the goats. 33 He will place the sheep at his right hand and the goats at his left. 34 "Then the King will say to those on his right, 'Come, you who are blessed by my Father, inherit the Kingdom prepared for you from the creation of the world.

Revelation 20,
10 Then the devil, who had deceived them, was thrown into the fiery lake of burning sulfur, joining the beast and the false prophet. There they will be tormented day and night forever and ever. 11 And I saw a great white throne and the one sitting on it. The earth and sky fled from his presence, but they found no place to hide. 12 I saw the dead, both great and small, standing before God's throne. And the books were opened, including the Book of Life. And the dead were judged according to what they had done, as recorded in the books. 13 The sea gave up its dead, and death and the grave gave up their dead. And all were judged according to their deeds. 14 Then death and the grave were thrown into the lake of fire. This lake of fire is the second death. 15 And anyone whose name was not found recorded in the Book of Life was thrown into the lake of fire.

Kids, you might be asked the question: how do I get my name in the Book of Life? You tell them when they are "born again" by the grace of God, their name will be put in the book.

"Then to the ones on his right again he will say; the Master said, 'Well done, my good and faithful servant.'" Kids, I don't have anything to add to these final words, except I am glad I am a sheep and not a goat, and I would like for my Father to say one day, well done!

What about you?

God loves you .

# MORE IMPORTANT, HEAVEN IS REAL ALSO
## February 28

Revelation 21:1–6
Now I saw a new heaven and a new earth, for the first heaven and the first earth had passed away. Also, there was no more sea.

2 Then I, John, saw the holy city, New Jerusalem, coming down out of heaven from God, prepared as a bride adorned for her husband.

3 And I heard a loud voice from heaven saying, "Behold, the tabernacle of God is with men, and He will dwell with them, and they shall be His people. God Himself will be with them and be their God. 4 "And God will wipe away every tear from their eyes; there shall be no more death, nor sorrow, nor crying. There shall be no more pain, for the former things have passed away."

5 Then He who sat on the throne said, "Behold, I make all things new." And He said to me, "Write, for these words are true and faithful."

6 And He said to me, "It is done! I am the Alpha and the Omega, the Beginning and the End. I will give of the fountain of the water of life freely to him who thirsts.

Jesus also said in John 14:2–3, "My Father's house has many rooms; if that were not so, would I have told you that I go to prepare a place for you? And if I go and prepare a place for you, I will come back and take you to be with me that you also may be where I am."

Hell is real, but more important, heaven is real also. Jesus is away, preparing a place for you, and Jesus knows you very well. Did you ever try to imagine what that place that He is preparing, especially just for you, will be like? A friend of mine is a Christian and a golfer, and he said, "Wouldn't it be great if we played golf in heaven?" I think he would like his place to be on a golf course. However, knowing him, he will be perfectly happy with whatever Jesus wants him to have, golf or no golf.

Listen, folks, you need to spread the word that not only is hell real, but heaven is real also.

In the story of the prodigal son, while the son was a long way off, his father saw him coming, filled with love and compassion, *he ran* to his son, embraced him, and kissed him.

Did you get that, *he ran* to his son! People this is Jesus telling this parable. If it were not true, He would not have said it!

He then prepared a banquet for him. God loves you more than we can imagine!

# THE TWELVE GATES WERE TWELVE PEARLS. March 1

These notes are from Chuck Swindoll on Revelation:

The New Jerusalem where God will reign will have twelve gates. Revelation 21:21 tells us that the twelve gates were made of pearls—each gate from a single pearl! And the main street was pure gold, as clear as glass. Wow that is a big pearl. But why a pearl? This is very significant, listen to what Phillips says about the pearly gates:

> All other precious stones are metals or stones, but a pearl is a gem formed within the oyster, the only one formed by living flesh, the humble oyster receives an irritation or wound, and around the offending article that has penetrated and hurt it, the oyster builds a pearl. The pearl, we might say, is the answer of the oyster, to that which injured it.

Something beautiful is made from an injury. The pearl represents pain resulting in beauty, suffering crowned with glory!

When we read of this symbol of the pearl eternally embedded in the doorways of heaven, it should remind us that Christ's suffering had an eternal purpose and opened heaven for us.

John saw a glorious city, an enormous city, a 1,500-mile cube with three gates on each side for a total of twelve gates. There will be plenty of room in heaven for all that believe in Him.

Above the twelve gates are the names of the twelve tribes of Israel, and on the foundation of the gates are the names of the twelve apostles. The city will be the dwelling place of all of God's people. The very things that we adore the most will be common things in heaven, like pearl gates and gold streets, and it will be adorned with every kind of jewel.

Yes, heaven is real, kids, and He will come back soon to take us there, keep looking up!

God loves you.

# STREETS OF GOLD. March 2

Revelation 21
The New Jerusalem;

And the street of the city was pure gold, like transparent glass.

22 But I saw no temple in it, for the Lord God Almighty and the Lamb are its temple.

23 The city had no need of the sun or of the moon to shine in it, for the glory of God illuminated it. The Lamb is its light.

24 And the nations of those who are saved shall walk in its light, and the kings of the earth bring their glory and honor into it.

25 Its gates shall not be shut at all by day (there shall be no night there).

26 And they shall bring the glory and the honor of the nations into it.

27 But there shall by no means enter it anything that defiles, or causes an abomination or a lie, but only those who are written in the Lamb's Book of Life.

Revelation 22, they shall see His face, and His name shall be on their foreheads.

5 There shall be no night there: They need no lamp nor light of the sun, for the Lord God gives them light. And they shall reign forever and ever.

6 Then he said to me, "These words are faithful and true." And the Lord God of the holy prophets sent His angel to show His servants the things which must shortly take place.

7 "Behold, I am coming quickly! Blessed is he who keeps the words of the prophecy of this book."

We will be walking on pavement of pure gold, and we will not need light because the glory of Jesus will be all we need to see by! There will be no more temptation, because guess who will not be there? That's right; Satan will be where he belongs.

Then Jesus says, "Behold I am coming quickly!"

We must be about the Lord's business; time is running out! God loves you.

# THE WILL OF GOD. March 3

Notes from the movie *The War Room*:

The best place in the world for any of us to be is squarely in the middle of God's will.

It is His perfect plan that will bring Him the most pleasure. It is not only what's best for us, but it is what will yield God the most glory, and thankfully, He has promised His children that we can live in His perfect will.

God's will be not a mystery. The first thing you need to do to find out what God would have you do and what His perfect will is for you in any situation is to pray about it: "Lord not my will but your will be done." Going in you have to know that His will shall ultimately glorify God.

John the Baptist knew what his life was all about, so he spent time preparing the folks for the coming of Christ. And when he saw that Jesus was beginning His ministry, he said, "*He must increase* and I must decrease."

Why can't that be our prayer for our lives as well? Lord, You increase in my life, and please help me to decrease. If He increases in me and I get out of the way and decrease my dumbness, then it will be much easier to find the will of Him who lives in me, who is wise beyond imagination.

Then begin to look for open and closed doors. He will direct your path, and if you listen and be aware of little nudges, you will know when to go left and when to go right.

He loves you and wants the best for you, and the best is always His perfect will for you!

The open door may well be the hardest route for you to take, but if it is in God's will for you to take it, He will be there with you through whatever you face.

Proverbs 2:1–5 says search for His wisdom as if you were digging for treasure, and you will find what you are looking for. If you search for God's will, like digging for treasure, you will find it, and the outcome will be perfect for you.

God loves you, have a great day today!

# TRUST IN THE LORD. March 4

Proverbs 3
My child, never forget the things I have taught you.

Store my commands in your heart.

2 If you do this, you will live many years, and your life will be satisfying.

3 Never let loyalty and kindness leave you!

Tie them around your neck as a reminder.

Write them deep within your heart.

4 Then you will find favor with both God and people,

And you will earn a good reputation.

5 Trust in the LORD with all your heart;

Do not depend on your own understanding.

6 Seek his will in all you do, and he will show you which path to take.

7 Don't be impressed with your own wisdom. Instead, fear the LORD and turn away from evil.

8 Then you will have healing for your body and strength for your bones.

Solomon wanted his kids to know the correct way to live, and that is my desire as well.

Kids, some of you are about to set off on a new chapter of your life. I desperately want for you what Solomon wanted for his children. He wanted them to understand before they made unnecessary mistakes, that they should trust in the Lord and seek His will for their lives. You need him to help you in all things. Read proverbs and then read it again, and when you are done, read it one more time.

Common sense says look at the world and do as they do, but Proverbs is *un*common sense. It is the right way—God's way.

I love you, kids, and pray for you always.

# JUDGING OTHERS. March 5

1"Do not judge others, and you will not be judged.
2 For you will be treated as you treat others the
standard you use in judging is the standard by
which you will be judged" (Matthew 7).

Pop, what are we talking about here? How do we judge others?

One word meaning for judge is to be a critic. Okay, get the
message now? Every time you are critical of someone's clothes,
shoes, car, hair, or appearance, you are judging them. Unless you
have walked in their shoes, how can you be critical of them?
Do not conduct your life in a spirit of condemnation of others.

Who died and made you the shoe inspector or the makeup
inspector or the clothes inspector? No one, that's who! Envy,
pride, and or jealousy, are the driving forces in most of the critical comments.

Remember the way you treat others is the standard by which
you will be judged by the real Judge, Jesus Christ. Do unto
others as you would have them do to you!

Please have a good, noncritical day.

God loves you.

# WHAT HAPPENED? March 6

Parents, why are we not teaching our kids about God?

Think about the Israelites in the times before Christ; fathers and grandfathers and maybe even great grandfathers, while working in the fields or taking care of the livestock, would talk to their kids about God. The moms would tell them when their fathers were off to work or war.

Before World War II, both Mom and Dad would take the kids to church on Sunday and tell them Bible stories at night. What happened after that? Both moms and dads went to work, and the kids were left to themselves in many cases, so they watched TV or listened to boom boxes, and Satan had his way with them—in the music, in their own imagination, and on the tube.

God was not a focus; the world was the focus, and Satan smiled. When parents went to church, they would leave it up to the SS teachers to tell the Bible stories, and Satan smiled. Today parents can't tell the children about Bible stories because they don't know them, either, and Satan is smiling about it.

So, what do we do to change this madness? Bottom line, parents and grandparents, you are accountable! If your kids grow up and know little to nothing about the Bible and God, it is my fault and your fault! Kids, when you get to the age of accountability, it is your fault if you don't make an effort to learn.

Remember a few days ago I said we will all stand before God and answer for what we did and didn't do? I think this will be high on the list. Satan will have a distressed look on his face then.

Today is the first day of the rest of your life. There is time to make a change, so start today. Make a plan and then work the plan; it won't happen by accident.

God loves you.

# WHAT HAPPENED? Part two. March 7

Proverbs 3:5–8—Trust in the LORD with all
your heart and do not lean on your own understanding. In all your ways acknowledge Him,
and He will make your paths straight. Do not be
wise in your own eyes; fear the LORD and turn
away from evil. It will be healing to your body
and refreshment to your bones.

Many moms and dads want to start teaching their children
the Bible. Yet, those same parents sometimes get paralyzed and
never take their first step. The reason is simple—they just don't
know where to start. Here is one place you could start. The book
of Proverbs is filled with wisdom for life and parenting. They
can become the centerpiece of your kitchen table discussions
and a tour guide for difficult conversations.

By the way, another reason we don't talk to our kids about
Bible stories is eating out all the time.

The book of Proverbs is arguably the most practical book
in the entire Bible because the wisest man that ever lived other
than Jesus, of course, wrote them. So, as you search for a place
to start in the teaching and instruction of your children, why
not start in a place that will make immediate impact? And that
impact is not limited to your children; it will happen in Mom
and Dad, too.

Then in your personal Bible study time, either in the morning
or before you go to bed, alternate between New Testament and
Old Testament so that when you come to a great story, and you
will, you can share it with your kids.

This is not rocket science, but it takes effort on your part.
What could possibly be more important?

Think about it and pray about it and then put action to
your prayers.

God loves you.

# A PARABLE OF SOIL. March 8

Jesus was a master storyteller. He used parables to teach his followers and to baffle the Pharisees. How many times when someone says to you, "Let me tell you a story," do you get disinterested? I would think not many. People love to hear stories. Here is a parable Jesus taught about four kinds of soil that a farmer planted seeds in. In those days, you planted seeds if you wanted to eat, so almost everyone knew what He was talking about. Jesus is speaking:

> Listen! A farmer went out to plant some seeds. 4As he scattered them across his field, some seeds fell on a footpath, and the birds came and ate them. 5Other seeds fell on shallow soil with underlying rock. The seeds sprouted quickly because the soil was shallow.6But the plants soon wilted under the hot sun, and since they didn't have deep roots, they died. 7Other seeds fell among thorns that grew up and choked out the tender plants. 8Still other seeds fell on fertile soil, and they produced a crop that was thirty, sixty, and even a hundred times as much as had been planted!9Anyone with ears to hear should listen and understand."

This is what I want you to do, I want you to ponder this story all day today and see if you know what Jesus is talking about.

You can find it in Matthew 13. But don't just go and read it, ponder it. Then when you think you have it, check to see if you were right. When you think you have it, think about the application to you. We will talk more about it tomorrow.

I think it will be good to go through some of the parables in the coming days.

God loves you.

# THE SOIL EXPLAINED. March 9

Now listen to the explanation of the parable about the farmer planting seeds:

> The seed that fell on the footpath represents those who hear the message about the Kingdom and don't understand it. Then the evil one comes and snatches away the seed that was planted in their hearts. 20The seed on the rocky soil represents those who hear the message and immediately receive it with joy. 21But since they don't have deep roots, they don't last long. They fall away as soon as they have problems or are persecuted for believing God's word. 22The seed that fell among the thorns represents those who hear God's word, but all too quickly the message is crowded out by the worries of this life and the lure of wealth, so no fruit is produced. 23The seed that fell on good soil represents those who truly hear and understand God's word and produce a harvest of thirty, sixty, or even a hundred times as much as had been planted!

Now there are four different kinds of soil: the footpath, the rocky, the weeds and the fertile soil. I would suspect that the four covers everyone at one time or another in their life. Where would you put yourself today?

Many people have a hollow hole in the head from ear to ear; it goes in one ear and flies out the other. Many have allowed Satan to snatch their joy away. Many are so wrapped up in the weeds of life, they don't have time for even the necessities of life. They eat junk food all the time, so how would they ever find time to read their Bible?

And then there are the hearers of the word, they have much fruit to enjoy, love, joy, peace, kindness, faithfulness, and gentleness. They bear fruit with patience.

Are there changes you need to make?

God loves you.

# SHINE YOUR LIGHT. March 10

Matthew 5:14–16
You are the light of the world—like a city on a hilltop that cannot be hidden.15No one lights a lamp and then puts it under a basket. Instead, a lamp is placed on a stand, where it gives light to everyone in the house. 16In the same way, let your good deeds shine out for all to see, so that everyone will praise your heavenly Father.

What does it mean to shine your light? Jesus explained that no one turns a light on and puts it under a basket so that the light is no good; if your light is out, what good is it? A lamp is meant to be placed on a stand to give light to everything around it.

Whether you are timid or outgoing, you're called to be a light to the people around you. That is only possible if you are taking time to interact with people and cultivate relationships.

No one does this better than my beautiful wife, who never meets a stranger. You may say, yes but that is who she is, and I am the shy person, and I find it hard to reach out to folks, even though I know I should.

Galatians 6:12 says, "Carry each other's burdens, and in this way, you will fulfill the law of Christ," the law of love.

Do you think God does not know what you are like? He made you, didn't He? So that is not a good excuse.

Guess what, He can use you just the way you are; you don't have to become an extrovert, you probably couldn't anyway, but you have to be *willing* to serve.

Peter was an extrovert, so it came easy for him, but Timothy was apparently an introvert and God used both of them because they loved the Lord and they were willing to be used. Don't worry about those folks you can't help. Instead, trust God to lead you to those who would respond better to a person like you.

Also, prayer warriors are needed by extroverts. There are many things that you can do to serve our Lord other than working in a hospitality booth.

Talk to God about it; He will find you something to do.

God loves you.

# MILK, CHICKEN FINGERS, AND STEAK. March 11

Milk is what you feed babies. Chicken fingers is what comes next, and then we eat adult food, like squash, carrots, steak, cornbread, and all the good stuff. So, what does this have to do with the Christian life?

Do you remember when we said that a good portion of Christians only have one year of the Christian life that is repeated over and over? Would you believe there are folks in our area that have lived as Christians for many years and only have one year of Christian knowledge? You might ask, how could this happen? It is because they have only digested milk—no chicken fingers or steaks, just milk. When a baby doesn't grow up as they should, we begin to wonder are they *okay*.

Folks, you can't just learn what you need to follow Jesus by sitting on a pew, listening to sermons. Many folks get home from church, put their Bibles up, and don't touch it again until they pick it up to go to church again. And they don't participate in a small group where we learn and grow from each other. Listen to what Hebrews 5:12–14 says about it:

> You have been believers so long now that you ought to be teaching others. Instead, you need someone to teach you again the basic things about God's word. You are like babies who need milk and cannot eat solid food. 13For someone who lives on milk is still an infant and doesn't know how to do what is right. 14Solid food is for those who are mature, who through training have the skill to recognize the difference between right and wrong.

What is the spiritual milk? It is the more digestible truths of doctrine that are given to new believers. Solid food is the deeper features of the doctrines of scripture. The difference is not the kind of truth but the degree of depth. The basic difference (in the limitations of a daily message) is that there is a difference between a baby in Christ and a mature Christian when it comes to wanting to hear and learn anything new and also being comfortable sharing what you know about Jesus. Which, by the way, is what Christians are supposed to do. Christ said to go and make disciples. Guys, we need to be moving to the next level in our Christian growth.

Now dust off your Bible and go to learning! The Bible should be picked up and opened at least once a day, seven days a week. Christianity is not a one day a week relationship with Jesus, and then maybe you will start using your teeth to chew on some meat so you can share what you know.

God loves you.

# SOWING AND REAPING. March 12

Billy Graham says on the radio every day, "Whatsoever a man sow is what he will reap."

In Galatians 6:7–10, Paul said:

> 7 Don't be misled—you cannot mock the justice of God. You will always harvest what you plant. 8 Those who live only to satisfy their own sinful nature will harvest decay and death from that sinful nature. But those who live to please the Spirit will harvest everlasting life from the Spirit. 9 So let's not get tired of doing what is good. At just the right time we will reap a harvest of blessing if we don't give up. 10 Therefore, whenever we have the opportunity, we should do good to everyone—especially to those in the family of faith.

Today is the father of tomorrow! What we are today is the result of what we have been thinking and the way we have lived in the past. Those who act wisely today will have wisdom in the future to make wise decisions.

Every farmer knows this principle: we reap what we sow, more than we sow, and later than we sow. This is a law of life. It works both ways, for Christian and for unbelievers. The verse starts out with "Don't be deceived, God is not mocked."

The problem is there are many people who are deceived. They either do not believe the truth or they think they will somehow be the exceptions to God's law. They turn their nose up at God, thinking they can outwit Him or maybe even wait until the perfect time comes. God calls you only so many times, and then He gives you over to yourself. There is a statement that goes something like this: Either God's will be done in your life for all eternity or *your* will be done in your life for all eternity. Which one do you think is better?

The fact that we reap what we sow is great news for those who sow good deeds with Christian values.

But it is not such good news for those who sow things other than that which is pleasing to God. You can't sow crabgrass and expect a harvest of strawberries! We cannot sow disobedience to God and expect to reap His blessings. What we sow, we reap! Don't deceive yourself.

We will reap the harvest of the way we live—His will or your will be done.

Sow good seeds today, for tomorrow's harvest.

God loves you.

# DO YOU THINK FAILING CAN LEAD TO SUCCESS? March 13

> Proverbs 2:10 says, "For wisdom will enter your heart, and knowledge will fill you with joy."

Don't get bored about reading the Bible; don't let it get mundane.

Many people fail many times before they have success. Think of yourself—how many times have you set a goal to go through the Bible, and you got hung up in Deuteronomy or Numbers?

But you are not in control. He is, and He says to trust Him. We talked about being dependent on God. If we ask Him for His help, He will give us what we need to stay focused.

I think you will agree we always find the time to do what we really enjoy doing, even when we are our busiest. So why can't we find the time to do what will enhance our lives? Nothing you can do in a day is more important than taking a few moments to listen to God speak to you through His word.

In fifteen minutes a day, you can start your day off on the right track or end your day with a smile before you go to sleep. If you have not been taking a few minutes to study the Bible, what do you have to lose? Try it and see what God can do through you.

Who knows, you might learn something life changing!

God loves you.

# DIGGING FOR SILVER! March 14

How much value are you getting out of your Bible?

A Christian lady's son was in bad financial shape. He called his mom and asked her for some money, so she sent him a Bible and told him to read the Bible and pray, and it will help.

He got really ticked off when he received the Bible. He called his mom and said, "Mom I asked you for some money and you sent me a Bible. I was really disappointed." She said, "Read your Bible, son, and it will help," so he didn't talk to her for a long time. So, one day he called her and brought up the fact that when he was in dire straits and asked her for money, all she did was send him a Bible.

She asked him, "Son, did you read the Bible and pray like I told you?" and he said, "Yes, Mom, I did, but I needed money not a Bible." She said, "Oh really? Well, I don't think you did because there was a hundred-dollar bill in front of all sixty-six books of the Bible!" *

*Author unknown

So, the moral of the story is, how much value are you getting out of your Bible? Are you just scanning through it or are you digging in for the treasure?

Proverbs 2:1–5
1 My son, if you accept my words and store up my commands within you,

2 turning your ear to wisdom and applying your heart to understanding—

3 indeed, if you call out for insight and cry aloud for understanding,

4 and if you look for it as for silver and search for it as for hidden treasure,

5 then you will understand the fear of the Lord
and find the knowledge of God.

God loves you.

# BEING BORN AGAIN. March 15

John 1,
10 He came into the very world he created, but the world didn't recognize him. 11 He came to his own people, and even they rejected him. 12 But to all who believed him and accepted him, he gave the right to become children of God. 13 They are reborn—not with a physical birth resulting from human passion or plan, but a birth that comes from God.

What does being born again mean? It is not another physical birth, affecting your body. But it is a spiritual birth, affecting your soul, the eternal you! When your body is dead and turning back to dust, your soul, the very essence of who you are, will be in another place. If you have been born again, then you, your soul, will be with him in heaven. If you have not been born again, your soul will be in purgatory, waiting on the great Judgment Day.

Look at the story of Lazarus and the rich man:

Luke 16:22, the rich man also died and was buried, 23 and his soul went to the place of the dead. There, in torment, he saw Abraham in the far distance with Lazarus at his side. 24 "The rich man shouted, 'Father Abraham, have some pity! Send Lazarus over here to dip the tip of his finger in water and cool my tongue. I am in anguish in these flames.'

25 But Abraham said to him, 'Son, remember that during your lifetime you had everything you wanted, and Lazarus had nothing. So now he is here being comforted, and you are in anguish. 26 And besides, there is a great chasm separating us.

No one can cross over to you from here, and no one can cross over to us from there.'

When Jesus was speaking to Nicodemus, he told Him in John 3:5:

> Jesus replied, "I assure you, no one can enter the Kingdom of God without being born of water and the Spirit. 6 Humans can reproduce only human life, but the Holy Spirit gives birth to spiritual life. 7 So don't be surprised when I say, 'You must be born again.

Kids, this is a teaching lesson. You may be asked one day: how can I be born again? I want to go to heaven? Just remember, Jesus, our Creator and our Savior, said you must be born again!

Unbelievers will make fun of this phrase, but it is because they do not understand it.

Tell them when they accept Jesus as their Savior in their heart and repent of their sins, they are born again! And that comes with eternal life.

God loves you.

# THE PARABLE OF WHEAT AND WEEDS March 16

24Here is another story Jesus told: The Kingdom of heaven is like a farmer who planted good seed in his field. 25But that night as the workers slept, his enemy came and planted weeds among the wheat, then slipped away. 26When the crop began to grow and produce grain; the weeds also grew.

27"The farmer's workers went to him and said, 'Sir, the field where you planted that good seed is full of weeds! Where did they come from?'

28"'An enemy has done this!' the farmer exclaimed.

"'Should we pull out the weeds?' they asked.

29"'No,' he replied, 'you'll uproot the wheat if you do. 30Let both grow together until the harvest. Then I will tell the harvesters to sort out the weeds, tie them into bundles, and burn them, and to put the wheat in the barn.'"

Okay, kids, here is another parable; ponder this one and see what you think.

Try to determine who the players are. Who are the farmer and the workers? What does the seed and weeds represent? Who was the enemy? And most of all, how does it apply to you?

Now don't be reading in Matthew 13 and get ahead of us. I'll give the answers tomorrow.

God loves you.

# WHEAT AND WEEDS EXPLAINED. March 17

Jesus replied, "The Son of Man is the farmer who plants the good seed.38The field is the world, and the good seed represents the people of the Kingdom. The weeds are the people who belong to the evil one. 39The enemy who planted the weeds among the wheat is the devil. The harvest is the end of the world, and the harvesters are the angels.

40"Just as the weeds are sorted out and burned in the fire, so it will be at the end of the world. 41The Son of Man will send his angels, and they will remove from his Kingdom everything that causes sin and all who do evil. 42And the angels will throw them into the fiery furnace, where there will be weeping and gnashing of teeth. 43Then the righteous will shine like the sun in their Father's Kingdom. Anyone with ears to hear should listen and understand!

Well, did you get that one or did you have to read it to understand. We just went through a series on heaven and hell, so it should have been easy for you. The end times will be a big surprise for all the folks looking for rewards that are not biblical.

As many Bibles as there are on this earth nowadays, you would wonder how anyone could be surprised. But there will be many who do not have the answers to the parables about the Kingdom of heaven because they do not have ears to here. They have flow-through ears—in one side and out the other. They do not think eternity is important to them today. But when it comes, they will be the ones who say to Jesus, "I didn't think, I didn't know, I didn't read about you, but I, but I, how could you expect . . ."

Oh, but the children of God will be so blessed; they will be so happy in the Lord for the rest of eternity. Did I tell you how long eternity is? No? Well, it is because I can't count that high. There is no end to it.

Think about it!

God loves you.

# THE BOOK OF JOB. March 18

The book of Job is an interesting and sometimes hard to understand but very important book. I got some of this from D. Jeremiah.

God released Satan to test Job, a very righteous man, because Satan said to God, "Of course, he loves You; he has no reason not to. He is very blessed.

So, Satan took all his children and all his wealth away from him. Then he caused all kinds of physical problems for Job. So, Job was sitting around talking to his so-called friends and he said, "If only I had someone that could speak for me to God." Job realized that compared to God, he was nothing, absolutely nothing.

> No man can argue with God, because He is incomprehensible and invisible, if he walks by me I don't even know it. So how could anyone have an audience with Him, how could I even reason with Him? If I called on Him why would He take my call?

Job said if I could clean myself up the best I can, I would not be clean enough because I am only a man, and God is God and there is *no mediator*.

Job begs for someone to speak for him. Job said God is not a man, so how could I ever go before him? Job asked how a man can go before God the judge. A man can reason with a man but not an infinite perfect God who knows all and sees all (my paraphrase).

Do you have someone to speak to God for you? When you stand before the almighty God, who will speak for you? You will, you know. Every living soul that has ever been born and lived on this earth will stand before the Creator at the final judgment. You will need a mediator!

Because God is incomprehensible and invisible, and he can walk behind you and you would not know it, He knows all about you. Everything! Without a mediator, Jesus Christ, your sins would be exposed by His light and the worst words ever spoken would be spoken: "I never knew you"!

Hell would be real to you, without Jesus.

God loves you.

# IS JESUS YOUR MEDIATOR? March 19

Job asked who could speak to God for him. Job did not have the risen Savior, as his go between, *but we do*!

Jesus is the Man / God, He has one hand on us and one to God and we go through Jesus to get an audience with God.

In the great Judgment Day, which is nearer than we think, everyone will need a mediator, Jesus. If He knows you, you are heaven bound!

> Let me explain, Jesus said, "Not everyone who says to me, 'Lord, Lord,' will enter the kingdom of heaven, but only the one who does the will of my Father who is in heaven. 22 Many will say to me on that day, 'Lord, Lord, did we not prophesy in your name and in your name drive out demons and, in your name, perform many miracles?' 23 Then I will tell them plainly, 'I never knew you. Away from me, you evildoers!' (Matthew 7:21-23)

You will not get to God in heaven without your mediator, your Savior, your God/Man,

Jesus Christ, who came to us from heaven to be a man so that He could be the perfect sacrifice for all of our sins. You see, God is perfect, and if you have one little blemish, one little white lie, He can't look at you, and He can't accept you into His presence.

But God knew this, and that is why He sent His son to die for us. Now through Jesus,

God will accept you with open arms as one of His children.

P.S. Job did get his day before the judge. Read the book. God restored Job by giving him ten more children and ten times what he had before because Job's faith in God was unbreakable!

God loved and blessed him because he was a righteous man. God loves you.

# DEFINE FAITH! March 20

Hebrews 11:1 says, "Faith is the confidence that what we hope for will actually happen; it gives us assurance about things we cannot see."

Faith is not just hope! There is a lot of things we hope for. We can hope it doesn't rain, or we can hope it does rain. But because we don't know for sure, it is just a hope.

It is not just optimism! We can be optimistic about it raining or that something will come in the mail a certain day, but we don't know for sure; there are too many variables.

Faith is believing that God will do what He says He will, exactly when and how He says He will do it. That's where the confidence comes in—we believe it to be true. We have an assurance of it happening because God said it would happen, and He has an unquestionable track record. Whatever He has said would happen for thousands of years, happened exactly as He said it would.

We have not seen God, Jesus, or anything that we hope for, but we certainly have much evidence that He is, though we haven't seen Him with our eyes. And yet we have faith!

We are assured that what we believe is real and that what God says will happen, will happen! He said it and that is good enough for me. My faith tells me so.

But the strength of your faith is also important. How strong is your faith? Do you ever doubt your faith? How many would say, "There are times when I just don't know what I believe to be absolutely true"?

Peter the apostle denied Jesus three times, and he lived with Him for three years, ate with Him, and talked to Him, and yet he denied Him three times. How strong was his faith at that very moment? Not so much. But it grew to the point that he died for his faith.

I think the best way to strengthen your faith is to stay in His word daily. Worship every Sunday and fellowship with like-minded people. Work on it and build yourself an unmovable faith in our Lord Jesus, our God and Savior. Pray about it!

God loves you.

# JOSEPH AND THE BOSS'S WIFE. March 21

I suppose everyone knows the story of Joseph being the son of Israel, (Jacob), and the coat of many colors.

But do you know the story of Joseph and Potiphar's wife? Genesis 39

Potiphar's wife was "hot" as we might say today. Potiphar was very high up in the ranks of the Pharaoh of Egypt, and very wealthy, he would have had a very beautiful wife for sure.

Here is the story:

> From the time he put him in charge of his household and of all that he owned, the Lord blessed the household of the Egyptian because of Joseph. The blessing of the Lord was on everything Potiphar had, both in the house and in the field. 6So Potiphar left everything he had in Joseph's care; with Joseph in charge, he did not concern himself with anything accept the food he ate.
>
> Now Joseph was well-built and handsome, 7and after a while his master's wife took notice of Joseph and said, "Come to bed with me!"
>
> But he refused. "With me in charge," he told her, "my master does not concern himself with anything in the house; everything he owns he has entrusted to my care. 9No one is greater in this house than I am. My master has withheld nothing from me accept you, because you are his wife. How then could I do such a wicked thing and sin against God?" 10And though she spoke to Joseph day after day, he refused to go to bed with her or even be with her.
>
> One day he went into the house to attend to his duties, and none of the household servants was

inside. 12She caught him by his cloak and said,
"Come to bed with me!" But he left his cloak in
her hand and ran out of the house.

Okay kids what do think happens next?

Does he go back and get his coat and give in to her? Does he
keep running until he gets back to Israel? Or does he sit under a
big oak and try to figure out how to get out of this mess? Or none
of the above? Tune in tomorrow, to read "the rest of the story"!

Something to think about: Joseph said he would not sin
against God. Although it would have been a sin against Potiphar
and his wife, he was more concerned about sinning against God.
All sins we do are against God!

Love you

# JOSEPH AND THE BOSS's WIFE
## continued. March 22

You remember where we left off yesterday; what was your guess about Joseph's next move? Here is how it happened:

When she saw that he had left his cloak in her hand and had run out of the house, 14she called her household servants. "Look," she said to them, "this Hebrew has been brought to us to make sport of us! He came in here to sleep with me, but I screamed. 15When he heard me scream for help, he left his cloak beside me and ran out of the house." 16She kept his cloak beside her until his master came home. 17Then she told him this story: "That Hebrew slave you brought us came to me to make sport of me. 18But as soon as I screamed for help, he left his cloak beside me and ran out of the house."

When the master heard the story his wife told him, saying, "This is how your slave treated me," he burned with anger. 20Joseph's master took him and put him in prison, the place where the king's prisoners were confined.

But while Joseph was there in the prison, 21the Lord was with him; he showed him kindness and granted him favor in the eyes of the prison warden. 22So the warden put Joseph in charge of all those held in the prison, and he was made responsible for all that was done there. 23The warden paid no attention to anything under Joseph's care, because the Lord was with Joseph and gave him success in whatever he did.

When God is with you, wherever you are, He honors your faith you have in Him.

Joseph was wrongly accused of a very bad thing and was put in jail though he did not do the wrong thing and sleep with Potiphar's wife. God honored his decision. Now he was in charge of the jail, not quite as lucrative as a rich man's house, but he was still in a situation where he was running things. God knew Joseph was training for better things to come.

Joseph made the correct decision and had to go to jail. He chose jail instead of a very bad sin. Joseph was a good man, and this story is not nearly over. Think about this young man's willpower and integrity.

And think about this: God could have let it play out differently, but He didn't. He was with Joseph where he was, and He blessed him where he was. He does not always get us out of a jam, but He is always with us while we are in it. As you will see later in this story of a great man of God, He did not leave Joseph in the jail.

He blessed him with much!

God loves you.

# WHAT DID THE DONKEY SAY? March 23

Have you ever heard the story of the talking donkey? No, I didn't make it up, God actually gave the donkey the ability to rebuke his rider. Here is the story, and it is in Numbers 22. When the people of Israel were coming out of Egypt, they came to the land of the Moabites. The king was terrified, so he sent for a prophet to curse the Israelites, hoping they would move on and leave his people and land alone. The first time they asked the prophet Balaam, he said, "Absolutely not. The second time he said, "Well let me see if God has changed His mind." God did not change His mind, and He was angry about Balaam asking, but God told him to go with the men to the Moabite king. Then in verses 21–35 we read:

> So, the next morning Balaam got up, saddled his donkey, and started off with the Moabite officials. 22But God was angry that Balaam was going, so he sent the angel of the LORD to stand in the road to block his way. As Balaam and two servants were riding along, 23Balaam's donkey saw the angel of the LORD standing in the road with a drawn sword in his hand. The donkey bolted off the road into a field, but Balaam beat it and turned it back onto the road. 24Then the angel of the LORD stood at a place where the road narrowed between two vineyard walls. 25When the donkey saw the angel of the LORD, it tried to squeeze by and crushed Balaam's foot against the wall. So, Balaam beat the donkey again. 26Then the angel of the LORD moved farther down the road and stood in a place too narrow for the donkey to get by at all. 27This time when the donkey saw the angel, it lay down under Balaam. In a fit of rage Balaam beat the animal again with his staff. 28 Then the LORD gave the donkey the ability to speak. "What have

I done to you that deserves your beating me three times?" it asked Balaam. 29"You have made me look like a fool!" Balaam shouted. "If I had a sword with me, I would kill you!" 30"But I am the same donkey you have ridden all your life," the donkey answered. "Have I ever done anything like this before?" "No," Balaam admitted. 31 Then the LORD opened Balaam's eyes, and he saw the angel of the LORD standing in the roadway with a drawn sword in his hand. Balaam bowed his head and fell face down on the ground before him. 32"Why did you beat your donkey those three times?" the angel of the LORD demanded. "Look, I have come to block your way because you are stubbornly resisting me. 33Three times the donkey saw me and shied away; otherwise, I would certainly have killed you by now and spared the donkey." 34 Then Balaam confessed to the angel of the LORD, "I have sinned. I didn't realize you were standing in the road to block my way. I will return home if you are against my going."

35But the angel of the LORD told Balaam, "Go with these men, but say only what I tell you to say." So, Balaam went on with the King's officials.

You need to go to Numbers 22 and read the rest of the story; it is good and fun to read. Okay, so here is the question: who was the dummy, the donkey or Balaam?

Obviously, it was Balaam. Remember God can do whatever He wants or needs to do to get our attention, even using a talking donkey!

God loves you; by the way don't let anyone tell you that Numbers is just about a bunch of numbers.

# IS YOUR RESERVATION
# GUARANTEED? March 24

Did you ever make a reservation for whatever and have some reception person tell you they don't know you, never heard of you, there is no reservation in your name, and by the way they are all booked up? The last thing you want to hear after driving a long way is to get back in the car and go somewhere else. It has happened to me and probably some of you also.

There is one reservation you can absolutely count on being ready for you when you get there.

Listen to what Peter says in 1 Peter 1:3–6:

> All praise to God, the Father of our Lord Jesus
> Christ. It is by his great mercy that we have been
> born again, because God raised Jesus Christ from
> the dead. Now we live with great expectation, 4
> and we have a priceless inheritance — an inher-
> itance that is kept in heaven for you, pure and
> undefiled, beyond the reach of change and decay.
> 5 And through your faith, God is protecting you
> by his power until you receive this salvation,
> which is ready to be revealed on the last day for
> all to see.

Do you see what I see here? The moment you accepted Jesus as your Savior, your eternal Life began. Your inheritance is being kept in heaven for you and but not just kept but protected by God! Think of it: we have a reservation in heaven purchased by the blood of Christ and protected by God!

There won't be some celestial receptionist when you walk up to get your reservation that says, "Now what was your name again? I am so sorry we are booked, and I don't see your name here. Now how do you spell that again?"

No, after your long and painful journey in this life, you do not have to contend with nonsense. God is protecting your res-ervation in the place He has prepared just for you, and when He sees you coming, His arms will be wide open to accept you in to His eternal family as a child of His, forever!

Now here is the question: are you living every day with the expectation of receiving your inheritance that is protected and waiting for you?

Would you look forward to a reservation in a nice motel on a beach, all expenses paid? Yes, I am sure you would just as I would because you have seen the beach and enjoyed it. But it is nothing next to what is to come. The very best you have ever enjoyed is nothing to the reservation you have in His house.

Spend some time laying on your back, looking up at heaven some night, and try to imagine that glorious day!

God loves you.

# THE THIEF ON THE CROSS NEXT TO JESUS. March 25

Luke 23:39–43, 39-One of the criminals who hung there hurled insults at him: "Aren't you the Messiah? Save yourself and us!"

40-But the other criminal rebuked him. "Don't you fear God," he said, "since you are under the same sentence? 41-We are punished justly, for we are getting what our deeds deserve. But this man has done nothing wrong."

42-Then he said, "Jesus, remember me when you come into your kingdom."

43-Jesus answered him, "Truly I tell you, today you will be with me in paradise."

One thief repented, and one did not. One went to paradise, and one did not!

Now think about the thief who rebuked the other thief for persecuting Jesus while on the cross. His life was a shamble; he was a robber. He was probably one of many robbers who would wait just outside of town and rob unsuspecting travelers. Most all of the people walked or rode donkeys from town to town; the only folks that had horses were the Romans. They would not let the locals have horses for fear they would start an uprising.

But it does not say he was a murderer, so maybe he was a robber with a little compassion for his fellow man. But what matters is, while on his cross, he rebuked the person speaking badly about Jesus and he repented of his evil ways when he said we are getting what we deserve for our deeds. Then he asked Jesus if He would save him.

The good news is Jesus told him; that "this very day you will be with Me in paradise"!

What an awesome scripture that speaks to every soul that has ever lived.

> Luke 11:9, Jesus speaking, "So I say to you: Ask and it will be given to you; seek and you will find; knock and the door will be opened to you."

The thief knocked, and Jesus opened the door to paradise for Him.

God loves you.

# HE ENTERED JERUSALEM ON A DONKEY. March 26

Zechariah 9:9, Rejoice greatly, Daughter Zion!

Shout, Daughter Jerusalem! See, your king comes to you, righteous and victorious,

Lowly and riding on a donkey, on a colt, the foal of a donkey.

This was the prophecy that all of Israel waited for, their Messiah entering Jerusalem to rule as the King.

Luke 19, 35-They brought the donkey to Jesus, threw their cloaks on the colt and put Jesus on it. 36-As he went along, people spread their cloaks on the road. 37-When he came near the place where the road goes down the Mount of Olives, the whole crowd of disciples began joyfully to praise God in loud voices for all the miracles they had seen:

38-"Blessed is the king who comes in the name of the Lord!" "Peace in heaven and glory in the highest!" 39-Some of the Pharisees in the crowd said to Jesus, "Teacher, rebuke your disciples!"

40-"I tell you," he replied, "If they keep quiet, the stones will cry out."

The people were unable to present Him with costly gifts, but they spread their coats out as a carpet in His path for him to ride on, and they also spread out branches of the palm in the way. They waved the branches in order to honor a victorious leader entering the city—what a joyous occasion! This was a festive time in Israel because many people had come for the Passover, and everyone got caught up in the dream of a David-like king who would liberate Israel from the Roman devils who were oppressing their lives.

But the Pharisees told Jesus to rebuke these people for treating Him like a king (they did not believe), but Jesus told them if they don't, the rocks will!

But the same crowd would just as easily turn on Him in less than a week and shout out, *"Crucify Him!"*

We, the sinful people, are the reason for what would happen the rest of the coming week, but He loves us anyway!

# THEY BEAT HIM FRIDAY! March 27

The fact is, in order for us to get to Easter, we have to go through Friday. We have to think of what our Lord went through on Friday before we can rejoice on Easter Sunday.

First, He was flogged with a whip with steel balls and bones braided in the straps, probably thirty-nine or more times. When a Roman soldier was doing it, a normal person might not survive it. He would have been whipped from the shoulders, down the back and legs; it would cause heavy bruises and deep contusions. *

It was a demonic thing to do to a person.

After the beating, He was in critical condition from the loss of blood. *

The mere thought of having to go through a beating like this would cause a man to go into shock.

Remember Jesus is God, and he is omniscient, meaning all knowing. He knew about every lash for a long time and as a human in the garden before He was arrested, He prayed all night to see if this cup of suffering could pass—and for the strength to get through it—but He also said, "Father not my will but your will be done."

During this time, he was sweating blood, and this is not a metaphor; it is a medical condition, called hematidrosis. * It occurs when people are facing death or other highly stressful events. They can sweat blood.

So, He knew exactly what was going to happen on Friday, and yet because of His love for me and you, He went through this willingly. It was part of the salvation plan, the sacrifice for sin.

Obviously, He loves you.

*Notes from *The Case for Christ* by Lee Strobel

# THEY NAILED HIS HANDS, FRIDAY
## continued. March 28

After the hellacious beating that Jesus took from the Roman soldiers, He then had to carry His cross to Golgotha, the hill that they crucified Him on, as best as He could.

When He arrived, they would have laid Him down with His arms stretched out across the cross beam. Then they nailed his hands to the beam with five- to seven-inch spikes. They actually nailed his wrist because a spike in the palm would not have held up His weight; the hand would have ripped and He would have fallen off the cross. The place where they nailed Him is also the place where the median nerve runs, about an inch below the hand. The pain experienced by a spike going into the median nerve was indescribable, as a matter of fact; later on, they had to come up with a new word for the pain, "excruciating."

Origin of the English word *excruciating*: The word *excruciating* comes from Latin *excruciare*, from *cruciare*, to crucify. It means unbearably painful, or extreme agony. The word *excruciating* originates from crucifixion, that is, "a pain like the pain of crucifixion."

Think about that: there were no words in their language to describe the pain because it was so intense, so they invented a new word for the torture.

Most everyone has hit your funny bone, or the ulna nerve and experienced the pain from that; now think about cutting that nerve or twisting it with a pair of pliers. That would be similar to a spike in the median nerve in the wrist. *

Inflicting excruciating pain, the Romans were demon-possessed barbarians!

But Jesus knew what would happen, and because He loves us, He let them have their way with Him.

*The Case for Christ* by Lee Strobel

# THEN THEY NAILED HIS FEET, FRIDAY! March 29

They have nailed His hands to the cross. We said they actually nailed His wrist, in the language of the day this part of the wrist was considered the hand also. The pain was absolutely unbearable. At this point Jesus was raised up, and His feet were nailed with spikes to the vertical part of the cross. The spikes crushing nerves in his feet just as they did in His hands, once again, inflicting excruciating pain! Think of everything His body was going through at this point—cuts and bruises from the beating, hands nailed and feet nailed to the wooden beams. The physical stress on the body was at its peak! It would be hard to take a deep breath. He would have to push his body up with His feet (scratching his cut and bruised back on the wooden beam) that were nailed to the cross to exhale a breath.

Then the arms would begin to stretch until His shoulders became dislocated.

> Psalm 22, 14 I am poured out like water, and all my bones are out of joint. My heart has turned to wax; it has melted within me. 15-My mouth is dried up like a potsherd, and my tongue sticks to the roof of my mouth; you lay me in the dust of death. 16-Dogs surround me, a pack of villains encircles me; they pierce my hands and my feet.
>
> 17-All my bones are on display; people stare and gloat over me.
>
> 18-They divide my clothes among them and cast lots for my garment.

This was written about Jesus dying on the cross before this evil way of torturing a human being had been invented, and the Holy Spirit gave the psalmist the words of the sacrifice that would save all of our souls.

Why would God send His Son to be our sacrifice and go through this unbearable death?

Because God loves you and wants you to choose to live eternally with Him in the place He has prepared for you!

# FRIDAY, PETER DENIED HIM THREE TIMES. March 30

Simon Peter's denial of Jesus is recorded in all four Gospels. Jesus predicted that Peter would deny Him three times before the rooster's crow the next morning.

After they arrested Jesus and took Him to the chief priest, Peter was warming by a fire and over a short period of time, they kept asking him, "Aren't you one of the disciples?" Peter said, "No, I am not" three different times, and the last time he heard the rooster crow.

Think about it: Peter said just a short time before, "Lord I am ready to go to prison or even die for you!" Then one time after another, he said "Who me? I don't know Him!"

Satan thought he won that round; one disciple sold Him out, and another denied he ever knew Him.

This came after three years of living with Jesus and seeing one absolutely amazing miracle after another day after day. And yet, "I don't know him; not me, I was not with Him!"

Judas said, "I will take thirty pieces of silver." Satan was thinking, *I have them now.*

But God is said, "Carry on, Son, with My plan!"

Peter did not know at the time he denied Jesus that God's plan was unfolding as predicted—right on schedule. Peter's sins would be forgiven for the rest of his life.

His sins, along with yours and mine, would be covered by Jesus' blood dripping off the cross. Peter's faith was tested, and his spirit was very low, but soon it would be very strong when he led thousands to eternal salvation at the Day of Pentecost.

Do you want your spirit to be as strong as Peter's when he led all those people to Christ?

Well, do what he did; talk about Jesus to someone who is lost and needs Jesus Christ's salvation!

Christianity is a personal, one-on-one thing with Jesus, but then it becomes public, with you one on one with those who need what you received, salvation!

God loves you.

# DIRECT ACCESS TO THE FATHER. March 31

> Luke 23:44–46, 44-It was now about noon, and darkness came over the whole land until three in the afternoon, 45-for the sun stopped shining. And the curtain of the temple was torn in two. 46-Jesus called out with a loud voice, "Father, into your hands I commit my spirit." When he had said this, he breathed his last.

Have you ever wondered what the purpose of the curtain was that separated the Holy of Holies from the rest of the Temple?

Listen to Hebrews 9:7: "but only the high priest entered the inner room, and that, only once a year, and never without blood, which he offered for himself and for the sins the people had committed in ignorance."

No one else but the High Priest had direct access to the Holy of Holies. Anyone else who entered was killed. But that was before the Messiah, Jesus Christ came to dwell among us and be our sacrifice for all our sins.

So, the presence of God remained shielded from man behind a thick curtain during the history of Israel. But the curtain was torn from top to bottom. Only God could have carried out such an incredible feat because the veil was too high for human hands to have reached it and too thick to have torn it. Furthermore, the way it was torn was from top down, meaning this act must have come from above.

Now that Jesus has come and sacrificed Himself for us, we all have access to the Father through Jesus. So what purpose would the curtain serve now if they had a Temple? None what so ever! That is why God ripped it from the top down.

Jesus is the curtain, or Mediator, between us and our Father. We no longer need the curtain, the priest, or the Temple. Jesus is our Holy Priest and our bodies are the Temple of the Holy Spirit! We can speak directly to the Father or Jesus or the Holy Spirit anytime!

Thank you, Jesus, for the love you showed us and Your perfect sacrifice!

# JESUS IS ALIVE! EASTER SUNDAY! April 1

On Sunday morning, many people saw Him alive. Over the next forty days, over five hundred people saw Him alive. The tomb was empty. It was guarded by Roman soldiers, and yet Jesus left the tomb without moving the stone that sealed the tomb. An angel came down and rolled the stone away, not for Jesus to leave, but so that the woman could see that Jesus was gone.

But now Jesus was different. It wasn't like He was dead and then He came back to life, like Lazarus did when Jesus called him out of his grave only to die again.

Jesus was much different; he appeared and disappeared at will. Jesus was raised unlike anyone before Him. His body had been transformed from a human body to a glorified body. He would never die again. He could eat and drink, and yet walk through walls!

Many people touched Him!

He told Thomas to touch his side where the spear pierced His body.

He cooked a meal for Peter and some of His disciples and ate with them.

Then at the end of the forty days, he ascended into heaven while the disciples watched.

Every Easter, Christians make the claim that Jesus is alive!

He left heaven to be the perfect sacrifice. He came, and He lived a perfect sinless life so that we, the sinners that sent Him to the cross, can be saved to live eternally with our merciful Holy God and Savior.

Praise His Holy name!

When the women looked in the tomb, the angel told them, "He is not here, for *He has risen*, just as He said He would!"

# JESUS APPEARS TO MARY MAGDALENE! April 2

John 20:11-Now Mary stood outside the tomb crying. As she wept, she bent over to look into the tomb 12-and saw two angels in white, seated where Jesus' body had been, one at the head and the other at the foot. 13 They asked her, "Woman, why are you crying?"

"They have taken my Lord away," she said, "and I don't know where they have put him." 14-At this, she turned around and saw Jesus standing there, but she did not realize that it was Jesus.

15-He asked her, "Woman, why are you crying? Who is it you are looking for?"

Thinking he was the gardener, she said, "Sir, if you have carried him away, tell me where you have put him, and I will get him."

16-Jesus said to her, "Mary."
She turned toward him and cried out in Aramaic, "Rabboni!" (Which means "Teacher").

Can you just imagine the excitement at that instant when Mary realized it was Jesus standing there? Think of all the emotions Mary was feeling. She was devastated that Jesus was dead, and now she thinks someone has moved the body. She must have thought, who would do such a thing? Then maybe at her breaking point, Jesus said, "Mary!"

When have you felt Him near you? Anytime you feel you are right on the edge, Jesus is there.

"Mary," I AM is here!
*I AM! He is! He always was!*
*He will always, be there for you!*
Praise our Risen Savior! He loves us so!

# PETER WENT FISHING! April 3

While the disciples were sitting around, not really knowing what they needed to do, Peter said, "I am going fishing." This he knew how to do. So, he and several of the other disciples went and fished all night. John tells us the story in John 21:

> 4-Early in the morning, Jesus stood on the shore, but the disciples did not realize that it was Jesus. 5-He called out to them, "Friends, haven't you any fish?" "No," they answered.
>
> 6-He said, "Throw your net on the right side of the boat and you will find some." When they did, they were unable to haul the net in because of the large number of fish.

With Jesus all things are possible, but Jesus called Peter and the disciples to be fishers of men, not fishermen. What have you been called to do?

Going fishing can mean a lot of different things in today's world. These things are really called distractions. They are things we do when we are not sure what we are supposed to do, like going fishing! Are you doing what God has called you to do, or have you gone fishing? Be honest with yourself and God when you answer the question!

There are many times when we are not sure what we need to be doing, but instead of going fishing, why not go to the prayer closet?

When you get to a place where it is just you and the Lord, He will lay a name or a verse on your heart or whatever it is you are called to do. Peter went fishing, and Jesus came to where he was, and sent him out to feed the Lord's sheep.

A beautiful passage is at the end of chapter 21, where Jesus reinstates Peter. Remember he knocked himself down when he denied Jesus, but then Jesus picked him back up and sent him on his mission.

If you are gone fishing, speak to Jesus about it. He will pick you up, brush you off, and send you on your way.

God loves you so much!

# THE RESURRECTION! April 4

1 Corinthians 15, Bible Translation "The Message"

42–44 This image of planting a dead seed and raising a live plant is a mere sketch at best, but perhaps it will help in approaching the mystery of the resurrection body—but only if you keep in mind that when we're raised, we're raised for good, alive forever! The corpse that's planted is no beauty, but when it's raised, it's glorious. Put in the ground weak, it comes up powerful. The seed sown is natural; the seed grown is supernatural—same seed, same body, but what a difference from when it goes down in physical mortality to when it is raised up in spiritual immortality!

51–57 but let me tell you something wonderful, a mystery I'll probably never fully understand. We're not all going to die—but we are all going to be changed. You hear a blast to end all blasts from a trumpet, and in the time that you look up and blink your eyes—it's over. On signal from that trumpet from heaven, the dead will be up and out of their graves, beyond the reach of death, never to die again. At the same moment and in the same way, we'll all be changed. In the resurrection scheme of things, this has to happen: everything perishable taken off the shelves and replaced by the imperishable, this mortal replaced by the immortal.

58 With all this going for us, my dear, dear friends, stand your ground. And don't hold back. Throw yourselves into the work of the Master,

confident that nothing you do for him is a waste
of time or effort.

Inside your body is the blueprint for your resurrection body.
You may not be satisfied with your current body or mind, but
you'll be thrilled with your resurrection upgrades. With them,
you'll be better able to serve and glorify God and enjoy an eternity of wonders He has prepared for you.
God loves you so much!

# JESUS APPEARS TO DIDYMUS. April 5

John 20:24, Now Thomas (also known as Didymus) one of the Twelve, was not with the disciples when Jesus came. 25-So the other disciples told him, "We have seen the Lord!"

But he said to them, "Unless I see the nail marks in his hands and put my finger where the nails were, and put my hand into his side, I will not believe."

26-A week later his disciples were in the house again, and Thomas was with them. Though the doors were locked, Jesus came and stood among them and said, "Peace be with you!" 27-Then he said to Thomas, "Put your finger here; see my hands. Reach out your hand and put it into my side. Stop doubting and believe." 28-Thomas said to him, "My Lord and my God!"

29-Then Jesus told him, "Because you have seen me, you have believed; blessed are those who have not seen and yet have believed."

Who are those who have not seen and yet believed?

There are millions, and that includes you and me! We cannot see His physical glorified body yet, but I know I can see Him in a flower or in a beautiful bird soaring in the sky or the waves coming in to shore. There are so many ways to see our Lord and Savior in all the things He is doing in and through us.

Don't be like doubting Thomas! Thomas could not believe what others told him; he had to see it for himself.

He saw the excitement and the hope in their eyes and their smiles, but it was not enough for him; he needed proof!

"Blessed are those who have not seen Him, and yet still believe."

When you give your heart to Him, you will see Him everywhere and in everything you do in many different ways.

I see Him every day writing these daily letters through me. He is doing it, not me.

Thank you, Jesus, for loving us!

# THERE ARE MORE ON OUR SIDE THAN ON THEIRS. April 6

Once there was a king of Aram who was at war with Israel. God was telling the prophet Elisha the bad king's every move to the point the king thought, *we must have a traitor among us.*

> 2 Kings 6:11–23
> 11The king of Aram became very upset over this. He called his officers together and demanded, "Which of you is the traitor? Who has been informing the king of Israel of my plans?"12"It's not us, my lord the king," one of the officers replied. "Elisha, the prophet in Israel, tells the king of Israel even the words you speak in the privacy of your bedroom!"13"Go and find out where he is," the king commanded, "So I can send troops to seize him. And the report came back: "Elisha is at Dothan." 14So one night the king of Aram sent a great army with many chariots and horses to surround the city.
>
> 15When the servant of the man of God got up early the next morning and went outside, there were troops, horses, and chariots everywhere. "Oh, sir, what will we do now?" the young man cried to Elisha.
>
> 16"Don't be afraid!" Elisha told him. "For there are more on our side than on theirs!" 17Then Elisha prayed, "O LORD, open his eyes and let him see!" The LORD opened the young man's eyes, and when he looked up, he saw that the hillside around Elisha was filled with horses and chariots of fire.

18As the Aramean army advanced toward him, Elisha prayed, "O LORD, please make them blind." So, the LORD struck them with blindness as Elisha had asked. 19Then Elisha went out and told them, "You have come the wrong way! This isn't the right city! Follow me, and I will take you to the man you are looking for." And he led them to the city of Samaria. 20As soon as they had entered Samaria, Elisha prayed, "O LORD, now open their eyes and let them see." So, the LORD opened their eyes, and they discovered that they were in the middle of Samaria.

21When the king of Israel saw them, he shouted to Elisha, "My father, should I kill them? Should I kill them?" (They had them completely surrounded) 22"Of course not!" Elisha replied. "Do we kill prisoners of war? Give them food and drink and send them home again to their master."23So the king made a great feast for them and then sent them home to their master. After that, the Aramean raiders stayed away from the land of Israel.

Elisha, the prophet of God, asked God to blind the army, and he walked them right into a trap, which was the best thing that could have happened to them. Kids, listen: did you get the fact that there were chariots of fire with angels ready to be called down to destroy the bad king? One of the angels with his chariot of fire could have killed all of them. Remember, when you have God on your side, who could ever be against you? There are more with you than with them!
God loves you.

# THIS INCLUDES YOU. April 7

Colossians 1:20b, 21–23, 10, NLT

He made peace with everything in heaven and on earth, by means of Christ's blood on the cross.

21-This includes you who were once far away from God. You were his enemies, separated from him by your evil thoughts and actions. 22-Yet now he has reconciled you to himself through the death of Christ in his physical body. As a result, he has brought you into his own presence, and you are holy and blameless as you stand before him without a single fault.

23-But you must continue to believe this truth and stand firmly in it. Don't drift away from the assurance you received when you heard the Good News. The Good News has been preached all over the world, and I, Paul, have been appointed as God's servant to proclaim it.

10-Then the way you live will always honor and please the Lord, and your lives will produce every kind of good fruit. All the while, you will grow as you learn to know God better and better.

The best way I know to learn and grow is to study your Bible and meet with other believers on a regular basis. Then live it, and share the gospel. Have you dusted off your Bible yet?

God loves you.

# DO YOU THANK THE FATHER FOR THE HOLY SPIRIT? April 8

John 16:7–151
But now I am going away to the one who sent me, and not one of you is asking where I am going. 6Instead, you grieve because of what I've told you. 7But in fact, it is best for you that I go away, because if I don't, the Advocate won't come. If I do go away, then I will send him to you. 8And when he comes, he will convict the world of its sin, and of God's righteousness, and of the coming judgment. 9The world's sin is that it refuses to believe in me. 10Righteousness is available because I go to the Father, and you will see me no more. 11Judgment will come because the ruler of this world has already been judged. 12"There is so much more I want to tell you, but you can't bear it now. 13When the Spirit of truth comes, he will guide you into all truth. He will not speak on his own but will tell you what he has heard. He will tell you about the future. 14He will bring me glory by telling you whatever he receives from me. 15All that belongs to the Father is mine; this is why I said, 'The Spirit will tell you whatever he receives from me.'

I think every day we should thank God the Father and God the Son for sending us the Spirit of truth, our great God the Holy Spirit.

Think about it: how could you make it through some days, weeks, or months without Him holding you up?

He is the One who whispers in your ear which way to go or not go. He is our Comforter, and He cries with us and lets us know that it will be okay because God is in control! He gives us sweet encouraging words to share with others. These things He does for us are good, but we can't even think of what He does for us as an Advocate! Look at the words that describe advocate: supporter, fighter, proponent, promoter, spokesperson, crusader, campaigner, and backer! Get the idea? He is on your side, fighting for what is best for you and supporting the things you do. He is your helper, and most important of all of this—He is your God!

Thank you, Holy Spirit, for all you do for us, even those things you do that we are not even aware of. Thank you, Father God and Jesus our Savior, for sending Him to us!

God is in control!

God loves you.

# ARE THERE ALIENS ON EARTH? April 9

Yes, there are many aliens living here temporarily. They are strangers to this world, waiting for the day to come when they can go home.

Okay, Pop, have you been watching too many science fiction movies? Well what would you say if I told you I was one of them? Look at what Peter says about it in 1 Peter 2:11, "Dear friends, I urge you as aliens and strangers in the world, to abstain from fleshly desires, which war against your soul."

How could we be called aliens and strangers to this world?

This world is not our home! We do not belong here. We were once citizens of this world and its dark and evil ways, but now we are on a path to our new home. We are aliens here, a different people living among the people of this world. Suppose you flew into another country that spoke a foreign language. You could not communicate with them; you would not understand their TV or radio. But if you start to learn their language, you can communicate with them though you are still aliens to them. You can live among those in this world, but we are not to conform to their ways.

Yes, we are now citizens of God's kingdom called heaven. We were delivered from the darkness by the Light of this world, Jesus Christ. Therefore, Philippians 3:20 says, "for our citizenship is in heaven, from which we also eagerly wait for the Savior, the Lord Jesus Christ."

He is coming to take us home one day soon, so Peter says, "Do not be conformed to this world but abstain from fleshly desires that war against your soul."

Peter says to conduct yourselves honorably among the folks so that in case where they speak against you, they will by observing your good works and glorify God on the day of the visitation.

Be a good alien, but stay an alien, separated from the ways of the dark side!

God loves you.

# ELIJAH FED BY RAVENS. April 10

Once there was a very bad king of Israel named Ahab. He did evil things in the sight of the Lord above. He set up the worshipping of idols and violated the commandments of God. So, God told the prophet Elijah to tell the people that because of this terrible sin, it would not rain and there would be no dew on the ground until God said it would.

Then he told Elijah to leave town for a while because the king's anger would grow toward Elijah. Here is the story;

> 1 Kings 17:2–6
> Elijah, who was from Tishbe in Gilead, told King Ahab, "As surely as the LORD, the God of Israel, lives—the God I serve—there will be no dew or rain during the next few years until I give the word!"

> 2 Then the LORD said to Elijah, 3 "Go to the east and hide by Kerith Brook, near where it enters the Jordan River. 4 Drink from the brook and eat what the ravens bring you, for I have commanded them to bring you food."

> 5 So Elijah did as the LORD told him and camped beside Kerith Brook, east of the Jordan. 6 The ravens brought him bread and meat each morning and evening, and he drank from the brook.

We serve an awesome God. He can make donkeys talk, and He can feed a hungry man by using the birds.

Now when you get to thinking that your problem is too big for God or maybe you just think God is too busy to be bothered by your problems, look up and try to count the birds that He has at His fingertips if He needs them. God sent Elijah on a camping trip and provided all of his needs, in what we would consider a somewhat unusual way. But how many times have you seen the workings of God in a usual way? I would bet not many. His ways are not our ways.

He loves you very much and wants the best for you. Today when you see a bird, put a smile on your face!

God created the birds; what was to keep Him from using them. By the way He created you also, what is keeping Him from using you?

God loves you.

# GOD ALWAYS PROVIDES! April 11

Jesus said, "Why do you worry, look at the birds of the air: they do not sow or reap or store away in barns, and yet your heavenly Father feeds them. Are you not much more valuable than they?"

There is the story of Elijah in which God told Him to go and live with a widow woman and her boy. God said she will feed you. When Elijah got there, the woman was in the process of making her last loaf of bread because she was very poor and her supplies were running out. Here is the story:

> 1 Kings 17:8–16
> Then the LORD said to Elijah, 9 "Go and live in the village of Zarephath, near the city of Sidon. I have instructed a widow there to feed you." 10 So he went to Zarephath. As he arrived at the gates of the village, he saw a widow gathering sticks, and he asked her, "Would you please bring me a little water in a cup?" 11 As she was going to get it, he called to her, "Bring me a bite of bread, too. "But she said, "I swear by the LORD your God that I don't have a single piece of bread in the house. And I have only a handful of flour left in the jar and a little cooking oil in the bottom of the jug. I was just gathering a few sticks to cook this last meal, and then my son and I will die."13 But Elijah said to her, "Don't be afraid! Go ahead and do just what you've said, but make a little bread for me first. Then use what's left to prepare a meal for yourself and your son. 14 For this is what the LORD, the God of Israel, says: There will always be flour and olive oil left in your containers until the time when the LORD sends rain and the crops grow again!"

So, she did as Elijah said, and she and Elijah and her family continued to eat for many days. 16 There was always enough flour and olive oil left in the containers, just as the LORD had promised through Elijah.

Did you get that there was always enough for them to eat? God provided for their needs, just as He will provide for yours. When the widow looked in the jar of oil, there was just enough for the day, and when she looked at her flour there was just enough. There was never an overabundance but always just enough.

He will always give you what you need; are you not more valuable that the birds?

Now it did not say they had steak and salad and drove the best-looking chariot everywhere they went, but God provided for their needs. God loves His children and He will take care of us.

Have a great day, our God provides!

God loves you.

# THE CURTAIN WAS TORN IN TWO FROM TOP TO BOTTOM! April 12

The curtain in the temple was said to be sixty feet high and thirty feet wide. It was a magnificent piece of work. There is much debate as to how thick it was; most say about four inches thick. When it got soiled it took three hundred temple workers to maneuver it. It was replaced every year. Two very strong horses could not tear it apart.

Listen to what happened to it at the time Jesus died; it's in Matthew 27:50–54:

> And when Jesus had cried out again in a loud voice, he gave up his spirit.
>
> 51At that moment the curtain of the temple was torn in two from top to bottom. The earth shook, the rocks split 52and the tombs broke open. The bodies of many holy people who had died were raised to life. 53They came out of the tombs after Jesus' resurrection and went into the holy city and appeared to many people.
>
> 54When the centurion and those with him who were guarding Jesus saw the earthquake and all that had happened, they were terrified, and exclaimed, "Surely he was the Son of God!"

There is only one way the curtain could have been torn from top down—God did it!

The reason is because now we all have access to the Father. Before Christ's death, only the chosen priest could enter the place where the Ark was kept behind the curtain. This place was called the Holy of Holies. Once a year on Yom Kippur, the Day of Atonement, the priest would enter the Holy of Holies with the blood of the lamb to atone for the sins of the Jewish people.

Now there is no need for the temple or the Ark or the curtain. Now that the Son of God was sacrificed for all our sins by the shedding of His blood, if we accept Him into our hearts, we can have a relationship with the Father without the Ark, without the Temple, and without the curtain that stood between God and His people. We now have direct access to the Father through His Son. Jesus is our Priest and our Savior, and we can talk to Him anytime, anywhere, and about anything.

Have you thanked Him today for His sacrifice for you? You can you now because the curtain was torn from the top down, and you now have access to Him.

God loves you.

# THE LORD CONFUSED THE ARMY TO DEATH! April 13

There once was a leader of Israel named Jehoshaphat. He heard that there was a large army gathering to destroy Israel. So, he gathered all the people and prayed to God, and God told him not to worry. Here is the story;

2 Chronicles 20
King Jehoshaphat bowed low with his face to the ground. And all the people of Judah and Jerusalem did the same, worshiping the LORD. 19Then the Levites from the clans of Kohath and Korah stood to praise the LORD, the God of Israel, with a very loud shout.

20Early the next morning the army of Judah went out into the wilderness of Tekoa. On the way Jehoshaphat stopped and said, "Listen to me, all you people of Judah and Jerusalem! Believe in the LORD your God, and you will be able to stand firm. Believe in his prophets, and you will succeed."21After consulting the people, the king appointed singers to walk ahead of the army, singing to the LORD and praising him for his holy splendor. This is what they sang:

Give thanks to the Lord, His faithful love endures forever.

At the very moment they began to sing and give praise, the LORD caused the armies of Ammon, Moab, and Mount Seir to start fighting among themselves. 23The armies of Moab and Ammon turned against their allies from Mount Seir and killed every one of them. After they had destroyed the army of Seir, they began attacking each other. 24So when the army of Judah arrived at the lookout point in the wilderness, all they saw were dead bodies lying on the ground as far as they could see. Not a single one of the enemy had escaped.

25King Jehoshaphat and his men went out to gather the plunder. They found vast amounts of equipment, clothing, and other valuables—more than they could carry. There was so much plunder that it took them three days just to collect it all! 26On the fourth day they gathered in the Valley of Blessing, which got its name that day because the people praised and thanked the LORD there. It is still called the Valley of Blessing today.

How many of you would have thought, *to defeat these guys we have to confuse them and turn them against themselves?*

We do not think like God! He takes care of our problems in ways we cannot even think of. Praise your Father in heaven for His wonderful wisdom, and pray that He will gives you wisdom also!

God loves you.

# THE END TIMES OR THE NEW BEGINNING? April 14

When we think of the end times, all sorts of things come to mind, such as the Rapture, The thousand-year reign of Christ, the Judgment Day, the antichrist, the seven-year tribulation, and heaven and hell. What do think about when the end times comes up? According to David Jeremiah, everyone is asking, "Is this the end?"

One thing is absolutely sure about the end times, we are 2,000 years closer to it than the disciples were. Are you looking forward to it or are you afraid of it? Maybe you just don't care to think about it.

I would say, if you believe in the Rapture, you probably are looking forward to the end of time. As a matter of fact, you might even be saying, "Lord, please come today!"

If you are a Christian, is it the end of times or the new beginning of eternal life? Look at what Jesus says about the end of days:

> Matthew 24
> No one knows the day or hour when these things will happen, not even the angels in heaven or the Son himself. Only the Father knows.
>
> 37"When the Son of Man returns, it will be like it was in Noah's day. 38In those days before the flood, the people were enjoying banquets and parties and weddings right up to the time Noah entered his boat. 39People didn't realize what was going to happen until the flood came and swept them all away. That is the way it will be when the Son of Man comes.
>
> 40"Two men will be working together in the field; one will be taken, the other left.41Two

women will be grinding flour at the mill; one will be taken, the other left.

42"So you, too, must keep watch! For you don't know what day your Lord is coming. 43Understand this: If a homeowner knew exactly when a burglar was coming, he would keep watch and not permit his house to be broken into.44You also must be ready all the time, for the Son of Man will come when least expected.

Do you think the world is much like it was in Noah's time? I sure do; just look at the news.

Jesus says no man knows the day or hour, so you must be ready all the time.

When the end comes it will be the beginning for the Christians, the beginning of eternity with the Father and the Son and the Holy Spirit. What a glorious new beginning.

God loves you.

# WHAT CAN A SMALL GROUP DO FOR GOD? April 15

I knew a small group in Georgia years ago. They started out with a Bible study on Thursday nights. All they did was read through parts of the Bible and discuss it as they went. They prayed before and after each session. People were added to the group by invitation, and souls were saved. One night they begin to talk about what they could do to improve the Wednesday night service at their church; there was not at that time a Wednesday night meal. So, they chose to start one, thinking that a meal would make it easier for folks to bring the kids to Royal Ambassadors and Girls in Action. They started with fifty or sixty eating and several years after that, they were averaging over three hundred. RAs and GAs were booming, with kids having fun and learning about the Lord.

Listen to what God says about it; Isaiah 55:3–11:

> Come to me with your ears wide open. Listen, and you will find life. I will make an ever-lasting covenant with you. I will give you all the unfailing love I promised to David.
>
> 4See how I used him to display my power among the peoples. I made him a leader among the nations. 5You also will command nations you do not know, and peoples unknown to you will come running to obey, because I, the LORD your God, the Holy One of Israel, have made you glorious."6Seek the LORD while you can find him. Call on him now while he is near. 7Let the wicked change their ways and banish the very thought of doing wrong. Let them turn to the LORD that he may have mercy on them. Yes, turn to our God, for he will forgive generously. 8"My thoughts are nothing like your thoughts," says the LORD. "And my ways are far beyond

anything you could imagine. 9For just as the heavens are higher than the earth, so my ways are higher than your ways and my thoughts higher than your thoughts. 10"The rain and snow come down from the heavens and stay on the ground to water the earth. They cause the grain to grow, producing seed for the farmer and bread for the hungry. 11It is the same with my word.

I send it out, and it always produces fruit. It will accomplish all I want it to, and it will prosper everywhere I send it.

If God said it you better believe it!

Try it and see what God can do through you. Those people were blessed by God for saying, "We can do this with His help." And they did! They never imagined what God would do through them. Small groups studying God's word can change this city or state or even the nation if God wants them to! He is waiting for you to say, "I will!" Anyone can start a group; all you need is a Bible and a few willing people.

God loves you.

# THE SUN STOOD STILL FOR JOSHUA. April 16

Have you ever had a day that you thought, *if only the sun would last a little longer*? Maybe you were at the beach or by the pool. I am sure all of us have been in a situation where we were enjoying God's creation so much that we wished it would last a little longer. I know I have had days like that. Well, Joshua needed it to last for a different reason; here is the story:

> Joshua 10:12–14
> On the day the LORD gave the Israelites victory over the Amorites, Joshua prayed to the LORD in front of all the people of Israel. He said, "Let the sun stand still over Gibeon, and the moon over the valley of Aijalon."
>
> 13So the sun stood still and the moon stayed in place until the nation of Israel had defeated its enemies. Is this event not recorded in The Book of Jasharb? The sun stayed in the middle of the sky, and it did not set as on a normal day. 14There has never been a day like this one before or since, when the LORD answered such a prayer. Surely the LORD fought for Israel that day!

We know that the sun does not move around the earth, causing day and night, but rather the earth moves around the sun. I am not sure Joshua knew that in those days, but God did, and he answered Joshua's prayer anyway. God answered the spirit of the request. Don't you think it is cool that we don't have to know everything; we just need to know the Lord because He does know everything? If we ask God with a pure heart, He will answer. So, in essence, God stopped the earth, causing the sun to stay in place while the battle waged on. You see, Joshua was doing what God told him to do—take the land. Joshua did not know that God would slow down 6.6 sextillion tons of spinning gravel, sand, and water to give Israel the victory. But he did know the Lord.

Do you think it was a fairly big request Joshua made of God? Yes, I guess it was, but Joshua did not think so; he had a job to do, and he needed to see how to do it. That is why he asked God to leave the light on for him, and He did.

Joshua had a large and in-charge God. How large is God to you? Is He large and in charge, or do you have Him in a box? Think about it today.

God loves you.

# GOD DOES THE IMPOSSIBLE FOR US. April 17

We have been talking about some of the miracles that God does, like talking donkeys, armies confused to death, curtains torn from top down, a prophet being fed by birds, flour and oil that never runs out, and kids walking around in a fire. These are only a few of them; we will be talking about many more as we go forward. All of them are stories of the Bible days.

I heard Chuck Swindoll say that everyone is probably dealing with something in their life today that you think is impossible; there is just no way we can think of that this thing can get done or be worked out for us. And guess what? The enemy is whispering in your ear, "It's useless; forget it! It can't happen. God is not in the miracle business anymore; just forget it!"

God is whispering, "I am able," but with our finite mind we listen to the wrong whisperer because, you got it, it's impossible in our mind!

But God is still God. He does not change!

He loves us as much as He loved those guys way back when! And He is still very active in the miracle business. Think of it this way: what we think is a miracle is everyday business as usual for God. It is only a miracle to us. He spoke the universe in to creation, breathed life into man, made the woman out of his rib, brought folks back from the dead, and made the blind see and the lame walk. It was all in a day's work for our Holy God. If you were to ask Him, "How did you do that?" he would probably say, "It was nothing!"

Do you see what I am saying? God can easily do the impossible in ways we can't even imagine. All you have to do is ask Him. Try it, and you will see!

God loves you.

# THE POOR BUT COCKY KID. April 18

Once upon a time long ago, there was a poor little boy that was walking down the street in front of the king's palace. He was kind of a cocky little fella, so he walked up to the guard and said, "I demand to see the King." The guard not only didn't look at the kid, but he certainly did not take him seriously. So once again, he said, "Hey you, I said I demand to see the king." Well, just when he was about to say it again, a man walked up to him and said, "Come with me, son," and the guard looked at the man and opened the gate and let them in.

They walked through the corridors and hallways of the palace. The man looked down at the kid and asked, "What's your name son," and the kid was so amazed at what he was seeing he could hardly speak, but eventually he said, "William, Sir."

They continued walking down the magnificent halls until they walked right in the throne room and right up to the king. The man said, "Your Highness, this is William, and he would have a word with you." And the king said, "Well, William, what can I do for you?"

Now you might ask how that could happen to a young poor cocky little boy. Well, the man was the Prince of Wales! What's the moral of the story?

Like the little boy, we will never get to see the King of kings unless His Prince, His one and only Son Jesus Christ, takes us there! He will grab you by the hand and walk you into the throne room and introduce you to the Father as one of His children! Ponder this today,

God loves you.

# THE EYES OF THE LORD ARE ON YOU. April 19

All of us have heard the saying "Don't do that; God is watching." Well it is not just a saying; it is the truth. Listen to what Peter says about it:

> 1 Peter 3 9–12
> Don't repay evil for evil. Don't retaliate with insults when people insult you. Instead, pay them back with a blessing. That is what God has called you to do, and he will bless you for it. 10For the Scriptures say, "If you want to enjoy life and see many happy days, keep your tongue from speaking evil and your lips from telling lies.
>
> 11Turn away from evil and do good. Search for peace, and work to maintain it.
>
> 12The eyes of the Lord watch over those who do right, and his ears are open to their prayers.
>
> But the Lord turns his face against those who do evil

We are not to repay evil for evil.

> Look at Proverbs 25:21–22, which says, "If your enemies are hungry, give them food to eat. If they are thirsty, give them water to drink. 22You will heap burning coals of shame on their heads, and the LORD will reward you." If we are to treat our enemies this way, then certainly we should treat our brothers and sisters in Christ even better!

Listen, I know these teachings are hard, but it is a choice you have to make. Every day you make many choices; this should be one you make daily. Pray for those who mistreat you; they will not know how to respond to a person that repays kindness for mistreatment.

Pray about it!

God loves you.

# THE FIRE BURNS HOT WHEN THE LOGS ARE STACKED. April 20

The other day we talked about what a small group can do for God. Today, let's look at it different way. Look at a fire; when the logs are piled together, the fire burns really hot, but what happens to the log that falls off to the side? You got it; it slowly dies out until there is no more fire left in it.

Don't you see that is how we are also? When we are with like-minded people, our fire burns hot for the Lord. But when we fall off to the side, for whatever reason, if we are not really careful, our fire for the Lord will go out!

It happens all the time that something happens, which cause people to miss a Sunday and then another and another, and very soon, we begin to watch programs we know we should not watch and we may go places we know better than to go. Then Satan has the door wide open, so he waltzes right in and begins to dump a ton of guilt on you to the point where you begin to think what a lousy person you are. Satan says you will never be forgiven for the things you are doing now. You might as well just get in a corner and cry. Sound familiar? Satan loves to kick you when you are down. If he can make a Christian miserable, his day is made! He may have lost you for eternity, but he sure tries to defeat you while he can here on earth.

But the Holy Spirit is way more powerful than the evil one, and with His help, we can make it through each day. Put your armor on today; there is a war going on out there!

God loves you.

# THE KING ATE GRASS LIKE A COW. April 21

King Nebuchadnezzar had a very large kingdom, and He thought it was all because of what he had done. He was eaten up with pride, so God gave him a dream, and Daniel told him what it meant.

> Daniel 5 This is what the dream means, Your Majesty, and what the Most High has declared will happen to my lord the king. 25You will be driven from human society, and you will live in the fields with the wild animals. You will eat grass like a cow, and you will be drenched with the dew of heaven. Seven periods of time (7 years), will pass while you live this way, until you learn that the Most High rules over the kingdoms of the world and gives them to anyone he chooses. 26But the stump and roots of the tree were left in the ground. This means that you will receive your kingdom back again when you have learned that heaven rules.

> Twelve months later he was taking a walk on the flat roof of the royal palace in Babylon. 30As he looked out across the city, he said, 'Look at this great city of Babylon! By my own mighty power, I have built this beautiful city as my royal residence to display my majestic splendor.'

There were too many I's in his thought process; he thought he was the reason he was the king. He thought he was majestic!

That same hour, the judgment was fulfilled, and Nebuchadnezzar was driven from human society. He ate grass like a cow, and he was drenched with the dew of heaven. He lived this way until his hair was as long as eagles' feathers and his nails were like birds' claws. Wow! Can you just see this guy in the field, grazing like a cow and swatting flies with his arms because he did not have a tail?

What a humbling experience. Don't ever think God is not in control. He has a sense of humor. I think God got a chuckle out of old King Nebuchadnezzar.

Well the king came to his senses. His kingdom was restored, and he sent out to the whole world this proclamation:

> King Nebuchadnezzar sent this message to the people of every race and nation and language throughout the world:
>
> "Peace and prosperity to you! 2"I want you all to know about the miraculous signs and wonders the Most High God has performed for me. 3How great are his signs, how powerful his wonders!
>
> His kingdom will last forever, his rule through all generations.

Amen and Amen, God is in control!
God loves you.

# ARE YOU TRYING HARD. April 22

To read your Bible every day?
To live a good Christian life?
To run a five-mile marathon?

If you walked out your front door and tried as hard as you possibly could to run a five-mile marathon, could you do it? I think most would say no and pass out half way down the block from exhaustion; at least I would. So how do you run a five-mile run?

You got it—you will have to train and train and train some more until you get to where you are in shape enough to run that far. Don't you think that is what the Christian life is all about, training and training for that day when God says to you, "I need you to speak to this person in need, or go to a place I will tell you, or maybe just, give a big tip to this one"?

> First Timothy 4:8 says, "For physical training is of some value, but godliness has value for all things, holding promise for both the present life and the life to come."

How do you train yourself to read the Bible every day? You have to be disciplined, you have to see the value in it, and you ask the Lord to help you train yourself. How do you train yourself to live a good Christian life? You have to be disciplined, you have to see the value in it, and you have to ask the Lord to help you in this race.

Folks, just trying hard, won't do it for you. You will fall flat on your face!

It will be like a roller coaster, try hard, forget, try hard, and forget. This is not a good plan. What we have to do is *train* ourselves for the race. Then we have to run to win.

I think that is our goal also: to run the race and get the prize, the crown, so that you can lay it at Jesus' feet one day.

Kids, we need to get off the roller coaster and stay focused. We cannot take our eyes and our minds off the goal in life. I know, it is a daily battle, even an hourly battle, but you can do it with your armor on and His help! Pray for His help today.

God loves you.

# PRODUCE LASTING FRUIT April 23

Jesus was talking to His disciples at the last supper before He was arrested. He was telling them that He was the vine and they were the branches. He told them to remain in Him and they can bear much fruit. He told them if they did not bear fruit they would be cut off. Then He told them; whoever abides in Me and I in him, will bear much fruit for apart from Me, you can do nothing.

We are His disciples today. We are His branches, and we are to bear fruit, (make more disciples). Men and woman have been making disciples for 2,000 years.

Some will say, I don't know, I am not good at that sort of thing, I wouldn't know how to witness or make a disciple.

Do you love anyone? Jesus walked and talked and loved His disciples. He told them and showed them how to love one another. Listen to what else He said;

John 15,

> 12" This is my commandment: Love each other in the same way I have loved you. 13 There is no greater love than to lay down one's life for one's friends. 14 You are my friends if you do what I command. 15 I no longer call you slaves, because a master doesn't confide in his slaves. Now you are my friends, since I have told you everything the Father told me. 16 You didn't choose me. I chose you. I appointed you to go and *"produce lasting fruit"*, so that the Father will give you whatever you ask for, using my name. 17 This is my command: Love each other".

If you love anyone, teach them about Jesus, show them the love of the Father and the Son, and you will make a disciple. It is a matter of eternal life or eternal death. You are the branch attached to the Vine (Jesus), if you abide in Him, you can do this!

God loves you

# WHY IS JESUS CALLED THE "LAMB OF GOD"? April 24

Kids, I want you to take a moment to shut your eyes and think about the question.

It is a very important question. Do you know the answer? Do you know it well enough to share the answer? For those who are not completely sure we will go over the answer.

In order for us to be in the company of God in heaven, there had to be a blood sacrifice to cover our sins once and for all. As we have said before, God cannot look at sin.

In the Old Testament days, the blood of the Lamb was poured out on the altar for atonement for the sins of Israel. The lamb had to be a perfect lamb with no blemishes.

Jesus was God before He came to this Earth. When He came, He lived as man and had no sin. He lived as a child, then as a young man, and then an adult and did not commit one sin, before during, or after His life here. So, He was the perfect sacrifice for our sins.

He was the perfect lamb that was slain for our sins. He was the only person who has ever lived, or whoever will live that lived a perfect life. He is God, and He is man. He is the only sacrifice that could atone for all of man's sins. God Himself, the second person of the Holy Trinity, came to be the perfect sacrifice so that he could fellowship with us, His sinful people, for all eternity.

You may ask, "Why couldn't another good man do it instead of God; why did Jesus have to die?" Because no one else was perfect; every human who has ever lived has sinned in some way, except Jesus! How could a sinner atone for sin? You may ask, "Why did it have to happen?"

It was the only way we as sinners could ever be in the presence of Almighty God. We needed a sacrifice, the blood of a sacrificial Lamb, to cover our sins so that we would be clean enough to be with God. Jesus' blood washes us clean enough to be in His presence. Nothing but the blood of Jesus will ever get us there.

Thank your Lord and Savior today for what He did for you, so you could be with Him in heaven for all eternity.

God loves you.

or deaf, or seeing or blind? Is it not I, the Lord?
12 Now then go, and I, even I, will be with your
mouth, and teach you what you are to say!

2 Corinthians 12:9 My grace is sufficient for you,
for My power is made perfect in weakness.

Well, there you have it. I think all God needs from you is
our willingness to share. Saving lost souls is His job; all He
eds from you is your mouth, He will speak through it and say
at needs to be said at exactly the time it needs to be said. He
s everything under control.

So, don't worry, He made your mouth, and He can speak
rough it! It would be good if you filled your mind with His
rds also.

God loves you kids. Just be willing!

# GOD'S RETURN POLICY. April 25

How many can say they like nothing better than to stand in a
line at Walmart to return something, or Home Depot or Lowe's
or anywhere for that matter? I bet I could count the number of
people in the great city of Millbrook, Alabama on one finger,
who like to do a return. It normally is a dreadful thing to do.

Did you know that God has a return policy? Yes, He does,
and it is just about the most liberal return policy you have ever
seen. And we so need God to let us come back to Him sometimes.

The definition of backsliding is as follows: (1) To relapse
into bad ways; (2) lose one's resolve; (3) give into temptation;
and (4) go astray. These are all definitions of a common thing
that Christians call backsliding.

Look at what Jeremiah 14:7 says about it: "Your wickedness
will punish you; your backsliding will rebuke you. Consider
then and realize how evil and bitter it is for you when you forsake the Lord your God and have no awe of me," declares the
Lord, the Lord Almighty.

Backsliding can be caused by many things. However, whatever the sin might be that leads us away from God, it must be
dealt with honestly and brought before Him in repentance. God
loves us and wants us to be close to Him. Even when we sin
against Him, He promises to forgive.

Hosea 14 says:

> Return, Israel, to the Lord your God. Your sins
> have been your downfall!
>
> 2Take words with you and return to the Lord.
> Say to him: "Forgive all our sins and receive us
> graciously, that we may offer the fruit of our lips.
>
> And God says; I will heal their waywardness and
> love them freely, for my anger has turned away
> from them.

Then in Luke 15, Jesus told them this parable:

> 4 "Suppose one of you has a hundred sheep and loses one of them. Doesn't he leave the ninety-nine in the open country and go after the lost sheep until he finds it? 5 And when he finds it, he joyfully puts it on his shoulders 6 and goes home. Then he calls his friends and neighbors together and says, 'Rejoice with me; I have found my lost sheep.' 7 I tell you that in the same way there will be more rejoicing in heaven over one sinner who repents than over ninety-nine righteous persons who do not need to repent.

Can you think of a better return policy than that, God is waiting with open arms to receive you back into the family, all you have to do is humble yourself and ask?

We serve a wonderful, forgiving God that loves us very much. Thank you, Lord!

## ARE YOU SHARING THE HOPE W
## YOU? April 26

> 1 Peter 3:15 tells us: "Always be ready to g defense to anyone who ask you for a reaso the hope that is in you."

Do you have a first-aid kit in your car? How light? Jumper cables or flares? What about an ext good walking shoes? I know it's hot, but winter is always good to be prepared even if you own a ne never know when it might decide to let you down in Atlanta one time walking home barefooted in weather because she wore high heels to work, an prepared for snow on the roads. All of these thing have tucked away in your vehicle. Be prepared! W to be prepared for whatever life throws at us.

What about sharing your faith—does it make I heard my preacher, Jim Graham, last week say h palms sometimes when it is one on one. We all d first thing that comes to mind when the opportul "What if I say the wrong thing?" Don't forget Jesu and He knows what humans think. Listen to wl say about it:

> Matthew 10:21 do not worry about h respond or what to say, in that hour yo be given what to say. 20 For it will not l speaking, but the Spirit of your Father sp through you.

> Luke 12:11 Do not worry about how to yourselves or what to say. 12 For at that ti Holy Spirit will teach you what you shou

> Exodus 4:11 The Lord said to him, W made man's mouth? Or who makes Hir

# ONCE UPON A TIME LONG, LONG AGO. April 27

When men's hearts were evil and even every thought they had was an evil one because they were very wicked (very much like today), God looked down on them and was sorry he created man. So, he thought *I will destroy every living thing that takes a breath. Both man and beast.* But then God said, "I do have one man that is righteous in my eyes. I will let him and his family re-populate the earth after I destroy it. I will have him build a vessel that will afford his people and two of all the animals, both male and female, protection from my judgment. I will call it an ark, a vessel of protection." So, God spoke to Noah, and told him how to build the ark. It was very large and it took a very long time for him and his sons to build. When Noah finished the ark, God sent all the animals into it, and when all the animals and Noah and his family were safe inside, God shut them in and made it rain. God opened the windows of heaven, and water poured out. Then He poked holes in the earth to let the fountains of the deep spew the waters from below. Between the two sources of water came a great flood that covered the entire Earth, even the tops of the mountains. The rains fell for forty days and forty nights, and from the day they entered the ark until the day they walked out was 371 days. Every living creature that breathed and roamed the earth was drowned. Noah and those who were with him on the ark were all that remained alive. The water stayed on the earth for 150 days and the ark rested on the mountain Ararat. This story can be found in Genesis 6.

God's judgment for man's wicked ways was swift, true and fatal (as it will be again soon).

Noah and his family had a fresh new start on life!

God will continue to work his plan now because he knows what will happen with man. He did not think, "Well, okay now, Noah will get this thing in the right direction, and man will quit having evil thoughts and start only doing righteous things. No, no—He created us, and He knows us much better than we know ourselves. He knew Satan was around to entice men to reject

God, and He knew that many would follow Satan, just like what happen with one third of the angels.

*But god had a plan from the beginning*. Read John 3:16.
God loves you.

# HOW SOVEREIGN IS OUR LORD? April 28

We know that God predicted many, many things that happened in the Old Testament days. Daniel wrote about many of His predictions. Now, we call them predictions or prophecies because He spoke of things that would happen many years before they actually happened. All through the Old Testament, God told the prophets to proclaim this or proclaim that, and every time He said something, it always happened as He said it would. The difference in a prophet and a phony is when it comes to telling the future, God is always right, and the phony misses most of the time. God knows the future. He sees the future. He is the only sovereign God! Here is one of many cases of how accurate He is, spoken some 210 years before it happened:

Isaiah 45:1–7
This is what the Lord says to his anointed, to Cyrus, whose right hand I take hold of, to subdue nations before him and to strip kings of their armor, to open doors before him so that gates will not be shut: 2, I will go before you and will level the mountains, I will break down gates of bronze and cut through bars of iron.3, I will give you hidden treasures, riches stored in secret places, so that you may know that I am the Lord, the God of Israel, who summons you by name. 4, For the sake of Jacob my servant, of Israel my chosen, I summon you by name and bestow on you a title of honor, though you do not acknowledge me. 5, I am the Lord, and there is no other; apart from me there is no God. I will strengthen you, though you have not acknowledged me, 6, so that from the rising of the sun to the place of its setting people may know there is none besides me. I am the Lord, and there is no other. 7, I form the light and create darkness, I

bring prosperity and create disaster; I, the Lord,
do all these things.

Cyrus, who God told of, even calling his name, walked into
Babylon with his army and took the city 210 years later and later
freed the Jewish people, just as was predicted.

God is great!

He knew you before you were formed in the womb, and He
has a plan for you. Seek it and you will find it!

God loves you.

P.S. God made Cyrus king and used him to do His will. God
knows who will win the election, and if He didn't want whoever
to be in charge for whatever reason, it would not happen. Don't
worry! His divine plan will happen!

# MORE ON THE HOPE THAT IS WITHIN US. April 29

1Peter 3:15b instructs us: "But in your hearts revere Christ as Lord. Always be prepared to give an answer to everyone who asks you to give the reason for the hope that you have. But do this with gentleness and respect."

In the spiritual sense, are you prepared to respond when someone asks you why you believe what you believe? Today's believers need to be prepared to lovingly present the basis of their hope, not in a threatening way or in a condemning way, but in a caring and loving way.

Do you understand the hope that is within you?

The hope God gives us is not wishful thinking; it is not a shallow pie-in-the-sky pipe dream. God's gift of hope is the assurance of our being held in the sure grip of His grace for the remaining days of this life and for life beyond the grave, for all of eternity. Christian hope is grounded in God's faithfulness and sovereign ability, not in our limited strength and others' limited abilities.

And God is faithful to His word. Jesus said in Luke 20:37–38:

But now, as to whether the dead will be raised— even Moses proved this when he wrote about the burning bush. Long after Abraham, Isaac, and Jacob had died, he referred to the Lord as 'the God of Abraham, the God of Isaac, and the God of Jacob.' 38, so he is the God of the living, not the dead, for they are all alive to him.

Our hope is in the death, burial, and resurrection of our Lord Jesus Christ, He was resurrected to newness in life, and so will we be, as His followers. We celebrate every Easter His resurrection, but we should be celebrating it every day. Because He was resurrected, we can also be resurrected and be with Him in heaven for all eternity! There is an eternal life!

And as a Christian you are living it now and will be living it forever and ever.

More important than knowing all the answers is having the right lifestyle to raise the right questions from the nonbelievers!

Thank you, Father for the hope we have!

God loves you.

# WHAT WOULD JESUS DO? April 30

In 1997 over 20,000 bracelets were sold every month with the letters WWJD on them. Of course, it stands for "What Would Jesus Do?" I had one; what about you? Some young people report that wearing them makes them stop and think so that they don't rent an R-rated movie or engage in other sinful behavior. When you ask this question based on scripture, it is a very good idea.

Jesus Christ is the only one ever to live a perfect sinless life. He is our example for godly living. He lived in perfect submission to the Father and was always obedient to His will. In Luke 2:39–52, we have the only reference in scripture to the years between His birth and the beginning of His ministry when He was about thirty. And there is not much there, just a time when He got left behind at the temple. I wonder why the stories of His childhood were not listed for us, but I am sure we have all we need to know about Him. Maybe if you want to know about His younger years, you can ask Him about them when you see Him. I think there will be plenty of time.

Charles Simeon says, there is little related of Him to gratify our curiosity, but enough to regulate our conduct. The idea is that we know all we need to know to be able to imitate Him in our conduct. So, if we ask ourselves, what would Jesus do about this or that, and we know enough about Him to come to a wise answer, it is a good thing. But if all you know about Jesus is a bracelet on your arm, it won't do much good because you have nothing to base your answers to the question on. What would Jesus do?

If you don't know Jesus, how would you know what He would do? Before we can imitate Jesus, we need to learn as much about Him as we possibly can. Then, when you ask the question, you would have an idea what He would do.

But listen, we will never know Jesus in this life as well as we will 10,000 years from now, and even then, we will have much more to learn. He needs to be the focus of our life to the point where we will know without a doubt, what He would do in any situation and then follow our hearts.

So, the question is a very good one to ask in any situation: what would Jesus do?

Make a habit of studying His life, so you will know!

God loves you.

# WHAT ARE YOU ASHAMED OF? May 1

When I was about seventeen, I had a '53 Ford that was a stick shift on the column. It looked bad, so I had to make it cool some way, so I put in a floor shifter. I cut a hole in the floor and hooked it up. The car did not sound cool, so I got under the car with a screwdriver and a hammer and beat holes in the muffler until it had a nice rumble when you drove it. The problem was, with a hole in the floor for the shifter and holes in the muffler, smoke poured into the car through the hole in the floor to the point we had to ride with the windows down no matter how cold it was. I was dating Pat, and she did not like the smoke, and I was so ashamed of my dumbness and that smoky old Ford.

I am sure all of us have something we were or are ashamed of.

*There are many Christians who are ashamed that they are a Christian when they are around certain people or in a certain place. Have you ever experienced that? This is not a new problem or a rare one. Paul found it necessary to write Timothy two times, and it is very evident that this young man struggled with being ashamed of the gospel (See 2 Timothy 1:8, 12, 16). Even though he traveled with Paul, he was still tempted to "keep a low profile." Today Christianity is not very popular, either, and I fear many of our Christian youth try to keep a low profile also. They try to keep off the radar. I am saved, I am glad, and I will keep it to myself.

I wonder what Jesus would say about this wimpy attitude?

> Paul says in Romans 1:16, "For I am not ashamed
> of the gospel, for it is the power of God for sal-
> vation to everyone who believes."

Paul took a stand for Jesus with boldness and love for His fellow man—the men who needed the Lord, the people who were on the broad road and going in the wrong direction.

Kids, there are a lot of things we can be ashamed of, but the gospel of Christ is not one of them. We are to boldly proclaim our love for our Lord. Don't be a wimp! Have a bold day today!

God loves you.

*Notes from Bob Deffenbaugh

*A Father's Love* | 177

# HE WAS DESPISED AND REJECTED. May 2

The book of Isaiah is one of the most important books of the Old Testament. Isaiah is said to be one of the greatest prophets of them all. Isaiah told of things that would happen some seven hundred years later. He spoke of our Lord Jesus and what would happen to Him; his words came from our Father God. Listen to these words:

> Isaiah 53
> My servant grew up in the LORD's presence like a tender green shoot, like a root in dry ground.
>
> There was nothing beautiful or majestic about his appearance, nothing to attract us to him.
>
> 3He was despised and rejected—a man of sorrows, acquainted with deepest grief. We turned our backs on him and looked the other way. He was despised, and we did not care. Yet it was our weaknesses he carried; it was our sorrows that weighed him down. And we thought his troubles were a punishment from God, a punishment for his own sins! 5But he was pierced for our rebellion, crushed for our sins. He was beaten so we could be whole. He was whipped so we could be healed. 6All of us, like sheep, have strayed away. We have left God's paths to follow our own. Yet the LORD laid on him the sins of us all.

The word *despised* means to look down the nose at or to consider something worthless and of no value and then treat it accordingly. Do you think there are people in the world who that think this way? We know there were two thousand years ago because they did this to Him.

But what about today? Yes, there are many people that look down their nose at the Christian way of life. Remember we said that the road is broad and the gate is large to hell.

So how can we change their attitude? We have to quit worrying about what they might think of us and realize that the message we have can save their eternal life.

What is more important: what they think of us or where they might end up?

There is no end to eternal death!

Pray about it!

God loves you.

# HE HAD DONE NO WRONG. May 3

He had done no wrong and had never deceived anyone. But he was buried like a criminal; he was put in a rich man's grave. It was the Lord's good plan to crush Him and cause Him grief. Yet when his life is made an offering for sin, He will have many descendants. He will enjoy a long life, and the Lord's good plan will prosper in His hands. When He sees all that is accomplished by His anguish, He will be satisfied. And because of His experience, my righteous servant will make it possible for many to be counted righteous, for He will bear all their sins! Isaiah 53:9–11, NLT

While we survey the suffering of the Son of God, let us remember our long catalogue of transgressions (sins) and consider Him as suffering under the load of *our guilt*.

"*We are* the purchase of His blood and the monuments of His grace; for this, He continually pleads and prevails, destroying the works of the devil" (Matthew Henry).

Did you know that Jesus is pleading your case in heaven, against the devil? And what's more important, *He is winning*!

Jesus loves you so much that He took your sins and my sins and made them disappear so that the Father can look at us!

Thank you, Jesus!

God loves you.

# WHO IS WINNING THE WAR? May 4

Ephesians 6:10–12

Finally, be strong in the Lord and in his mighty power. 11Put on the full armor of God, so that you can take your stand against the devil's schemes. 12For our struggle is not against flesh and blood, but against the rulers, against the authorities, against the powers of this dark world and against the spiritual forces of evil in the heavenly realms.

Who is winning your war—the powers of the darkness or you?

Wow, Pop, how would we know? It really is pretty simple. Take a moment and ask yourself who is stronger? How could I know that? Easy—which gets fed the most? How many doors are you leaving open for the powers of the darkness to creep in?

There used to be cartoons where the skinny (looked like he was starving to death) guy was sitting on the beach with a beautiful girl and a strong muscular guy walks up, pushes the skinny guy down, and walks off with the girl. It was very easy for the strong guy because he was getting plenty of training and nourishment. Whoever gets the most nutrition will be the strongest.

It is the same thing in this war we are in. Whoever gets fed the most will win you over.

Now the question is, who are you feeding the most? Are you feeding the darkness by doing things or saying things or looking at things that are against the values you have committed to? Or are you feeding your mind with the words of God and socializing with like-minded people?

I am a strong believer in a daily read-through-the-Bible program. If you are on one, great! Keep it up and train yourself to be a good soldier for God. If you are not on one, I suspect there are too many doors left open for creepy things to slip in.

Start with John and then alternate one book in the Old Testament and then one in the New Testament until you have gone completely through the Bible. Then start over and do it again. By the time you have gone through the Bible three times, you won't be able to stop! You will realize that every word is divine and that you are having a conversation with God. That is as good as it can get!

God loves you.

# GOD WOOS YOU! May 5

Notes from John Phillips:

God woos; he does not abduct. He does not supply His creatures with wills of their own, with the power of choice and personal accountability for their behavior, and then act as if they did not have a free will. Some are asking, Pop, what does "woo" mean? It means God pursues you! God seeks you! God wants you to be in His family.

It is like you, Casey. Casey woos Hannah. You are trying to gain her love.

God does not want robotic worship. He wants you to love Him! When you accept Him on your own, He is waiting with open arms to accept you into the family!

Jesus said, "You did not choose me; I chose you," He was talking to His disciples that He chose for a special mission, just as He can and does choose many people for specific missions. Make no mistake, God chose us, all of us, but the world (the people) in darkness, chose the evil one.

Don't you know, it makes God very sad, when someone chooses darkness instead of His love?

He will not abduct you against your will into His Kingdom. He knows how all of this will end, and He knows by that time, who chose Him and who did not. He knows exactly how many people will accept Jesus. He knows who they are, when they accepted Him, where they live, the various circumstances of their lives, and how to fit them in His plan from now to eternity.

But we have a will to choose. We can choose to serve God or reject God. The fact that He knows who will and who won't choose Him as their Savior does not change the outcome.

He chose you and now He allows you to choose Him or not. He said, "For God so loved the world that He gave His only begotten Son that who so ever shall believe will not perish, but have eternal life" (be saved). It plainly says *whosoever*!

And in John 1:12, He says, "As many as received Him, to them He gave the power to become the sons of God."

We choose to receive or reject. God loves all people, and because of that love, He allows us to decide what we think is best for ourselves, knowing full well that a large majority would choose wrong because of temptation.

Like I have said before: His will be done, or our will be done. It is His will that all would come to Him, but He knows that all will not. Some will have their own way, and their will shall be done.

God will grieve enormously over you if you choose wrong, but it will be your choice.

I hope you choose wisely! And I know you did already.

God loves you.

# TO SOME, SUNDAY IS JUST ANOTHER OFF DAY! May 6

Do you believe there are many people living all around you who have never stepped a foot inside a church and have no idea what goes on inside? Case in point, I knew a kid one time who invited a girl he was dating to go to church with him. She agreed and after a few moments, it was very obvious that it was the first time she had ever been in a church. I was shocked that in the "Bible belt" there are many people that really have been brought up unaware that Sunday is anything but an off day to go to the lake or wash the car or sleep in. To them, it is just a weekend day off.

God is very much at work in this world, and few even know He is doing it. God is judging folks for their sin, and they don't even know it is happening. Unbelievers are unaware of God's judgment because they do not know God, and they are not aware of His presence and power in the world today. A commentator watching a Mardi Gras celebration in New Orleans made the comment, "It is sin and degradation, and we love it"! Sometimes Christians, rather than grieving over the sins of others as Lot did over the sins of Sodom and Gomorrah, are tempted to envy sinners as though they are privileged to enjoy pleasures we Christians are denied—as if God was withholding something good from us. We reconcile it with, "Oh well, we will have better times in heaven." We will but this is not a good comparison. But listen, folks, they really have no excuse for not knowing God. Listen to Romans 1:18–20, 25–26:

> But God shows his anger from heaven against all sinful, wicked people who suppress the truth by their wickedness.19They know the truth about God because he has made it obvious to them. 20For ever since the world was created, people have seen the earth and sky. Through everything God made, they can clearly see his invisible qualities—his eternal power and divine

nature. So, they have no excuse for not knowing God. They traded the truth about God for a lie. So, they worshiped and served the things God created instead of the Creator himself, who is worthy of eternal praise! Amen. 26That is why God abandoned them to their shameful desires.

So as a Christian, how does this make you feel? Will you say, "Oh well, it is what it is!" Or will you feel sad because many folks are lost?

What can we do about it? If you polled all of your friends and neighbors, would they know you were a Christian? Or are you one of God's "secret agents," working undercover? You do know that God does not have any secret agents, right? Do you think it would be a good place to start to turn your community around and make disciples out of them right there in your neighborhood?

Of course, it would, so what is holding you back? Start by making sure all of them know what you stand for, and how much you love the Lord! Have a great day, for "This is the day that the Lord hath made; we will rejoice and be glad in it."

God loves you.

# IS IT WELL WITH YOUR SOUL? May 7

What is the most important thing to you? Some will say my husband or wife, my mom and dad, or my kids.

What is it that is the most important thing you have? Could it be your soul, maybe? Your soul is forever, and what happens to it has to be very important. The spiritual, immortal part of who you arc is the part of you that will go to be with Jesus when you die.

The song writer says it better than me:

> My sin, oh, the bliss of this glorious thought
> My sin, not in part but the whole,
> Is nailed to the cross, and I bear it no more,
> Praise the Lord, praise the Lord, o my soul
> It is well (it is well)
> With my soul (with my soul)
> It is well, it is well with my soul! *

Is it well with your soul? Can you sing that song with head and hands held high in adoration to your Lord and Savior? How can you be sure? Well, when you think about it, are you absolutely sure of where your soul will go when it leaves your body? It will go from this world to the next, either heaven or the other place, the place no one wants to talk about. Are you sure? Or would you say, "Well I hope so," or "I think so"?

You do not have to guess! If you have Him in your heart, *it is well with your soul*! Now say it out loud, right now; don't be ashamed. Shout it out! *It is well with my soul*! Now didn't that feel good? You know you can do that any time you feel like it?

The devil is in charge of doubt, not God. God wants you to feel safe.

God loves you.

*Song written by Horatio G. Spafford

# WHAT IS GRACE? May 8

Grace is a constant theme in the Bible, and it culminates in the New Testament with the coming of Jesus Christ.

We can all extend grace to others, but when the word *grace* is used in connection with God, it takes on a more powerful meaning. Grace is God choosing to bless us rather than curse us, as our sin deserves. It is His benevolence to the undeserving.

According to the dictionary; it is the free and *unmerited* favor of God, as manifested in the salvation of sinners through His Son Jesus Christ and the bestowal of blessings.

It is the love and mercy given to us by God because God desires us to have it.

It is a *gift from our Lord*. It is not because of anything we have done to deserve it—a loving gift from our Father. We can do nothing to earn it. God's grace is not like, "Here I give you a gift, and you give me one."

It is an unmerited gift! All that is required is for you to accept it. You do not have to take the gift; you have the ability to reject the grace gift and, sad to say, many will reject it. But how sad is it that our Creator has His hand out with a precious gift of eternal life in paradise, and many will turn their nose up at it, walk away, and not take it out of His hand?

Ephesians 2:8 says, "For by grace are you saved, through faith, and that not of yourself."

The only way any of us can enter into a relationship with God is because of His grace toward us. God is the instigator of grace, and it is from Him that all grace flows.

God shows mercy and grace, but they are not the same. Mercy withholds a punishment we deserve; grace gives a blessing we don't deserve. God extends grace to us; He offers us forgiveness, reconciliation, abundant eternal life, His Holy Spirit, and a place in heaven with Him some day when we accept His offer and place our faith in His Son.

Grace is God giving the greatest treasure to the least deserving—which is all of us!

Thank God for His grace today.

God loves you.

# GOD IS STILL GOD. May 9

He is still on the throne, He is still omnipotent, He is still omniscient, He is still omnipresent, He is still the Creator, and He is still the faithful Jehovah, the absolutely dependable Triune God! He is God the Father, God the Son, and God the Holy Spirit, three persons—one God.

What is omnipotence? Omnipotence is basically a compound word that means all (omni) powerful (potent), and if you have read enough of the Bible, you can clearly see that God is indeed omnipotent; all powerful. It means that God has unlimited authority and infinite power!

> First Peter 4:19 says, "Wherefore let them that suffer according to the will of God commit the keeping of their souls to him in well doing, as unto a faithful Creator."

No one said it better than Job, who had suffered the loss of children and fortune: "Though He slay me, yet will I trust in Him," and Peter would have said amen to that!

We have an omnipotent God. He has the ability and power to anything. This power is exercised effortlessly. A good example of God's omnipotence is in the name El Shaddai, which means "self-sufficient" or "almighty." God's power is unlimited. A proper definition is given by Thiessen: "God is all-powerful and able to do whatever he wills.

> Matthew 19:26, And looking at them Jesus said to them, "With people this is impossible, but with God all things are possible."

> Genesis 18:14, Is anything too difficult for the LORD? At the appointed time I will return to you, at this time next year, and Sarah will have a son.

Sarah was ninety years young and Abraham was one hundred!

Luke 1:37, for nothing will be impossible with God."

Acts 26:8, why is it considered incredible among you people if God does raise the dead?

Jeremiah 32:27, Behold, I am the LORD, the God of all flesh; is anything too difficult for Me?"

God is all powerful, if He wills it, it will happen. He is Omnipotent! Praise our El Shaddai (Almighty) God, our Creator! Hope this helped; God loves you.

# WHAT DOES IT MEAN THAT GOD IS OMNISCIENT? May 10

Omniscience is defined as "the state of having total knowledge, the quality of knowing everything." For God to be sovereign over His creation of all things, whether visible or invisible, He has to be all-knowing. His omniscience is not restricted to any one person in the Godhead—Father, Son, and Holy Spirit are all by nature omniscient. God knows everything (1 John 3:20). He knows not only the minutest details of our lives but those of everything around us, for He mentions even knowing when a sparrow falls or when we lose a single hair (Matthew 10:29–30). Not only does God know everything that will occur until the end of history itself (Isaiah 46:9–10), but He also knows our very thoughts even before we speak them (Psalm 139:4).

> Psalm 147:5, Great is our Lord and abundant in strength; His understanding is infinite.

> Psalm 139:4, even before there is a word on my tongue, Behold, O LORD, You know it all.

> Psalm 147:4, He counts the number of the stars; He gives names to all of them.

> Psalm 139:1–4, O LORD, You have searched me and known me. You know when I sit down and when I rise up; you understand my thought from afar. You scrutinize my path and my lying down, and are intimately acquainted with all my ways. Even before there is a word on my tongue, Behold, O LORD, You know it all.

> Psalm 44:21, would not God find this out? For He knows the secrets of the heart.

Isaiah 40:28, do you not know? Have you not heard? The Everlasting God, the LORD, the Creator of the ends of the earth does not become weary or tired His understanding is inscrutable.

Isaiah 46:9–10, Remember the former things long past, For I am God, and there is no other; I am God, and there is no one like Me, Declaring the end from the beginning, and from ancient times things which have not been done, Saying, 'My purpose will be established, And I will accomplish all My good pleasure'

Enough said today; God knows everything about you, and He loves you anyway, so much so that He died for you!
God is all knowing; He is Omniscient!
God loves you.

# WHAT DOES IT MEAN THAT GOD IS OMNIPRESENT? May 11

The word *omnipresence* is a compound word and comes from the words *omni* (all) and *presence* (present) and so God is present everywhere at all times with no exceptions. There is no place you can be that God is not also there. He is always everywhere in all places and at all times. He is omnipresent.

God's presence is continuous throughout all of creation. The Bible reveals that God can be both present to a person in a manifest manner (Psalm 46:1; Isaiah 57:15) and present in every situation in all of creation at any given time (Psalm 33:13–14).

> Proverbs 15:3 states, "The eyes of the Lord are in every place, keeping watch on the evil and the good."

This is very similar to Job 34:21, but the difference here is that God is seeing all the evil that takes place on the earth, even under the cover of darkness, and even if no one else sees someone's evil doing, God does! He also sees every good thing done that no one else sees, and that is because "The eyes of the Lord are in every place."

> Jeremiah 23:24 asks, "Can a man hide himself in secret places so that I cannot see him? Declares the Lord. Do I not fill heaven and earth? Declares the Lord?"

Jeremiah asked a rhetorical question with an obvious answer; there is no place you can be that God is not also there and aware of someone's presence. God declares that He fills both heaven and earth, and so there is nowhere that humans can go that God is not already there—before they even get there.

Omnipresence is God's characteristic of being present to all ranges of both time and space. Although God is present in all time and space, God is not locally limited to any time or space.

God is everywhere and in every now. No molecule or atomic particle is so small that God is not fully present to it and no galaxy so vast that God does not circumscribe it.

God is everywhere all the time; He is Omnipresent!

Praise His Holy Name today!

Hope this helped; God loves you.

# A MIRACLE IN AN OIL JAR. May 12

Did you know that in the Old Testament days, if you owed money and you could not pay, your landlord or banker or whoever you owed the money to, could make you a slave to them until you paid off the loan? How do you think that would go over in the United States today—probably not so good. Listen to 2 Kings 4:

The Widow's Olive Oil

1 The wife of a man from the company of the prophets cried out to Elisha, "Your servant my husband is dead, and you know that he revered the Lord. But now his creditor is coming to take my two boys as his slaves."

2 Elisha replied to her, "How can I help you? Tell me, what do you have in your house?"

"Your servant has nothing there at all," she said, "accept a small jar of olive oil."

3 Elisha said, "Go around and ask all your neighbors for empty jars. Don't ask for just a few. 4 Then go inside and shut the door behind you and your sons. Pour oil into all the jars, and as each is filled, put it to one side."

5 She left him and shut the door behind her and her sons. They brought the jars to her and she kept pouring. 6 When all the jars were full, she said to her son, "Bring me another one."

But he replied, "There is not a jar left." Then the oil stopped flowing.

7 She went and told the man of God, and he said, "Go, sell the oil and pay your debts. You and your sons can live on what is left."

Olive oil was very valuable in those days.

This is just another example of how God is El Shaddai. He is all powerful. He made the olive oil continue to pour out of the small jar until all the jars they could find were full. Can you just picture the kids looking at the small jar and wondering what is going on here? God can take care of your problems in so many ways, and most of them you can't even imagine. We don't even think that way. Whatever your issue is, never underestimate our El Shaddai Lord! He does things in ways we are not privileged to know about.

Pray to your Father today about whatever!

He loves you!

# WHAT IF JESUS CAME TO DINNER? May 13

Let's think about it, for a few minutes. What if Jesus sent a messenger to speak to you, and he told you your Lord and Savior would be coming to dinner tomorrow night. You might say that wouldn't happen. Oh no, Jesus sent many messengers to tell His people different things that was going to happen. One example is:

> Matthew 28, 5Then the angel spoke to the women. "Don't be afraid!" he said. "I know you are looking for Jesus, who was crucified. 6He isn't here! He is risen from the dead, just as he said would happen. Come, see where his body was lying. 7And now, go quickly and tell his disciples that he has risen from the dead, and he is going ahead of you to Galilee. You will see him there. Remember what I have told you.

There are many examples of the angels giving messages to His people! Okay, so you are told Jesus is coming to dinner.

The question is, what would you do to prepare for your dinner? What would you cook and who would you invite to eat dinner with the Savior? Would you ask believers or nonbelievers? Would you make it a celebration dinner with current Christians or an evangelical dinner?

Who would have the most to gain? Who do you think Jesus would want there? When you read about Him, what kind of people did He hang out with? I think He came to save the lost; don't you think so?

A lot of hypothetical stuff here, Pop, yes maybe, is it possible? Could Jesus come to your dinner?

What does omnipresence mean? Surely you have not forgotten already, if you have, go back and look at the message on omnipresence. It means He is in all places all the time!

> Matthew 18:20 (KJV) states, "20 for where two or three are gathered together in my name, there am I in the midst of them."

So, He is invited to your dinner if there are two or more gathered together in His name. Do you pray in His name? Maybe we should set a chair for him.

Okay, we have established that He will be there; now, who will you invite to your home where Jesus will be for dinner? Wow! What a great way to evangelize your neighbors! Is it important? You bet it is! So, what are you cooking, and who are you inviting? Have a great time sharing your main guest to all the others!

God loves you.

# ARE YOU APPLYING WHAT YOU READ? May 14

Chuck Swindoll says if you don't apply what you know about Jesus it is a sin!

Listen to what Thomas Brooks says:

> Reader if it be not strong upon thy heart to Practice what thou read, to what end do you read, to increase your own condemnation? If your light and knowledge be not turned into practice, the more knowing person thou art, the more miserable person thou will be on the day of accountability! *

Doing is just as important as knowing (Brooks). Those are very strong words from Brooks. But listen to what James 4:17 says, "Therefore to him that knows how to do good and does it not, to him it is a sin."

Just a couple of reasons we don't apply what we know we should:

It is not comfortable!

Too many distractions!

We have too many excuses!

Maybe we are confused!

And maybe a little bit of uncertainty.

Read back over this list and see if anything fits you. Now think about what it is that fits your circumstances and then get out from under your circumstances! Start applying what you know about your Lord and Savior today! There are folks out there who need what knowledge you have about Jesus!

Think of it this way, even if you are a brand-new Christian, what you know that made you a Christian is more than the unbelievers know. Remember we said not to worry about what to say; the Holy Spirit will speak through you. All you have to do is give Him a chance.

God loves you.

*oChristian.com

# THE WORST WORDS THAT WILL EVER BE SPOKEN TO SOMEONE. May 15

On a scale of one to ten, these words will break the scales. I would say they rank a hundred times ten. I am not even sure that there is a number above 10, high enough that would satisfy just how miserable these words will be to some:

> Revelation 20:11Then I saw a great white throne and him who was seated on it. The earth and the heavens fled from his presence, and there was no place for them. 12And I saw the dead, great and small, standing before the throne, and books were opened. Another book was opened, which is the Book of Life. The dead were judged according to what they had done as recorded in the books. 13The Sea gave up the dead that were in it, and death and Hades gave up the dead that were in them, and each person was judged according to what they had done. 14Then death and Hades were thrown into the lake of fire. The lake of fire is the second death. 15Anyone whose name was not found written in the Book of Life was thrown into the lake of fire.

Have you figured out what the words are yet? They will be surprising words to many people. The people at that day that will have their heads held high, waiting in the line to proclaim to the Lord, all that they have done! However, Jesus says, in Matthew 7:21–23:

> 21"Not everyone who says to me, 'Lord, Lord,' will enter the kingdom of heaven, but only the one who does the will of my Father who is in heaven.22Many will say to me on that day, 'Lord, Lord, did we not prophesy in your name and in your name drive out demons and, in your name,

perform many miracles?' 23Then I will tell them plainly, 'I never knew you. Away from me, you evildoers!

There it is: the worst words Jesus ever spoke to a human being: *I never knew you, away from me, you evildoers!* Those turned away will include cultists of false religions and many very religious people who don't truly believe what they profess because behind the façade is a world of sin.

The Pharisees were the most biblically oriented religious people, but they epitomized what Jesus was warning about. They knew the Bible well, but knowing and doing are different things! These people were in the fast lane of the broad road.

God loves you.

# THE PHARISEES. May 16

The Lord's obvious contempt for the Pharisees must have sent shock waves, or you might even say will be sending shock waves through every religion! For there are many very religious people in every religion that live their whole lives for their religion but miss the point of religion: Jesus. They were the most respectable, seemingly upright, and ardently devoted holy men in the Roman Empire.

They were quite confident that they deserved heaven because they had worked very hard to enforce the Ten Commandments, along with all the other religious laws that were added. But in the process of enforcing the laws, they conveniently forgot about the welfare of the widows and children and the poor citizens that they took advantage of. They enforced the law, but they, themselves could not follow the law.

The sins that they committed were in secret, well hidden from the folks, but not from the all-knowing, omniscient God. They were obsessed with what the people saw in them and how they wanted the people to act, but they neglected the important issues like pride, lust, and greed that festered in their own hearts.

> 27"Woe to you, teachers of the law and Pharisees, you hypocrites! You are like whitewashed tombs, which look beautiful on the outside but on the inside are full of the bones of the dead and everything unclean. 28In the same way, on the outside you appear to people as righteous but on the inside, you are full of hypocrisy and wickedness.
>
> Matthew 23:27–28

Jesus spoke about their hypocrisy because He knew their hearts. Did you get that, they thought they deserved heaven because of their works, but Jesus knew their hearts!

Heaven will be obtained by the amazing grace of God, not by any works we will do here on Earth!

God loves you.

# GO AND SIN NO MORE. May 17

John 8:3–11

As he was speaking, the teachers of religious law and the Pharisees brought a woman who had been caught in the act of adultery. They put her in front of the crowd.

4"Teacher," they said to Jesus, "this woman was caught in the act of adultery. 5The Law of Moses says to stone her. What do you say?"

6They were trying to trap him into saying something they could use against him, but Jesus stooped down and wrote in the dust with his finger. 7They kept demanding an answer, so he stood up again and said, "All right, but let the one who has never sinned throw the first stone!" 8Then he stooped down again and wrote in the dust.

9When the accusers heard this, they slipped away one by one, beginning with the oldest, until only Jesus was left in the middle of the crowd with the woman. 10Then Jesus stood up again and said to the woman, "Where are your accusers? Didn't even one of them condemn you?"

11"No, Lord," she said.

And Jesus said, "Neither do I. Go and sin no more."

The Pharisees were always trying to catch Jesus in saying or doing something they could condemn Him for. This is another example of how bad Satan wants to prove that He was not God. But when He was done talking, they were all gone. Take note of the fact that what the woman did was wrong, but her accusers were guilty of sin also, probably as bad or worse, and that is the reason they left. When Jesus looked at them, He looked at the heart; then they were ashamed of themselves.

Jesus did not come to condemn the world; He came to save it! Note also that He told her to go and sin no more! Turn around and begin to follow Him and stop doing what is not pleasing to our Lord. Do not live a life of sin.

It is a good lesson for all of us because we all have things we need to get forgiven for. Get on your knees and ask Him, and you will feel better! Then go and don't do the thing you asked forgiveness for anymore.

God loves you.

# GOD IS YOUR EVERYTHING. May 18

You in me? Who can understand? I only know that when I walk and You are not leading, I stumble, and if I continue walking without You, I fall! But when You are leading, my way is clear!

When I speak and You are not there, what I say makes no sense. But when You are speaking for me and through me, the words are understandable and can be used for Your glory.

When I try to listen and You are not there, I am rude and do not hear what is being said, but when You are there, I hear what is being said clearly, and Your wisdom shows in my response!

When I try to rest and You are not there, I toss and turn and the sleep is not restful, but when You are there, my rest is refreshing, and when I wake the day looks brighter!

Lord, help me to know at all times that You are my everything! I am useless without You! Please keep me close to You and do not let the evil one near me. Help me to resist the evil one so that you can lead me always.

I don't understand it but I know when I look back I can clearly see when You were with me and when I was on my own. I never want to be, on my own again, please, Lord.

This is my psalm to our loving God.

In your quiet time, think about writing one to your Savior. Just open your heart and put the words on paper. Share it with someone who needs some encouragement.

God loves you.

# THE BOOK OF LIFE. May 19

How long has God known you?

I read a commentary one time, not sure from whom, that said: There is a book in heaven called the Book of Life, where the names of the believers are recorded. Now this much I knew because Revelation 21:12, 27 tells us that at the Judgment Day, God will open it.

But this is what I found interesting: the book was written before humankind was created, and God wrote the names of His children in this book. The Book of Life is a kind of family photo album. It will have all the names of the believers who are heaven bound because they have given their life to Christ.

Here is the thing about this that shouted out to me: God had your name in the book before creation! Think about that for a moment or two. God knew you before you were you, and He had already written your name in the book! Hard to wrap your mind around, I know. Maybe this will help:

> Psalm 139,
> 16Your eyes saw my unformed body; all the days ordained for me were written in your book before one of them came to be. 17How precious to me are your thoughts, God!
>
> How vast is the sum of them! 18Were I to count them, they would outnumber the grains of sand — when I awake, I am still with you.

Guess what, God does not have an eraser on His pen, if He put your name in the Book of Life, it is there! How do I know? If He knew you before you were you, don't you think He knew you when you get done being you here on this earth?

All I can say is God is God, and I am just a human being who doesn't know anything about this because I can't think His way! But I do believe it because I know God, and I have faith that He is what He says He is, and I love Him for it!

And God loves you.

# SATAN IS LIKE A ROARING LION. May 20

1 Peter 5,
8 Be alert and of sober mind. Your enemy the devil prowls around like a roaring lion looking for someone to devour. 9 Resist him, standing firm in the faith, because you know that the family of believers throughout the world is undergoing the same kind of sufferings.

If you are a member of the body of Christ, get ready to face a mad devil. You may not want to think about it or even accept it—but if you have determined to follow Jesus with all your heart, Satan has marked you for destruction, and he's going to flood your life with troubles of all kinds.

The apostle Peter warns, "The end of all things is at hand: be ye therefore sober, and watch unto prayer" (1 Peter 4:7).

He is saying, in other words, "This is no time for lightness. You have to get sober-minded about spiritual matters. It is an issue of life and death."

Why the need to be so serious? The end of time is near—and our enemy has turned up the heat. He is stalking us like a lion, hiding in the grass and waiting for an opportunity to pounce. He wants to devour us—to utterly destroy our faith in Christ.

Some Christians say we shouldn't even talk about the devil, that we're better off just ignoring him. Others try to reason him out of existence. *

But understand this: If the owner of the house had known at what hour the thief was coming, he would not have let his house be broken into. Jesus is coming back, and Satan knows his time is short, so be alert. Peter says to be alert at all times and be serious about it. He says Satan is like a hungry lion.

Keep your armor on every day, please!

God loves you.

*notes by David Wilkerson

# LAZARUS AND THE RICH MAN. May 21

Then Jesus told a tragic parable that highlights the hopeless horror of hell and the infinite regret that will eternally haunt well to do and self-righteous people whose wealth of religion or other earthly advantages that have insulated them from the reality of the need for amazing grace. This parable confronts us with things we don't like to talk about but desperately need to take seriously.

> Luke 16:19–31, There was a rich man who was dressed in purple and fine linen and lived in luxury every day. 20 At his gate was laid a beggar named Lazarus, covered with sores 21 and longing to eat what fell from the rich man's table. Even the dogs came and licked his sores. 22 "The time came when the beggar died and the angels carried him to Abraham's side. The rich man also died and was buried. 23 In Hades, where he was in torment, he looked up and saw Abraham far away, with Lazarus by his side. 24 So he called to him, 'Father Abraham, have pity on me and send Lazarus to dip the tip of his finger in water and cool my tongue, because I am in agony in this fire.' 25 "But Abraham replied, 'Son, remember that in your lifetime you received your good things, while Lazarus received bad things, but now he is comforted here and you are in agony.26 And besides all this, between us and you a great chasm has been set in place, so that those who want to go from here to you cannot, nor can anyone cross over from there to us.' 27 "He answered, 'Then I beg you, father, send Lazarus to my family, 28 for I have five brothers. Let him warn them, so that they will not also come to this place of torment.' 29 "Abraham replied, 'They have Moses and

the Prophets; let them listen to them.' 30 " 'No, father Abraham,' he said, 'but if someone from the dead goes to them, they will repent.' 31 "He said to him, 'If they do not listen to Moses and the Prophets, they will not be convinced even if someone rises from the dead.' "

Obviously, the rich man heard the worst words ever to be spoken to a human: "I never knew you" because he was in the eternal fire being tormented. In other words, he was in hell. If hell were not real, why would Jesus talk about it?

No one in the Bible had more to say about hell than the Savior of sinners, the Lord Jesus Christ. Jesus was very vivid and profoundly shocking about the things He said about hell. He said, for instance, hell would be full of religious people. He also indicated that most of the world's religious activity is nothing more than a highway to hell.

He talked about it because He doesn't want you to go there. God loves you.

# LAZARUS AND THE RICH MAN,
## continued. May 22

The parable deals with several extreme opposites: terror and comfort; death and life; and hell, and heaven. Even the characters are opposite, the rich and the poor, whose fortunes are reversed in the end. Jesus was warning the Pharisees and urging them to repent before they wound up like the rich man. He obviously did not tell the story for anyone's amusement. This is a warning that came through loud and clear from the rich man who wanted Lazarus to go and tell his brothers of the horror of hell and tell them to repent and change their ways.

If this story causes you any shock or worry, that was precisely Jesus' intent. This is hard teaching, on purpose! This is truth spoken by Jesus for a serious reason: to cause you to reflect on your own life and decide what you need to do with the knowledge of the story.

Truth is not judged by how it makes you feel; that only happens in politics.

Why is the subject of hell taboo in today's world? Because hell is an embarrassment to those who want Christianity to fit the modern way of life, full of tolerance and universal goodwill. There are those who just want the message to always be cheerful to unchurched people.

Jesus told it like it was and will be, not how people want it to be.

There are many leaders today who promote the love of God and downplay what the Bible says about hell. Why? Because the things of hell are not popular. Hell is just a meaningless curse word to most. Actually, the word is used a lot but not in the right context by many unbelievers, and it is hush-hush to many believers.

Guess what, that is exactly how Satan wants it—hush-hush.

The parable tells us that people in hell want their loved ones to know about hell and to do everything possible to stay away from there.

Christians must not remain silent about hell! We must tell of the horrors and the very real threat it poses to those who live in unbelief and unrepentant sin.

Jesus told of the reality of the terror of eternal hell, of eternal death. Many think that they can live like they want to live, and at the end they will just be snuffed out. Nothing could be further from the truth! Your soul will never die!

> 2 Corinthians 5:10–11, Paul speaking, 10For we must all stand before Christ to be judged. We will each receive whatever we deserve for the good or evil we have done in this earthly body.11Because we understand our fearful responsibility to the Lord, we work hard to persuade others.

God knows we are sincere, and I hope you know this, too. God loves you.

# LAZARUS AND THE RICH MAN, part three. May 23

Why is the rich man in hell? After all he was apparently a religious man. Jesus does not charge him with any gross or notorious sins. In fact, the story does not mention any of his sins or evil deeds. He was just a typical citizen in that society, or he could have been from our society. It is clear of course that he was selfish, uncaring, and stunningly oblivious to the needs of his neighbors because he did nothing to help poor Lazarus, whom he and his brothers knew well and called by name. He even allowed him to eat the scraps from his table—what a guy!

But he didn't throw him off his property or abuse him as far as we know. He is not put forth as an uncommonly cruel man or a harsh evildoer, as if hell were only for the Hitlers of the world. That is not the point!

Notice if you will, when the rich man finds himself in hell, he is not surprised by being there. He does not say, "Hey there must be some mistake." And he does not ask, "Why am I here?" All of that was stripped away, and he understands why he is there; his only concern is for his brothers. He knows he deserves to be in hell. He just wants a hint of relief for himself, just a drop of water.

In hell, all hope is gone! The guilty conscience takes over and torments forever!

> Revelation 22:11 states, "He who is unjust, let him be unjust still: he who is filthy, let him be filthy still."

Hell fixes the destiny and the character of the reprobate forever!

We can never say too much about hell; it is a real place, the road to which is wide and the gate is large to it. Why? Think about it—if the road is narrow to heaven and wide to hell, what does that tell you?

God loves you.

Notes on this series is from John MacArthur's book on Parables.

# PHILLIP AND THE ETHIOPIAN. May 24

Phillip was a relatively new Christian, but he was out preaching what He knew about Jesus. He was able and willing and an angel appeared to him:

> Acts 8:26 As for Philip, an angel of the Lord said to him, "Go south down the desert road that runs from Jerusalem to Gaza." 27 So he started out, and he met the treasurer of Ethiopia, a eunuch of great authority under the Kandake, the queen of Ethiopia. The eunuch had gone to Jerusalem to worship, 28 and he was now returning. Seated in his carriage, he was reading aloud from the book of the prophet Isaiah. 29 The Holy Spirit said to Philip, "Go over and walk along beside the carriage." 30 Philip ran over and heard the man reading from the prophet Isaiah. Philip asked, "Do you understand what you are reading?" 31 The man replied, "How can I, unless someone instructs me?" And he urged Philip to come up into the carriage and sit with him. 32 The passage of Scripture he had been reading was this: "He was led like a sheep to the slaughter. And as a lamb is silent before the shearers, he did not open his mouth. 33 He was humiliated and received no justice. Who can speak of his descendants? For his life was taken from the earth." 34 The eunuch asked Philip, "Tell me, was the prophet talking about himself or someone else?" 35 So beginning with this same Scripture, Philip told him the Good News about Jesus. 36 As they rode along, they came to some water, and the eunuch said, "Look! There's some water! Why can't I be baptized?" 38 He ordered the carriage to stop, and they went down into the water, and Philip baptized him. 39 When they came up out of the

water, the Spirit of the Lord snatched Philip away. The eunuch never saw him again but went on his way rejoicing. 40 Meanwhile, Philip found himself farther north at the town of Azotus. He preached the Good News there and in every town along the way until he came to Caesarea.

Again, Phillip was willing to do whatever the Lord needed him to do.

I wonder how many people this high-ranking Ethiopian told about Jesus when he returned to his own country. I bet he led many people to the Lord. Are you ready and willing? You may not know how many, the one you tell about Jesus will tell and lead to the Lord until you meet them in heaven!

God loves you.

# GOD WANTS ALL TO COME TO HIM. May 25

2 Peter 3:8–13

8But do not forget this one thing, dear friends: With the Lord a day is like a thousand years, and a thousand years are like a day. 9The Lord is not slow in keeping his promise, as some understand slowness. Instead he is patient with you, not wanting anyone to perish, but everyone to come to repentance.

10But the day of the Lord will come like a thief. The heavens will disappear with a roar; the elements will be destroyed by fire, and the earth and everything done in it will be laid bare.

11Since everything will be destroyed in this way, what kind of people ought you to be? You ought to live holy and godly lives 12as you look forward to the day of God and speed its coming. That day will bring about the destruction of the heavens by fire, and the elements will melt in the heat. 13But in keeping with his promise we are looking forward to a new heaven and a new earth, where righteousness dwells.

Some will ask, why is Jesus waiting to come back, but to God it has only been a couple of days, (verse 8, a thousand years is like a day). Peter says, God does not want any to perish! God is so amazing. In the middle of all that is going on in this awful world, God is waiting for those who will accept Him to do it. And when the last one whose name is in the Book of Life who will be saved before the Rapture bows down and accepts him in their heart, we will hear a loud shout, and Jesus will appear in the air. There we will meet Him. What a wonderful day that will be for all the folks who have Jesus in their hearts. Keep looking up it could be any time now.

God loves you.

# A NICE CALM OCEAN. May 26

Hey kids I am at the beach at St George's Island. This morning when I got up and looked out the window, I saw something absolutely mind changing—a nice calm ocean! There was no confusion, there was no uncertainty, no politics, and no worries because everything was just as it should be. The waves were rolling up to the beach as they have since God filled the ocean.
Listen to Job 38:2–11:

2 Who is this that obscures my plans, with words without knowledge?

3 Brace yourself like a man; I will question you, and you shall answer me.

4 "Where were you when I laid the earth's foundation? Tell me, if you understand.

5 Who marked off its dimensions? Surely you know! Who stretched a measuring line across it?

6 On what were its footings set, or who laid its cornerstone—

7 while the morning stars sang together and all the angels[a] shouted for joy?

8 "Who shut up the sea behind doors, when it burst forth from the womb,

9 when I made the clouds its garment and wrapped it in thick darkness,

10 when I fixed limits for it, and set its doors and bars in place,

11 when I said, 'This far you may come and no farther; here is where your proud waves halt'?

God is in control; he told the waves where to stop. When you let Him completely take control of your life, what do you have to worry about? The world looks like it is spiraling out of control, but I think God has it going in the direction He wants it to go!

Everything is just falling into place. God was here in the beginning, and He will be here in the end. He is omnipresent!

God loves you.

# HOW NOT TO READ YOUR BIBLE? May 27

Most of us at one time or the other has said, "I am going to read through the entire Bible."

Why would we *not* want to read the Bible? It is our instruction book on how to live in the messed-up world we live in. There is a right way to begin, and there are a few ways that are not recommended.

Here are a few that are not recommended:

1. Use it as a buffet where you pick and choose only to glean "the stories" that interest you.
2. Set a goal of reading through the whole thing by reading a book a day.
3. Don't take time to pray before you start; you got this!
4. You don't need one of those reading plans; again, you got this, no problem.
5. Only read the parts where Jesus is speaking.
6. Read it so you can be smarter than anyone else about the Bible.

Well I think you get the idea; these are not good ideas.

Reading your Bible is the most important thing you can do for yourself and the people around you. Why? Because God wrote it! He wrote you and me and everyone else a book of love that from the beginning to the end is all about His Son and the way you can be with Him forever. It tells us how to live, and react to the people around us.

When you read, He will speak to you directly in ways you can't imagine. They will be so timely that you will think He just wrote it to you. If it was the only book ever published, it would be all we would ever need to live by. It is the most important book ever written!

When you read it, expect your Lord and Savior to speak to you; He will. I promise!

If you don't achieve anything else in your life time, do this: read the Book that your Creator left for you. Pray about it, put action to your prayers, and do it!

God loves you.

# A FRIENDLY REMINDER. May 28

2 Peter 1:12–15,
12So I will always remind you of these things,
even though you know them and are firmly
established in the truth you now have. 13I think
it is right to refresh your memory as long as I
live in the tent of this body, 14because I know
that I will soon put it aside, as our Lord Jesus
Christ has made clear to me. 15And I will make
every effort to see that after my departure you
will always be able to remember these things.

Peter knew that he would soon die and be with His Savior.
He was writing during the time of Nero the Emperor of Rome.
Nero was murdering Christians whenever he could find them.
This was the time that many scholars believe that Peter and Paul
both were martyred for their faith in the Lord Jesus Christ. Peter
says, "I know I won't be here much longer so I want to make
sure you know what you need to know so that you can sustain
yourself in the faith." He wanted to be sure they remembered
what he had told them.

I, too, want you to know everything you need to know to
live in this awful world. The world is full of false teachers, and
there are and will be people who do not take these things seriously anymore. The world will treat these things like a joke and
make their own religion to fit their own whims and lusts. There
are many like this today.

There will be more and more opportunities for you to share
your faith because we are getting closer and closer to the end
times—if we are not already in them. Go after the ones going
the wrong way; be tender with the lost but not soft on sin. Throw
them a life vest, and do all you can to get them in the boat.

Read your Bible daily!

God loves you.

# GOD LOVES US VERY MUCH! May 29

Romans 8:38–39
38 For I am convinced that neither death nor life, neither angels nor demons, neither the present nor the future, nor any powers, 39neither height nor depth, nor anything else in all creation, will be able to separate us from the love of God that is in Christ Jesus our Lord.

Ephesians 2:4–5
4 But because of his great love for us, God, who is rich in mercy, 5 made us alive with Christ even when we were dead in transgressions—it is by grace you have been saved.

Zephaniah 3 17
17 The Lord your God is with you, the Mighty Warrior who saves.

He will take great delight in you; in his love he will no longer rebuke you, but will rejoice over you with singing."

1 John 3
1 See what great love the Father has lavished on us, that we should be called children of God! And that is what we are! The reason the world does not know us is that it did not know him. 2 Dear friends, now we are children of God, and what we will be has not yet been made known. But we know that when Christ appears, we shall be like him, for we shall see him as he is.

Kids, the Bible, God's love letter to His children, speaks of the great love God has for us. We have talked a lot about what will happen to the folks who absolutely refuse to accept the love that God offers them; to me it is beyond comprehension. "Saving us is the greatest and most concrete demonstration of God's love, the definitive display of His grace throughout time and eternity" (David Jeremiah).

God loves you guys!

# THE FENCE. May 30

There was a large group of people. On one side of the group stood a man, Jesus. On the other side of the group stood Satan. Separating them, running through the group of people was a fence. The scene set, both Jesus and Satan began calling to the people in the group, and one by one, each having made up his or her own mind, followed either Jesus or Satan, depending on the choices they had made. This process kept going. Soon enough, Jesus had gathered around Him a group of people from the larger crowd, as did Satan. But there was one man that did not join either group. He had climbed the fence that was there and sat on it. Then Jesus and His people left and disappeared. So, too, did Satan and his people. And the man on the fence sat alone. As the man was sitting, Satan came back, looking for something, which he appeared to have lost. The man on the fence said, "Have you lost something?"

Satan looked straight at him and replied, "No, there you are. Come with me."

"But," said the man, "I sat on the fence. I chose neither you nor Jesus."

"That's okay," said Satan. "I own the fence." *

You just can't win sitting on the fence!

There are only two choices: Jesus or Satan. You can either go and be with Jesus in a place He has prepared for you, or go with Satan to a place God has prepared for him and his followers.

Get off the fence, and follow Jesus!

God loves you.

*unknown

# THE LORD IS MY SHEPHERD! May 31

Psalm 23
1 The Lord is my shepherd, I lack nothing.

2He makes me lie down in green pastures,

He leads me beside quiet waters.

We have the Lord God looking over us and seeing after our every need. He makes us happy. He gives us green pastures to lie down in with nice quiet waters beside us. As a sheep, what could possibly be better than a lush green pasture and sweet, still waters? That's right—absolutely nothing! It is your happy place.

When God is your shepherd and you are following Him, there are no worries; you are in your happy place. Happiness is something the world cannot give you, and if God is your shepherd, the world cannot take your happiness away from you.

There are three sections of the 23rd Psalm; the first part is the secret of a happy life; in the next, he gives us a happy death; and the third is a happy eternity.

God loves you.

# THE DEVIL HAS NO HAPPY OLD MEN! June 1

Psalms 23:3, KJV He restoreth my soul: he leadeth me in the paths of righteousness for his name's sake.

Someone once said that the devil has no happy old men. He decided to put it to the test and for a week asked every old man he met if he was happy. He found it was true—the devil has no happy old men. He helped one old man carry a suitcase up a hill. The man thanked him, but when the man asked him if he was a happy old man, the old man swore at him. He found only one happy old man. He helped an old blind man across the street, and halfway across, he asked him if he was happy. The man said he was, sure enough, a Christian. *

I think by the time a man gets old without Jesus in his heart, he gets bitter at the world.

The Lord Jesus shares His life with us, He puts all of His resources at our disposal, He gives us restfulness, He gives us green pastures and still waters, He restores our souls. When a sheep wanders off, he cannot find his way back, and it takes our Shepherd to bring us back home. Remember the Good Shepherd left the ninety-nine to find the one that was lost.

He gave His life for us and bears the scars of Calvary. He loves us very much!

God loves you.

*Phillips commentary on Psalms

# I WILL FEAR NO EVIL. June 2

23rd Psalm
4Yea, thou I walk through the valley of the
shadow of death,
I will fear no evil; for thou art with me;
Thy rod and thy staff, they comfort me.

Instead of talking about the Shepherd, now David is talking to Him. He says, "Thou art with me." Notice that this is only the valley of the shadow of death. The shadow of a dog cannot bite you, the shadow of a sword cannot harm you, and the shadow of death cannot harm a child of God. Don't forget where there is a shadow, there is the Light. The Light, Jesus Christ, is what makes the difference between the death of a believer and an unbeliever. The unbeliever goes out in the darkness forever, but the believer goes out into the beautiful Light. You will fear no evil; you will be happy to see your Lord and Savior, for He is with you!

God loves you.

# THY ROD AND THY STAFF THEY COMFORT ME! June 3

Psalm 23:4 Yea, though I walk through the valley of the shadow of death, I will fear no evil: for thou *art* with me; *thy rod and thy staff they comfort me.*

Okay, Kids, I understand how a shepherd's staff can provide comfort for the sheep. The shepherd protects the sheep from all the wild animals that are in a mood for lamb chops. As we have said before, the lamb is the only animal that cannot make it in the wild. They have to have a protector, so a sheep, seeing the staff in his Shepherd's hand, would say, "Yeah, baby, now we talking. Lay into those bad guys with that stick." They would be happy to see it.

But did you know what the rod was for? It was to keep the sheep in line. Proverbs says, "Spare the rod and spoil the child." So how many of you sheep out there would be glad to see the shepherd with a rod in his hand? Not me, if what I saw when I saw it in the hand was a switch. I don't think so!

So, what did David mean by he would be comforted by the rod? Because he is stupid; sheep are dumb animals, and they have to be guided along the path or they will wander off. There is much danger out there when you wander off; you can become someone's lamb chops!

So yes, be happy to see the rod because it will keep you safely on His road, the paths of righteousness in the light so that you can bring honor to His name.

God loves you guys.

# THOU PREPAREST A TABLE BEFORE ME IN THE PRESENCE OF MINE ENEMIES June 4

Thou anoint my head with oil; my cup runs over (Psalm 23:5).

Think about the Israelites running away from the Egyptians. They got through the Red Sea and headed for the desert. And there it was: a table set in defiance of their foes. There was the table in the Tabernacle and there was a carpet of manna on the desert sands. The table was to sustain and satisfy them on the way to the Promised Land. We have talked about the great banquet that Jesus is preparing for His children when we get home; can you imagine the spread on that table? Ladies, I know you guys are good, but I got to believe that will be a table that will trump anything you have ever thought about—and it is prepared just for you! Whatever you think is the best there is, won't hold a candle to this table.

This will be a grand banquet we will share with our Lord! And there will be an abundance. David says, "My cup runs over," enough for myself and my friends.

Think about it, we will have a table set for the children of the King of kings!

Have a great day.

God loves you.

# THOU PREPAREST A TABLE BEFORE ME IN THE PRESENCE OF MINE ENEMIES, Cont. June 5

"Thou anointest my head with oil; my cup runs over" (Psalm 23:5).

Picture this in your mind; you are about to go to war, against a very large army. It will be a fierce battle, but God is outside your tent preparing a banquet. You can see the enemy's army on the other side of the field. He is setting the table, filling it with all the things you love.

Got the picture? Good. What do you think is going through your mind, eating a hardy meal or staying alive? Then how does this make sense? The only person that could eat a banquet-sized meal before a hard battle is a person that is not worried about the outcome of the battle.

We don't think like this, but God does!

If God be with you, who can be against you? If He is your God and He is in charge of you, mind body, and soul, then eat up and enjoy the banquet in front of your enemy! If He is not worried and He thinks it is time to relax and enjoy a good meal when an important battle is at hand, then what are you worried about? God is either in control or you are! He has it! Turn it loose and let Him be in control!

God loves you.

# A HAPPY ETERNITY. June 6

"Surely, goodness and mercy shall follow me all
the days of my life and I shall dwell in the house
of the Lord forever" (Psalm 23:6).

We are given two glimpses of what lies ahead. We are given
a glimpse of the King's highway, for we are on journey, and hard
on our heels comes God's two great ambassadors, goodness and
mercy. Goodness takes care of my steps; Mercy takes care of
my stumbles. Mercy and goodness are what get us through this
life journey.

Then He gives us a glimpse of His home where we shall
dwell forever. There it is, a "happy eternity." Jesus said, "In my
Father's house are many mansions," and He said, "I go to prepare a place for you."

All this and heaven, too — wow. We serve an Awesome Master! *

This is a wonderful psalm that takes us from a happy life to
a happy death and on to a happy eternity. When you are feeling
down and out and Satan has done a number on you, ponder on
the 23rd Psalm and the great hope it gives us from now through
all of eternity.

Do you have it memorized? You should be able to quote it
to the devil whenever!

God loves you.

*Notes on this series was from Phillips on Psalms.

# THE LORD'S PRAYER, MATTHEW
## 6:9–13. June 7

Luke tells us that when the disciples saw Jesus praying one day, one of them asked Him to teach them how to pray, just as John taught his followers to pray. And He said to them, "When you pray say this," and He went on to quote the Lord's Prayer.

Can you say the prayer; do you know it by heart? If you don't, now you know where to find it—in Matthew chapter 6. Think about it: His followers asked Him, how they should pray and He told them. Shouldn't we also want to know how to pray? This was God telling them how to pray. Matthew says that Jesus said when you pray, get by yourself in a dark place. He said a closet, where it is just you and Him, no interruptions, no phones, no noise, just you and Him.

Now I know we have a relationship with Jesus, and we can talk to Him anytime about anything and we should. But I think this prayer is directed to Almighty God, the Creator of heaven and Earth because it starts with, "Our Father." What an intimate, personal, family way to approach God.

Could it be that He actually regards me as His child? Does He care enough to see me as His son? That in itself is a startling concept. But that is exactly what Jesus, the Second Person of the Triune God told us. Jesus called Him the Father more than seventy times. And He told us to do the same. So, get your Bible out, or go to Bible Hub, or Bible Gateway or whatever phone app you use, and find it and repeat it over and over until it is written on your mind. There are only five verses; you can memorize that. Over the next several days, we will look at it and see how to make it personal: for instance, "My Father," instead of Our Father, forgive me my sins.

He is our Father, but when you are in your quiet place, it is just you and Him, so address Him as such.

God loves you.

# OUR FATHER. June 8

Do not do as some do and try to relate God to what we experienced from our fathers when we were growing up. There is no comparison accept by the word *father*.

Our earthly fathers were not gods. Some may have thought they were, but they were not. I know it is hard to think of God as father without thinking of something that may have happened to you as a kid, good or bad. But that is not the way to see your Father in heaven. Nor is He a condemning judge standing over us, shaking His head from side to side, as He looks down on us. Do not forget what it says in Psalm 139:16: "You fashioned me before I was born and every day of my life was recorded before a day had passed." He knows us very well, He knows our comings and our goings, He knows when we get up and when we lay down. We cannot hide from him, even when we know we have done wrong.

Because He knows you, you cannot surprise Him, He knew it before you did it. And somehow, He still loves you and me. We are His children, and we can address Him as "our Father," two short words that set the tone for this prayer. We are praying to a loving Father who knows more about us than we do and loves us still!

Do you know Him as Your Father? You can!

God loves you.

# WHO ART IN HEAVEN? June 9

God is omnipresent. He is anywhere and everywhere, in all times. He reigns in heaven.

How can He be in heaven and everywhere else at the same time? Our minds cannot conceive the power of God. But I believe it because the Bible tells me so! Let's look at what the Bible tells us about heaven; the first thing is Satan; our archenemy will not be there. So, there will be no temptation.

We will have a quiet contentment, we will be at home without a restless spirit, and we will be at rest. There will be no tears, no death, no more sorrow, no more crying, and we will not have to cry out for God because we will be with Him. There will be no more pain because we will have our glorified bodies. No more sun or moon and no clocks because time will not be what rules us. There will be no perversions and nothing to cloud our thoughts—no falsehoods, lies or dishonesty. Life there will be abundant with our Father who art in heaven!

But we are not there yet, so seek to know God as your Father here. Let heaven begin now in this life as you grow daily to get closer to Him. The closer your walk with Jesus, the more of heaven you will experience. As a born-again Christian, your eternal life has already begun, so now is the time to learn as much as possible about our Lord.

God loves you.

# HALLOWED BE THY NAME! June 10

What does hallowed mean? Well the dictionary says honor as Holy, sacred, blessed, greatly revered or respected. A whole world of respect, reverence, awe and appreciation for the person of God the Father.

So enormous was the ancient Hebrews' respect even for the name of God that they wouldn't speak His name. But Jesus taught us that He was our intimate Father. His name is holy, and we should respect it. One of Ten Commandments says, "Thou shalt not take the Lord your God's name in vain," which means do not use His name to no avail! His name is holy! Do not use his name fruitlessly. Do not speak it except in praise or worship. It is not an adjective to a curse word, ever!

When God was asked by Moses, who should I say sent me? God said, "Tell them 'I AM' sent you." Ponder the thought that God calls Himself, I AM.

He said, "I AM THAT I AM." Think of what that means. Putting it into plain language, what Jesus is saying in this prayer is, "Father, may Your Person, Your Identity, Your Character, Your Reputation, Your very being always be honored." *

Everything that was created and made was made by God,

Sweetheart, you need to get us all some bracelets that say's "Made by God." Then maybe we will understand what "Hallowed Be Thy Name" really means. His name be hallowed!

God loves you.

*Keller, on the Lord's Prayer

# THY KINGDOM COME. June 11

Who is King of your life? Most if not all of us become supreme experts in selfish, self-centered living where all of life revolves around the sovereign Me, I, and Mine. So, when I sincerely ask the King of kings to come into my life and establish His Kingdom in my life, naturally there will be a great conflict between the King and my ego. So, when you pray that thy kingdom come, you have to be willing to give up your kingship to Him. *

That's easy to say, but we all find it harder to do on a day-to-day basis. Because giving up making decisions for my own affairs and letting God the Holy Spirit make decisions for me is what it means to let Him rule your life.

Our idea of freedom that has been pounded in our brains conflicts with living under a King's rule in a Kingdom.

First Corinthians 3:16 says, "Know ye not that ye are the temple of God, and that the Spirit of God dwells in you?"

So here it is: Oh Lord God, come and establish Your sovereignty in my heart while I am on earth and then soon on this earth itself, when you come back!

I accept You as King of my life! You are all knowing and know me better than I know myself; you are in charge of me, and I give my whole self to you, mind, body, and soul!

Now if indeed the King is within your castle, then make sure there is nothing that enters that will offend Him. Do not allow anything in the castle that would grieve the King of kings and Lord of lords!

Lord, Thy kingdom come.

God loves you.

*notes by Keller

# THY WILL BE DONE. June 12

What is God's will? Can our Father's will be known? Does the will of God become important to strong-willed men and women? God's will simply put: it is His intentions for our lives. It is what He wants for us, His plan for us. Great, Pop, but how do we know that?

How could you know God's will if you don't take time to know God?

> God has a plan for all of us, His will for us. But He will allow you to do your will, and it probably won't be what He has planned. It can be His will be done or your will be done—which do you choose? He tells us in Isaiah 55:8 "My thoughts are not your thoughts, and He says, "I know the thoughts which I think toward you." Jeremiah 29:11 KJV

> His will for us is gracious and generous. "11For I know the plans I have for you," declares the Lord, "plans to prosper you and not to harm you, plans to give you hope and a future" (Jeremiah 29:11 NIV).

Why would we not want to know His plan is? Then it follows that if we want to know what His plan is, we need to read His book. He also tells us in Matthew 7:7–8, "Ask and it will be given to you; seek and you will find; knock and the door will be opened to you. 8For everyone who asks receives; the one who seeks finds; and to the one who knocks, the door will be opened."

If you want to know God's will for you, then do as He says A=ask, S= seek and K= knock (ASK) him. Read His guidebook, your Bible, and have a burning desire to know the Will of God, and you will!

God loves you.

# IN EARTH AS IT IS IN HEAVEN. June 13

When will His will be done in earth? Can it be done on earth with so much evil in the world? His will cannot be done when the hearts and minds of so many reject His very existence, can it? Here on earth? Simple answer to all questions—yep! Remember, He is all knowing, omniscient.

There are no surprises. He is not fooled; Satan does not win, God is in charge, "I am the Alpha and the Omega, the First and the Last, the Beginning and the End" (Revelation 22:13). If He says My Will be done, it will!

The word of God says obey and be blessed, disobey and meet disaster, obey and live, disobey and die. It is a fairly simple plan and an easy plan: believe and be saved!

John 14:23 says (Jesus speaking) "If a man loves me, he will keep my words.)

When He comes back, His will shall be done on earth, and everything is falling into place just as God planned. Woe be unto those who reject His plan. That place has been prepared also

> 28, there will be weeping there, and gnashing of teeth, when you see Abraham, Isaac and Jacob and all the prophets in the kingdom of God, but you yourselves thrown out. 29People will come from east and west and north and south, and will take their places at the feast in the kingdom of God. Luke 13.

Some obeyed and some did not. Tomorrow, give us this day our daily bread

God loves you.

# GIVE US THIS DAY OUR DAILY BREAD. June 14

Do you think we take our daily bread for granted? Jesus said give us our daily needs; He did not say, "Give me all I can consume today." That is just a thought.

He gave us all we can ever want, though. Think of this great world that He has provided for us. Psalm 54:4 says, "Surely God is my help; the Lord is the one who sustains me."

He has given us very much, but He told Adam, "Thou shall earn thy bread by the sweat of your brow." So, don't pray the prayer and sit on a corner and wonder why you don't have something to eat. You don't see birds sitting on limbs looking up to the sky with their mouths open, waiting for God to drop seeds down their throats. They work from sun up to sun down, gathering what God has provided for them. He has provided, but we have to do our part. He also tells us that "Man shall not live by bread alone, but by every word that proceeds out of the mouth of God" (Matthew 4:4).

He is Jehovah Jireh; the LORD will provide.

> Genesis 22:13–14 "And Abraham lifted up his eyes, and looked, and behold behind <him> a ram caught in a thicket by his horns: and Abraham went and took the ram, and offered him up for a burnt offering in the stead of his son. {14} And Abraham called the name of that place Jehovah Jireh.

So, do we need bread, of course. Do we need spiritual food from heaven, yes, of course? What we need is our daily food for our mind, body, and our souls from heaven. The saying goes, you are what you eat! Are you eating the bread of life, food for your soul, every day?

Don't sit on a limb, looking up with your mouth open, waiting for God to drop knowledge of Himself in your brain. Do like the birds and work for it: ask, seek and find. It is like the

Promised Land God provided for the Israelites; He gave them the land, but they had to fight for it.

Praise the Name of Jehovah Jireh, (our provider!)

God loves you.

# AND FORGIVE US OUR DEBTS. June 15

What are our debts? Sin is represented here under the notion of a debt, and as our sins are many, they are called debts here. God made man that he might live to His glory and gave him a law to walk by. When he does anything that tends not to glorify God, he contracts a debt with divine justice; Romans 3:23 says, "For the wages of sin is death," meaning eternal death.

The question is, do most of us really come to the Father feeling indebted to Him? After all, we live a better life than, "old what's-his-name next door," don't we?

That has to count for something! And it would, if "old what's-his-name," was the norm that we are compared by, but he is not. Jesus Christ is, and He lived a perfect life!

The whole concept of comparing ourselves to others or even to Christ is not what was intended. The fact is, the Bible leads us to believe that forgiveness is the issue, not comparisons. The other question is, who is going to pay off your debt? You can try, and you will spend eternity in hell trying, but it won't happen. Or you can choose your Champion to pay it for you. Jesus Christ has paid it already; all you have to do is accept Him as your Savior.

Second Corinthians 5:21 says, "God made him who had no sin to be sin for us, so that in him we might become the righteousness of God."

God loves you.

# AS WE FORGIVE OUR DEBTORS. June 16

This part of the prayer is ongoing. Why? Because not only do we continue to sin but those around us will continue to sin against us. So, Jesus said, forgive me *as* I forgive others. It is not a one-time deal. Many of us have prayed the prayer and not made any effort to forgive that person or persons that have wronged us. So how can you ask Him to forgive you if you don't do your part? Is there someone that you harbor hate for deep down in the recesses of your mind? Guess what? It is not hidden from God no matter how far you have pushed it away. You need to write that old debt off by way of forgiveness. Do not lie to yourself or God; do the forgiving before you do the praying.

> John 4:24, 24, God is spirit, and his worshipers must worship in the Spirit and in truth."

> Eph. 4:32, be kind to one another, tender-hearted, forgiving one another, as God in Christ forgave you.

> Luke 23:34, Father, forgive them; for they know not what they do. He harbored no hate even for those who killed Him.

> John 8:32, then you will know the truth, and the truth will set you free."

Do the forgiving and then do the praying or while you are praying!

God loves you.

# AND LEAD US NOT INTO
# TEMPTATION. June 17

Satan does not come at us with a red face and horns on his head; he comes at us presenting himself as everything we could ever want. He knows your weakness and that is where he hits you the hardiest. And Jesus knew this; He had experienced it in the wilderness for forty days. He knew because He won the battle between Him and Satan. We are not God-men, like Jesus, and we are weak, and we give in to temptation. Listen to what Paul says about it in,

> Romans 7:14, 14: "So the trouble is not with the law, for it is spiritual and good. The trouble is with me, for I am all too human, a slave to sin. 15, I don't really understand myself, for I want to do what is right, but I don't do it. Instead, I do what I hate."

There is a battle going on in all of our lives. Just remember, what can help you win is the fact that Jesus won the battle already! Normally, it is not God leading you into temptation, it is you where you have given in to secularism and started to depend on self. After all, you can do anything; you don't need anyone beyond yourself. *Glory to you in the highest!*

But if God does it, is for your own good, He will always provide a way out, but you have to recognize it and escape. There would be something for you to learn in the temptation— maybe humility.

> Remember 1 John 4:4 that says, "Greater is He that is in you, than he that is in the world."

The decision as to whether or not we overcome the temptation is ours. We will decide to give in or run away. God loves you and wants you to run away from sin as fast as you can. He knows with the Spirit's help, you can win the battle, so be strong and listen to Him, not self.

God loves you.

# BUT DELIVER US FROM EVIL. June 18

All of us know full well where our weak points are. We know those places where we are most likely to fall for Satan's tricks. We know the people who most likely would lead us off track. So, if we really want to be good strong Christians for Jesus, it is madness to go to those places or allow ourselves to be influenced by those people.

Look at what Joseph did in,

> Genesis 39. One day he went into the house to attend to his duties, and none of the household servants was inside. "12 She caught him by his cloak and said, 'Come to bed with me!' But he left his cloak in her hand and ran out of the house."

Did you get that, kids? *He ran out of the house.* Do not even go close to the places or people who will affect your walk with the Lord.

> James 4:7 says, "Resist the devil and he will flee from you."

He will move on to an easier target.

When we know full well, what is right and proper and in accord with the Father's wishes, then we need to be courageous and stand firm, and then keep on standing! The Holy Spirit will help you to stand for what is right and good!

> Jude 24–25,
> 4To him who is able to keep you from stumbling and to present you before his glorious presence without fault and with great joy—25to the only God our Savior be glory, majesty, power and authority, through Jesus Christ our Lord, before all ages, now and forevermore! Amen.

God loves you.

# FOR THINE IS THE KINGDOM, AND THE POWER AND THE GLORY FOREVER. AMEN June 19

This is a praise benediction to the prayer.

We opened with "Hallowed be thy name," and we close with His Kingdom, power, and glory. It is appropriate and very proper that this prayer that Jesus taught us should finish with exultation and praise of our Father God. *

> Col. 1:19–22, For God in all his fullness was pleased to live in Christ, 20, and through him God reconciled everything to himself. He made peace with everything in heaven and on earth by means of Christ's blood on the cross. 21, this includes you who were once far away from God. You were his enemies, separated from him by your evil thoughts and actions. 22Yet now he has reconciled you to himself through the death of Christ in his physical body. As a result, he has brought you into his own presence, and you are holy and blameless as you stand before him without a single fault.

What an amazing thought: we who are the worst of sinners can stand before God blameless because of what Jesus has done for us. What an awesome God we serve!

Father, may all who pray this wonderful prayer, pray it now with more understanding of how great Thou Art. Thank you, Father God!

God loves you.

*Notes on this series is from Keller's book, a layman's look at the Lord's Prayer.

# SATAN IS ON THE ATTACK! June 20

A certain man had several sons who were always quarreling with one another, and try as he might, he could not get them to live together in harmony. So, he determined to convince them of their folly by the following means. Bidding them to fetch a bundle of sticks, he invited each in turn to break it across their knee. All tried and all failed. Then he undid the bundle, and handed them the sticks one by one, which they had no trouble breaking over the knee. "There, my boys," he said. "United you will be more than a match for your enemy, but if you quarrel and separate, your weakness will put you at the mercy of those who attack you." *

This is exactly what happens when we as Christians drift away from the Lord and begin to quarrel and separate. The enemy walks in the open door and wreaks havoc.

We have a great example, in our family, of what a group of Christians with like intentions praying can do when the enemy attacks. He is beaten by the Spirit of God through the unity of the Christians.

1 + 1 + God is a majority. If you have drifted and are trying to run solo, shut the door and get back to your first love.

Shut Satan out! Union is strength!

God loves you.

*Aesop

# BE STRONG, COURAGEOUS, AND SUCCESSFUL. June 21

God has given us a pathway on which to walk that ends in success in this life and the next.

Listen to what God told Joshua:

> Joshua 1,
> 8 Keep this Book of the Law always on your lips; meditate on it day and night, so that you may be careful to do everything written in it. Then you will be prosperous and successful. 9 Have I not commanded you? Be strong and courageous. Do not be afraid; do not be discouraged, for the Lord your God will be with you wherever you go."

Now I don't think I would interpret this verse to read, like most of us actually do. This is *not* what God said, "Now, Josh, when you feel like you are in the mood and you have nothing else to do, sit down and scan through the Good Book, and if you see anything that looks interesting, spend a moment or two reading my word." He also did not say, "Josh here is another good idea: hold the Bible on its end and let it open, and I will make it open to what I want you to read. What do you think?"

*God did say*; keep the Book always on your lips, think about it day and night, and study the word so that you may do everything in it! *And I will be with you!*

You must establish a Bible-reading plan, and it should never be a second thought. It should be at the top of your list of things to do! How will you ever be able to think about His word day and night if nothing comes to mind? Put something worthwhile up there, so it can rattle around and give you something good to think on.

Home school yourself about God, and read His love letter systematically. Pray about it and put action to your prayer!

God loves you.

# ARE YOU A CHRISTIAN ALL THE TIME? June 22

Or just when you are in the mood to be one, you know, when something spiritual happens?

We have talked about that, it is called being a part-time Christian. That is like being a Christian on Sundays or when you are around other Christians only.

Here is the question that you have to ask yourself: Am I a Christian at work, at school, on the ballfield, or at all of my neighbors' houses? Am I blending in or standing out? Would everyone who knows me agree that I am sold out for Jesus? Everyone?

If not, does that mean there are times when I don't want to be a Christian? What kind of thinking is that?

Listen to what Paul told the people of Colossae:

> Colossians 3:1, since, then, you have been raised with Christ, set your hearts on things above, where Christ is, seated at the right hand of God. 2, Set your minds on things above, not on earthly things. 3, for you died, and your life is now hidden with Christ in God. 4, When Christ, who is your life, appears, then you also will appear with him in glory. (When Jesus comes back)

> 5, Put to death, therefore, whatever belongs to your earthly nature: sexual immorality, impurity, lust, evil desires and greed, which is idolatry. 6, Because of these, the wrath of God is coming. 7, you used to walk in these ways, in the life you once lived. 8, but now you must also rid yourselves of all such things as these: anger, rage, malice, slander, and filthy language from your lips. 9, do not lie to each other, since you have taken off your old self with its practices 10, and have put on the new self, which is being renewed in knowledge in the image of its Creator.

Paul said it best. Set your mind on eternal things. God loves you.

# WHO IS OUR WORST ENEMY? June 23

Matthew 16:23 says, "Jesus turned and said to Peter, "Get behind me, Satan! You are a stumbling block to me; you do not have in mind the concerns of God, but merely human concerns."

Peter was worried about Jesus. Jesus said to Peter, "Get thee behind me Satan." Did this mean that Peter was possessed by Satan? No, it was Peter's mouth; he was the rebel. Does that mean that we can cause ourselves to stumble and that it is not always Satan making me sin? Yes, as a matter of fact, *we* are sometimes our worst enemy! Paul had a lot to say about how self can lead you down the broad road to destruction in Romans.

> Romans 7:18, For I know that good itself does not dwell in me, that is, in my sinful nature. (Or old self), for I have the desire to do what is good, but I cannot carry it out. 19, For I do not do the good I want to do, but the evil I do not want to do—this I keep on doing. 20, now if I do what I do not want to do, it is no longer I who do it, but it is sin (self) living in me that does it.

So, Paul says the old self, or flesh, or whatever you want to call your sin nature:

> The part of you that came from Adam and Eve,

> The stubborn part of you, the hard-headed part of you,

> The rebel you, the side of you that wants to be fun loving and fancy free, no rules no consequences,

> The part of you that says, "You don't want to be a goody two shoes, do you?"

is the part of you that Jesus died for, I repeat, the part of you that Jesus died for, the part of you that needs to listen to the good part of you? It is the part of you that makes you do what you don't want to do because you know better and the part of you that wants you to blend in and not stand out. This part of you is the one that has been defeated by Jesus along with Satan. Yes, Satan is an enemy and a fierce one, but *you* are sometimes your worst enemy.

The good news is the Holy Spirit that lives within you will keep that part of you shut out—if you let Him. You just have to listen to Him; He will always suggest the right way. Listen to Him instead of self! His will, not yours.

God loves you.

# JEHOVAH-RAPAH, THE LORD WHO HEALS! June 24

These verses are for those that are ill;

Exodus 15:26 "And God said, if thou wilt diligently hearken to the voice of the LORD thy God, and wilt do that which is right in his sight, and wilt give ear to his commandments, and keep all his statutes, I will put none of these diseases upon thee, which I have brought upon the Egyptians: for I <am> the LORD that healeth thee."

Psalm 103:3 "Who forgiveth all thine iniquities; who healeth all thy diseases;"

Psalm 107:20 "He sent his word, and healed them, and delivered <them> from their destructions."

Isaiah 41:10
10, so do not fear, for I am with you; do not be dismayed, for I am your God.

I will strengthen you and help you; I will uphold you with my righteous right hand.

Psalm 41:2–3
2, The Lord protects and preserves them—they are counted among the blessed in the land—

He does not give them over to the desire of their foes.

3, The Lord sustains them on their sickbed, and restores them from their bed of illness.

Mark 5:34

34, Jesus said to her, "Daughter, your faith has healed you. Go in peace and be freed from your suffering.

Christians, if this is from Satan, as in the form of attack on your sweet spirit, he has made a grave error, for he has unleashed a group of true born-again spirits praying for you that will cause him much grief. Jesus Christ defeated him already!

*God's will be done!*

God loves you.

# THE FATE OF SATAN AND UNBELIEVERS! June 25

Revelation 20:10, and the devil, who deceived them, was thrown into the lake of burning sulfur, where the beast and the false prophet had been thrown. They will be tormented day and night for ever and ever.

Revelation 14:11 And the smoke of their torment will rise for ever and ever. There will be no rest day or night for those who worship the beast and its image, or for anyone who receives the mark of its name." 12This calls for patient endurance on the part of the people of God who keep his commands and remain faithful to Jesus.

Listen guys, I don't know about you, but this is and should be the scariest verse in the Bible (the smoke from their torment will rise forever). This is an eternal burning death; this is the second death. The Bible says in Hebrews 9:27, "Just as people are destined to die once, and after that to face judgment."

If you follow Jesus, you will only die once unless you are alive when He returns, but then you will be with Him eternally in heaven, unlike the unbelievers who will die once and then the judgment, and following that, eternal torment in hell where the smoke of their torment will rise forever. Like we have said before, we live on earth only a moment or two, compared to eternal life.

We should always have eternity in mind with everything we do. Dying is one thing; dying eternally by fire is something else completely.

Do not live here on earth as if you have plenty of time to do the "Jesus thing" because you don't. You need to get about doing what God has for you to do! God has a plan for you.

And if you are reading this and have not made the choice to follow Jesus, then do it now. Bow your head and do it right now. It will be between you and Jesus; repent of your sins, and ask Him into your life.

God will bless you with life if you do.

God loves you.

# THE FATE OF UNBELIEVERS
## CONTINUED. June 26

What constitutes an unbeliever?
Jesus said, in John 3:16–18:

> 16-For God so loved the world that he gave his one and only Son, that whoever believes in him shall not perish but have eternal life. 17-For God did not send his Son into the world to condemn the world, but to save the world through him. 18-Whoever believes in him is not condemned, but whoever does not believe stands condemned already because they have not believed in the name of God's one and only Son.

But you see, you can believe that Jesus is the Son of God, like Satan and his demons do; they believe it also, but they don't believe *in Him*. They do not and do not want to follow Him, and they do not want Him to be the Lord of their lives and their Savior. They do not believe that He died for their sins. Satan and his cronies don't care that He died; they were mostly responsible for it. They wanted Him dead, but they did not want Him to rise again after three days; that constituted their death in hell.

Jesus defeated death!

It has been justly said that every sin is an act of ingratitude or rebellion against the Father. So, everyone needs a Savior, and that is what you need to know and believe about Jesus, to *believe in Him*. Accept it on faith that if you ask Him, He will be your Lord and Savior.

God loves you.

# WHAT DOES IT MEAN TO
# DIE TO SELF? June 27

Look at these verses where Jesus speaking, and ponder the meaning. We will discuss this over next few days.

> Luke 9:23, 23 and he said to all, "If anyone would come after me, let him deny himself and take up his cross daily and follow me.

> Mark 8:35, for whoever would save his life will lose it, but whoever loses his life for my sake and the gospel's will save it.

> John 12:24, 24 truly, truly, I say to you, unless a grain of wheat falls into the earth and dies, it remains alone; but if it dies, it bears much fruit.

> Matthew 10:38, 38 and whoever does not take his cross and follow me is not worthy of me.

> 1 Peter 2:24, 24 He himself bore our sins in his body on the tree, that we might die to sin and live to righteousness. By his wounds you have been healed.

> 2 Corinthians 5:17, Therefore, if anyone is in Christ, he is a new creation. The old has passed away; behold, the new has come.

The Bible clearly tells us that we must die to self and follow Jesus, but what does that mean? And how do I do it?

Here is a good question to ponder: what have you personally given up for Jesus? What in your life has changed? Have you said to Jesus, "Lord, here I am; what I need is You as the icing to my cake." If so, Jesus might tell you, "Find someone else."

He does not want to be the icing. He wants to be the whole thing—none of you, all of Him! Die to self!

God loves you.

# DIE TO SELF, continued. June 28

What kind of thoughts and things were part of the old you? Before Christ, what were you like? Were you selfish, greedy, and self-satisfying? What did the old you look like? Was your life full of sin? What did you care about besides yourself? Look at Ephesians 4:20–24:

> But that is not the way you learned Christ! — assuming that you have heard about him and were taught in him, as the truth is in Jesus, to put off your old self, which belongs to your former manner of life and is corrupt through deceitful desires, and to be renewed in the spirit of your minds, and to put on the new self, created after the likeness of God in true righteousness and holiness.

There has to be a change, the Lord says put away the old self and put on the new self, or new you, Christ in you, so that means there must be a change in you! You must think differently; you must be different.

Jesus did not tell us to add the new to the old. He said, in Mark 2:22, "And no one pours new wine into old wineskins. Otherwise, the wine will burst the skins, and both the wine and the wineskins will be ruined. No, they pour new wine into new wineskins." You cannot maintain the old you and just add the new you. If you do, there will be a war going on inside of you all the time.

You need to bury the old you and put Jesus on, like you would new clothes, and live for Him! He has to be the center of all of your attention. This is what baptism represents; you bury the old and when you come out of the water, you come out the new you in Christ.

If you have not given anything up for the Lord, are you really following Jesus?

Pray about it.

God loves you.

# DIE TO SELF part three. June 29

You might say, "Well, I ain't perfect, and you would be correct; none of us are. We all have a problem with the old self rearing its ugly head now and then. But it should not be a continued way of life as you did before you ask Christ into your heart.

Then you might say, "Well, I am under grace, so no worries. But listen to what Paul says about that in Romans 6:1–7, 13–14:

> What shall we say, then? Shall we go on sinning so that grace may increase? 2-By no means! We are those who have died to sin; how can we live in it any longer? 3-Or don't you know that all of us who were baptized into Christ Jesus were baptized into his death? 4-We were therefore buried with him through baptism into death in order that, just as Christ was raised from the dead through the glory of the Father, we too may live a new life. 5-For if we have been united with him in a death like his, we will certainly also be united with him in a resurrection like his. 6-For we know that our old self was crucified with him so that the body ruled by sin might be done away with, that we should no longer be slaves to sin—7-because anyone who has died has been set free from sin.

> 13-Do not offer any part of yourself to sin as an instrument of wickedness, but rather offer yourselves to God as those who have been brought from death to life; and offer every part of yourself to him as an instrument of righteousness. 14-For sin shall no longer be your master, because you are not under the law, but under grace.

All the times Paul mentions dying in these verses, he is speaking about dying to self, burying the old you so that you can live in the new you, in Christ.

No, we are not perfect, but we should be growing in Christ every day.

God loves you.

# DIE TO SELF, part four. June 30

Laodicea was the worst of the seven churches that John wrote a letter to, in Revelation from the Lord Jesus. This church was neither hot nor cold, they were lukewarm. Look at Revelation 3:14–20:

> To the angel of the church in Laodicea write: These are the words of the Amen, (Jesus Christ), the faithful and true witness, the ruler of God's creation. 15-I know your deeds, that you are neither cold nor hot. I wish you were either one or the other! 16-So, because you are lukewarm—neither hot nor cold—I am about to spit you out of my mouth.
>
> 19-Those whom I love I rebuke and discipline. So be earnest and repent. 20Here I am! I stand at the door and knock. If anyone hears my voice and opens the door, I will come in and eat with that person, and they with me.

Lukewarm, what do you suppose that meant? I wonder could it have meant that they had not died to self. They were cold about things they needed to be hot about, and they were hot about unimportant things. They were living in the old self and not the newness of Christ to the point that if they did not change, Jesus would spit them out. What a horrible thought. But just like the Lord, He was giving them a second chance, He warned them to change.

I wonder if they were religious on Sundays and back to old self Monday through Saturday. Hot and then cold! Lukewarm!

Don't be like them! Die to self! And follow Jesus, twenty-four hours a day and seven days a week!

God loves you.

# WHAT IS A DISCIPLE? July 1

Who were the original disciples? Let's look at them to decide what a disciple is.

A definition of a disciple is; a follower or student of a teacher, leader, or philosopher. It is also a term used for the twelve apostles that Jesus called to follow Him. Jesus later told them to go and make disciples in all the world. He used three action words: go, baptize and teach, with the core meaning to make disciples.

Who were these men? They were ordinary laboring men. There were no professional men except what knowledge they needed for their vocation. They were an average cross section of the society of that day. They were certainly not the group one would have thought could win the world for Christ, but the one who thought that would have been wrong. Look at Acts 4:13 that says, "When they saw the courage of Peter and John and realized that they were unschooled, ordinary men, they were astonished and they took note that these men had been with Jesus."

Key words—they had been with Jesus! They were Jesus followers. Even though they were lacking in higher education and were somewhat unpolished, Jesus chose them, and they followed Him. Jesus taught them how to be disciples and how to make disciples, followers of Christ. The Holy Spirit came on them when Jesus went to the Father. There were a lot of people following Jesus, but the twelve were called disciples because some of the others were just along for the show; Luke said the others were just "going along" with Him with no real commitment. Lukewarm folks. He did not meet their expectation of Him; they were looking for a king to rid them of the Romans. Instead, He would have given them eternal life. Some folks are funny that way. No commitment. Lukewarm.

God loves you.

# WHAT IS A DISCIPLE? part two. July 2

First of all, you need a personal relationship with Jesus.

In fact, He expects people to choose Him over mother, father, and brothers and sisters if it comes to that (Luke 14:26). So, don't let it come to that kind of choice; lead your family to the Lord and there won't be a choice to make. If there is a choice, choose Jesus.

Here is the point, disciples have no higher priority in their lives than Jesus Christ. Jesus will be number one in the life of a disciple, even over the family! Second, there has to be a high level of commitment. A disciple will replace his own selfish goals and desires with God's desire for them.

God, your will be done in my life, not mine! They will sacrifice their way for His way.

> Philippians 2:3–4, 3-Do nothing out of selfish ambition or vain conceit. Rather, in humility value others above yourselves, 4-not looking to your own interests but each of you to the interests of the others.

> John 6:38, 38-For I have come down from heaven not to do my will but to do the will of Him who sent me.

A disciple does not make decisions without asking, "What would Jesus have me to do?"

God loves you.

# WHAT IS A DISCIPLE? part three. July 3

What about personal possessions?

Luke 14:33 says, "In the same way, those of you who do not give up everything you have cannot be my disciples."

This sounds like dying to self; if we die to self, are we not giving up everything that we were? By the way, who does your possessions belong to anyway? Yep, you are right—the Creator of all things. What we have is just on loan from the Father. Jesus is not saying that we can't possess anything; we just can't let anything possess us. Corrie ten Boom once said she had learned how to hold everything loosely in her hands; that way when the Lord pried it out of her hand, it would not hurt much. Disciples should hold on to things loosely. Can you think of anything that you have that has a hold on you? Let it go, and turn it over to him. Look at what the disciples did in Matthew 4:18–22:

> 18-As Jesus was walking beside the Sea of Galilee, he saw two brothers, Simon called Peter and his brother Andrew. They were casting a net into the lake, for they were fishermen. 19-"Come, follow me," Jesus said, "and I will send you out to fish for people." 20-At once they left their nets and followed him. 21-Going on from there, he saw two other brothers, James son of Zebedee and his brother John. They were in a boat with their father Zebedee, preparing their nets. Jesus called them, 22-and immediately they left the boat and their father and followed him.

All four left everything they had and followed Jesus. That is a real commitment!

A disciple will walk away from whatever Jesus calls him to walk away from. A disciple is called to be a servant of the Lord and obey His commands. Many of us are certainly Christians, but what about discipleship? *

That is a costly subject that the Lord requires all of you. He requires you to be an empty vessel that He may come in and fill up. We tend to want to give him a half or three quarters of a full vessel—some, or a lot of me, and a top off of Jesus, but He wants a full commitment, not a lukewarm one. But you know what? If you come to Him with an empty vessel, and allow Him to fill you up with Himself, you will never be the same again. I think the term is *in Christ*!

They dwell in Him, and He dwells in them. He is the source of their life, and it shows in everything they do. "The peace of Christ rules in their hearts," "the power of Christ is made perfect in their weakness," and "the life of Christ is made manifest in their mortal flesh." *

God loves you.

*notes on this series from Chuck Swindoll's book *Strengthening your Grip*.

# LOVE FROM THE HEART AND SOUL. July 4

Joshua had led the Israelites in defeating the Canaanites and in taking the Promised Land; now it was time for the Israelites that had taken the land east of the Jordan River to go home. This is what he told them in Joshua 22:5:

> But be very careful to keep the commandment and the law that Moses the servant of the Lord gave you: to love the Lord your God, to walk in obedience to him, to keep his commands, to hold fast to him and to serve him with all your heart and with all your soul.

This is also a great verse to memorize because we should be doing the same thing. This is very close to what Jesus said: Love your God with all of your heart soul and mind. Walk in His ways and keep all His commandments. Then Joshua said to remain faithful to Him as you serve Him. The words *heart* and *soul* highlight the need to be "all in."

Are you "all in" for Jesus?

If you love God, intellectually, emotionally, and spiritually, then you can serve God faithfully. Nothing else but total commitment would suffice, and that is what God expects!

Joshua's solemn charge to the eastern tribes provides a wonderful guideline for believers today. We can fulfill no greater commandment than to love the Lord our God with all we are. Then we will walk in His ways and keep His commands.

I would add for us, if I may, because we now have the word of God, to stay in His word. To me meditating on His words is what will help us to be faithful and keep His commands!

Has anyone made a commitment to read through His word this year?

God loves you.

# MOE AND THE TRICYCLE. July 5

One night in a Bible study in the neighborhood we lived in Marietta, Georgia, one of our friends, Moe, told a story that left us all speechless. He said he was driving on one of the winding hilly roads of north Georgia. One day, and he admitted he was probably driving a little fast for a two-lane country road, when he was climbing a hill, his car shut down. The motor stopped, and he started coasting. He said just as he peaked the top of the hill, he saw a little tot riding his tricycle in the middle of the road. He easily stopped before he got to the little fellow and made sure he got back in his own yard. When he got back in his car to leave, it started up as if nothing had been wrong with it. He said while he sat there with the car running, he realized what happened to the car. An angel or the finger of God or whatever had stopped the engine of the car to save the life of the little boy and Moe probably. As he said, had he run over the little guy while speeding on a country road, he would not have been able to live with himself. There was no doubt in Moe's mind that God had intervened in saving the boy. There are those who would say, no, it was just his lucky day, but Moe knew it was not luck; it was God.

Listen to Psalm 91:9–14:

> If you say, "The Lord is my refuge," and you make the Most High your dwelling,
>
> 10-no harm will overtake you, no disaster will come near your tent.
>
> 11-For he will command his angels concerning you to guard you in all your ways;
>
> 12-they will lift you up in their hands, so that you will not strike your foot against a stone.

13-You will tread on the lion and the cobra; you will trample the great lion and the serpent.

14- "Because he loves me," says the Lord, "I will rescue him; I will protect him, for he acknowledges my name.

God loves you, and will protect you!

# IN CHRIST. July 6

The expressions "in Christ," "in the Lord," and "in Him" occur 164 times in Paul's letters alone.

Kids, to be in Christ, does not mean to be inside Christ, as tools are in a tool chest or forks in a drawer, but it is to be like a limb on a tree. If Jesus is the tree, then being in Christ is you being the limb of the tree. The limb cannot survive or live without the tree. This is also having a personal relationship with Jesus. Listen to Jesus speaking in John 5:

> 4-Remain in me, and I will remain in you. For a branch cannot produce fruit if it is severed from the vine, and you cannot be fruitful unless you remain in me. 5- "Yes, I am the vine; you are the branches. Those who remain in me, and I in them, will produce much fruit. For apart from me you can do nothing. 6-Anyone who does not remain in me is thrown away like a useless branch and withers. Such branches are gathered into a pile to be burned. 7-But if you remain in me and my words remain in you, you may ask for anything you want, and it will be granted! 8-When you produce much fruit, you are my true disciples. This brings great glory to my Father.

All around us are people that do not feel fulfilled, they are asking,

What am I here for and what am I supposed to do?" They are always searching for satisfaction, for happiness.

They do not have the living water or the bread of life, Jesus Christ! They are not attached to the living Christ. They are not "In Christ." There is an inner emptiness that only He can fill.

Everyone is born with it, and only those who have Jesus as their vine to feed them, realize the inner peace of being, "In Christ."

God loves you.

# IN CHRIST, part two. July7

There are several different kinds of people in today's world that we can see from what we learned in the book of Joshua. Most people are still in bondage in Egypt; they never left to go to the Promised Land, and they need to be delivered by faith in Jesus Christ.

Others have trusted Christ and have been delivered from bondage but are still wandering in the wilderness of unbelief because they won't enter into their inheritance by faith.

Still others have sampled the inheritance but prefer to live on the borders of the blessing.

Finally, there are those who follow Jesus and enter the Promised Land and claim their inheritance. They are "in Christ."

Crossing the Jordan and going into the Promised Land is not a picture of dying and going to heaven; it is a picture of dying to self, our old life, and entering into our spiritual inheritance now, in this life, and enjoying the fullness of God's blessings as we serve the Lord and glorify Him.

A great need today is for God's people to see how much they are missing by wandering in the desert of unbelief or by living on the borderline of the blessings. *

This is a great day for people to access where they are, still in Egypt, in the wilderness, on the border, or in Christ in the Promised Land.

When you decide where you are, then pray about it. God wants all His people to follow Jesus. Jesus said in John 15:8, "When you produce much fruit, you are my true disciples. This brings great glory to my Father."

God loves you.

# IN CHRIST, part three. July 8

Galatians 3:26, So in Christ Jesus you are all children of God through faith, 27-for all of you who were baptized into Christ have clothed yourselves with Christ. 28-There is neither Jew nor Gentile, neither slave nor free, nor is there male and female, for you are all one in Christ Jesus. 29-If you belong to Christ, then you are Abraham's seed, and heirs according to the promise.

Being in Christ means brotherly unity.

Those who are *in Christ* enjoy a unity with one another which transcends nation and denomination, race and rank, class and culture. Friendships between the friends of Jesus is unlike any other friendship, and this is evidence that Jesus has continually been active in men and woman's lives. It is proof that being *in Christ* is to be radically transformed. Paul said if anyone is in Christ, he is a new creation. Paul is speaking of dying to the old way of life and having been risen to the new life with Christ. Thus, you have a new lifestyle with a new value system with new moral standards, which will be plain to those around you. Which, by the way, is very different than the world's standards. The world admires the powerful; it is concerned with appearances with a philosophy of "only love those who love you" and "repay evil for evil."

But Jesus says love your enemies and pray for those who persecute you, and do good to those who hate you, overcoming evil with goodness. Those *in Christ* will bear much fruit and glorify the Father in Jesus' name. Amen

God loves you.

# BEAR MUCH FRUIT IN CHRIST. July 9

Think of a fruit tree, any fruit tree—plums, pears or peaches. What do you see?

Most likely you see in your mind a colorful tree full of whatever fruit you are thinking about. Yes, but how does this relate to Jesus saying—He is the vine and we are the branches? Branches are what bears the fruit that is fed by the tree. So, if Jesus is the tree, He is feeding us His words when we need them to witness to someone. Remember He said, "Don't worry about what you will say; I will give you the words to say." God said that to Moses and many other prophets, and Jesus told us the same thing. Like the tree feeds the branches and the branches feed the fruit, He will feed you and tell you what to say and do. Imagine the tree again: the fruit is beautiful. What other fruits can you bear? What are the fruits of the Spirit?

> Galatians 5:22–23 says, "But the fruit of the Spirit is love, joy, peace, forbearance, kindness, goodness, faithfulness, 23 gentleness and self-control. Against such things there is no law."

All of these things are on the tree, like fruit, being fed to you by Jesus when you are in Christ and when you need them. You need self-control today, Jesus says, "Here, it is flowing through you." "You need joy? Here, it is yours for the taking."

"Yes, I am the vine; you are the branches. Those who remain in me, and I in them, will produce much fruit. For apart from me you can do nothing" (John 15:5, Jesus speaking_.

Have a great day in Christ.

God loves you.

* SERIES notes from *In Christ* by John R. W. Scott

# LOVE MUST BE SINCERE. July10

Romans 12:9–13

9-Love must be sincere. Hate what is evil; cling to what is good. 10-Be devoted to one another in love. Honor one another above yourselves. 11-Never be lacking in zeal, but keep your spiritual fervor, serving the Lord. 12-Be joyful in hope, patient in affliction, faithful in prayer. 13-Share with the Lord's people who are in need. Practice hospitality.

One of the differences between Christians and the world is our ability to love. This love comes solely from God and stems out of the fact that He first loved us. First John says, "Dear friends, let us love one another, for love comes from God. Everyone who loves has been born of God and knows God" (1 John 4:7). Our capacity to love is much more than a natural response to a feeling; our capacity is supernatural because we are children of God and God lives in us (1 John 4:7–21).

We are in Christ, and He is in us. In today's passage, Paul tells us that love must be sincere. It must be genuine—the real thing. It must be without hypocrisy. In our natural selves, this is hard to do. It is not always easy to show love and compassion to one another, but this is the mark of a born-again believer. Our love for one another should speak louder than any words we can express. It is no mystery that love is the very first fruit of the Spirit listed in Galatians 5. This fruit is the characteristic of God that was deposited in our born-again spirit.

These things were given to us at salvation and prove that we are children of God when we allow them to operate in our lives. We have been given a supernatural ability to love one another. Love is the anchor to every fruit of the Spirit because God is love and his love is the driving force behind everything he has done. In the same way, since God loved us, we should love one another and allow His love to flow through us (1 John 4:11). *

God loves you.

*Author unknown

# SINCERE LOVE, part two. July 11

It is important to understand that living and operating in love is not something that we must work at; it is a natural byproduct of being born again and walking by the Spirit of God.

Paul told us in Romans 8, "Those who live according to the sinful nature have their minds set on what that nature desires; but those who live in accordance with the Spirit have their minds set on what the Spirit desires" (Romans 8:5).

> By simply walking in fellowship with the Lord and renewing our minds to the truth of God's word, we will see these things manifested in our lives supernaturally (Romans 12:2).

> This is the beauty of living by the Spirit of God; the changes that occur are effortless because in the process God changes our hearts to align with His heart. His characteristics become our characteristics as evidenced by the fruit of the Spirit operating in our lives. Walking by the Spirit of God, we will love deeply and gravitate toward everything good because his Spirit leads us. He is the vine, and we are the branches. This is the way He designs us to function, not by trying in our own efforts and failing, but His spirit living within us.

What an amazing thing to love in the same way we are loved by God. Today, may this revelation of God's love for you overflow into your love for one another. May your love show you to be a child of God today. Amen. *

God loves you.

*Author unknown

# JESUS IS COMING BACK SOON. July 12

Matthew 24:40-Two men will be working together in the field; one will be taken, the other left. 41-Two women will be grinding flour at the mill; one will be taken, the other left.

42- "So you, too, must keep watch! For you don't know what day your Lord is coming. 43-Understand this: If a homeowner knew exactly when a burglar was coming, he would keep watch and not permit his house to be broken into. 44-You also must be ready all the time, for the Son of Man will come when least expected.

We do not talk enough about the return of our Lord. But not talking about it will not change the outcome. The reason is obvious; it is not popular to hear that the Lord will soon come back and collect His children and then the judgment. It is like in Noah's days; people were going about their everyday life, not paying any attention to God, and then one day He had enough of their indifference and the rains came.

There is only One who knows when Jesus is coming back, and that is the Father. So, we don't know when, but we do know that we are 2000 years closer than the disciples were, and they expected it to happen in their lifetime.

Listen to Matthew 16:27: "For the Son of Man will come with his angels in the glory of his Father and will judge all people according to their deeds."

God loves you.

# JESUS' SECOND COMING. July 13

Much of the Bible is dedicated to the theme of the second coming of our Lord Jesus. There are over 1500 prophecies of Jesus' second coming. For every prophecy of His first coming mentioned in the Old Testament, there are eight predicting His second coming. Think about it, that is a lot of discussion about Jesus' second coming. Jesus' return is mentioned once in every five verses in the New Testament, according to the net. Chuck Swindoll says one out of every thirty in the Bible.

Wouldn't you agree that it is a topic that we are expected to talk about?

Can you say that for every five sermons you have heard, one of them was on the return of Jesus?

I know I could not say that. The Bible warns us of a period of great trouble and tribulation just before the second coming. The second coming is not necessarily good news for all people, as the Bible warns that those who have rejected Jesus will *run from Him* at His appearing. Look at Matthew 24:30–31:

> And then at last, the sign that the Son of Man is coming will appear in the heavens, and there will be deep mourning among all the peoples of the earth. And they will see the Son of Man coming on the clouds of heaven with power and great glory.31And he will send out his angels with the mighty blast of a trumpet, and they will gather his chosen ones from all over the world from the farthest ends of the earth and heaven.

Always be looking up.
God loves you.

# THE RAPTURE. July 14

There are two comings of Christ in the future. The first is when He will be coming for us, and then next He will be coming back with us. The first of these comings is to the air for the Church, the Rapture, and the next He will come to the earth for the Judgment.

Many will say, "Where do you find the word *rapture* in the Bible?" It may not be found in the Bible, but the truth of it is not invalidated, any more than the absence of the word *Trinity* invalidates the triune Godhead.

We get the word *rapture* from the phrase, "caught up," "taken away," or "snatched up."

There is a good example of the resurrection in nature. Look at the caterpillar; it begins life crawling around eating leaves, and at that point in his life, would he ever think of soaring in the wind? Probably not, but then it weaves a coffin, crawls inside, and dies to this world and the life he knew. Then, suddenly, it hears a resurrection call, and it leaves its coffin and emerges as a beautiful butterfly. It metamorphosed, it is caught up, and it spreads its wings and soars in the sky. And that is what will happen to the dead in Christ. They lie in the grave, asleep in their coffin, and then one day they will hear a shout, and they will be resurrected in to a glorious new body and meet the Lord in the air at the time of the rapture.

> 1 Thessalonians 4, 15-According to the Lord's word, we tell you that we who are still alive, who are left until the coming of the Lord, will certainly not precede those who have fallen asleep. 16-For the Lord himself will come down from heaven, with a loud command, with the voice of the archangel and with the trumpet call of God, and the dead in Christ will rise first. 17-After that, we who are still alive and are left will be caught up together with them in the clouds to meet the Lord in the air. And so, we will be with

the Lord forever. 18-Therefore encourage one another with these words.

God loves you.

# PARADISE TO COME. July 15

Paul called the Rapture of the church "the blessed hope" in Titus 2:13: "while we wait for the blessed hope — the appearing of the glory of our great God and Savior, Jesus Christ."

Every true child of God anticipates not the grave but the glory, not some kind of afterlife as a ghost, but as a full-bodied, glorified immortal body to live eternally in heaven or "paradise" as Paul called it.

Google *paradise* and see how it is described. You will find that Paradise is the term for a place of timeless harmony. The Abrahamic faith associates paradise with the Garden of Eden, that is, the perfect state of the world prior to the fall from grace and the perfect state that will be restored in the world to come, heaven. By all accounts, it denotes peace and tranquility.

Think of a place here on this earth that you would call paradise. There are some very beautiful places, but the best you can come up with, will be lacking in many things.

Jesus is preparing a perfect place for you, personally. You couldn't even do that if you had His resources because He knows you better than you know yourself. He created you!

Paul's glimpse of heaven and its glory made it clear to him that what awaits us is far better than anything we have down here,

> as he said in Philippians 1:23, "I am torn between the two; I desire to depart and be with Christ, which is better by far, but it is more necessary for you that I remain in the body."

The great hope of the church is that Christ will come and rapture us up to heaven before death intervenes, but even if death comes first, the soul will go on to be with Him and then we will be resurrected and given glorified bodies like Jesus has when He comes to get the Church.

Are you ready for Jesus to come today? He could, you know! God loves you.

# WHAT IS THE BLESSED HOPE OF CHRISTIANS? July 16

Titus 2, 12It teaches us to say "No" to ungodliness and worldly passions, and to live self-controlled, upright and godly lives in this present age, 13while we wait for the blessed hope—the appearing of the glory of our great God and Savior, Jesus Christ.

The word *blessed* can mean "happy," or "beneficial"; our hope is blessed in that Jesus' return will be an amazing joyful experience for the believer in Christ. The trials and sufferings of this life will be over.

The word *hope* does not communicate uncertainty, as in "I hope that something may occur"; rather, it is glad assurance that something *will* take place. Jesus is our *hope*, and no one can take that hope away. Look at Romans 5:5 that says, "And hope does not put us to shame, because God's love has been poured out into our hearts through the Holy Spirit, who has been given to us."

The blessed hope, then, is the joyful assurance that God will extend His benefits to us and that Jesus Christ *will* return. Jesus said He would return, the angels said He would return, and the Bible in many, many times says that He will return. Jesus could come back at any time now.

Jesus' imminent return should motivate the believer to live godly in an ungodly world. And it should motivate the unbeliever to become a believer in Christ.

Always be looking for our Lord to return.

God loves you.

# THE SHOUT AND THE TRUMPET. July 17

1Thessalonians 4:16, New Living Bible, says,
"16-For the Lord himself will come down from
heaven with a commanding shout, with the voice
of the archangel, and with the trumpet call of
God. First, the Christians who have died will rise
from their graves."

The trumpet will sound the alarm for the world at large.
They will be alerted that the day of grace is over, the Day of
Judgment has come, and the great seven-year tribulation has
begun. Everyone on earth will be affected by the Rapture. The
Christians will leave the Earth, and all nonbelievers in Christ
will experience seven years of hell on earth. Some people will
say, "Well, I am already experiencing hell on Earth." I would
say they may be to an extent, but nothing like what will happen
in the seven-year tribulation. Here is a taste of what is to come:

Revelation chapter 6,
12-I watched as the Lamb broke the sixth seal,
and there was a great earthquake. The sun
became as dark as black cloth, and the moon
became as red as blood. 13-Then the stars of the
sky fell to the earth like green figs falling from
a tree shaken by a strong wind. 14-The sky was
rolled up like a scroll, and all of the mountains
and islands were moved from their places.

Wow! You do not want to be on earth during this time.
God loves you.

# IN THE TWINKLING OF AN EYE. July18

I have, in the past, wondered how quick a twinkling is, but not anymore. When my wife, Pat, got new lenses for her eyes because of cataracts, one of the first things I noticed that happened was not only could she see without her glasses, but she also gained a distinct twinkle in her eyes. And you don't really have to look hard to see it; it is always there. She looks at you, and not only does she smile, but her eyes twinkle. Let me tell you, it is quick. It is faster than a blink.

> Look at 1 Corinthians 15:51–52, Paul talking to the Christian brothers and sisters, "51-Listen, I tell you a mystery: We will not all sleep, but we will all be changed—52in a flash, in the twinkling of an eye, at the last trumpet. For the trumpet will sound, the dead will be raised imperishable, and we will be changed."

We will be fitted in an instant, (a twinkling of an eye) with our new immortal body, our glorified body, and we will meet the Lord in the air.

Have you ever seen iron jump up to attach itself to a magnet? Think about a giant magnet moving along the earth; the magnet is Jesus, and all the Christians will be attracted to him, like iron to a magnet. And just as all the gold, silver, copper, and lead will not be drawn to Him, many will be left behind. Only the iron will go. You know why only the iron, Christians, will be drawn to Him? Because the iron has the same "nature" as the magnet. When Jesus comes, He will draw to Himself only one kind of person, the born-again Christian. Not necessarily the religious, the moral, the church member or the theologian, but just the kind of person who has the same "nature" as Himself, only the born again.

> Jesus told Nicodemus, "Ye must be born again"!
> John 3:3

So, the all-important question I need to ask myself is this: Have I been born again? Not am I well liked, like gold, or silver. Or am I a church member or a very moral person, like copper, but do I have the "nature" of Jesus Christ? Have I been born again? Will I jump up to Him like iron to a magnet, or will I be left behind?

Please make sure; I will assure you, you will not want to be left behind!

God loves you.

# MORE ON THE RAPTURE. July19

Someone might ask, "I understand that the dead will rise and meet up with their souls in the air, but what happens to the Christians who are alive when Jesus comes for the Church?" Look at what Paul says about it.

> 1 Thessalonians 4:17, Then, together with them, we who are still alive and remain on the earth will be "caught up," (raptured), in the clouds to meet the Lord in the air. Then we will be with the Lord forever. 18, so encourage each other with these words.

> 1 Corinthians 15:51, But let me reveal to you a wonderful secret. We will not all die, but we will all be transformed! 52, It will happen in a moment, in the blink of an eye, when the last trumpet is blown. For when the trumpet sounds, those who have died will be raised to live forever. And we who are living will also be transformed. 53, For our dying bodies must be transformed into bodies that will never die; our mortal bodies must be transformed into immortal bodies.

> 58, So, my dear brothers and sisters, be strong and immovable. Always work enthusiastically for the Lord, for you know that nothing you do for the Lord is ever useless.

God loves you.

# THE TEN BRIDESMAIDS. July 20

Matthew 25:1–13, Jesus speaking, "Then the Kingdom of heaven will be like ten bridesmaids who took their lamps and went to meet the bridegroom. 2-Five of them were foolish, and five were wise. 3-The five who were foolish didn't take enough olive oil for their lamps, 4-but the other five were wise enough to take along extra oil. 5-When the bridegroom was delayed, they all became drowsy and fell asleep.

6-At midnight they were roused by the shout, 'Look, the bridegroom is coming! Come out and meet him!' 7-All the bridesmaids got up and prepared their lamps. 8-then the five foolish ones asked the others, 'Please give us some of your oil because our lamps are going out.'

9-But the others replied, 'We don't have enough for all of us. Go to a shop and buy some for yourselves.' 10-But while they were gone to buy oil, the bridegroom came. Then those who were ready went in with him to the marriage feast, and the door was locked. 11-Later, when the other five bridesmaids returned, they stood outside, calling, 'Lord! Lord! Open the door for us!'

12- "But he called back, believe me, I don't know you!" 13-So you, too, must keep watch! For you do not know the day or hour of my return."

This is a parable about the second coming, Jesus is telling the story.

In this parable how many can guess what the oil represents?

There were five foolish and five wise bridesmaids; five had the extra oil and five did not. Five was able to go in, and five were left behind.

What do you think? Find out tomorrow.

God loves you.

# THE OIL FOR THE LAMP. July 21

In the Bible days the lights were either a torch, candle, or an oil lamp. In the parable yesterday, we had five wise and five foolish bridesmaids; when the Bridegroom came the foolish bridesmaids had no oil for their lamps, so they were left behind. How many figured out that the oil they were missing was symbolic of your faith and of the Holy Spirit. Outwardly, all ten bridesmaids were the same. They all had lamps, and they all fell asleep; the only thing different was the oil supply. An oil lamp will not burn without oil; it is a useless lamp. They had the language of a believer but not the life of a believer.

A person who professes to be a Christian but has not been born again and does not have the Holy Spirit in their heart is nothing but a foolish bridesmaid who will be left outside when the wedding banquet begins between Jesus and His Church. The foolish bridesmaids were pretenders. At the end, they wished that they had the oil they needed for their lamps, but they did not. The wise bridesmaids had the oil and was invited to the wedding banquet. What a marvelous banquet it will be.

At the end times, there will be many people that will wish that they were born again into God's kingdom so that they would be invited to the wedding feast, but they will be left into the darkness where there will be weeping and gnashing of teeth.

What about you? How is your oil supply?

God loves you.

# THE DAY OF THE LORD! July 22

1 Thessalonians 5:1–5

But of the times and the seasons, brethren, ye have no need that I write unto you. 2For yourselves know perfectly that the day of the Lord so cometh as a thief in the night. 3For when "they" shall say, Peace and safety; then sudden destruction cometh upon "them," as travail upon a woman with child; and "they" shall not escape. 4But "ye," brethren, are not in darkness, that that day should overtake you as a thief. 5Ye are all the children of light, and the children of the day: we are not of the night, nor of darkness.

The Rapture will be the prelude to the coming "Day of the Lord," that terrible day when God will send judgment on this world because of its rejection of His Son, Jesus Christ!

To understand the verses above, look at the personal pronouns, "ye, we, and us" (who were raptured) and "they and them," who were left behind. These verses of scripture prove that the church will not be left behind. The sudden destruction is not directed to ye and we and us, but to they and them. *

We are gone, and they are left behind! The church will be gone and the remaining people will rush into the arms of the devil's messiah. For three and a half years, there will be somewhat prosperity and peace, but then all of a sudden, the devil's man will mobilize the world against the Jews and all hell will break out on the earth; the great tribulation will begin. This "Day of the Lord" will bring much judgment on the earth. "Them and they" will go through all the terrible things we read about in Revelation. Many things are very hard to read and understand, but just know, you certainly do not want to be around to experience it. You want to be part of the "we and us," not the "they and them"!

But you don't have to be here; you can choose not to. We all have a choice!

God loves you.

•notes on this series are from the great writer of commentaries, John Phillips', book, *The Future*.

# JESUS WEPT. July 23

John 11:33-When Jesus saw her weeping, and the Jews who had come along with her also weeping, he was deeply moved in spirit and troubled. 34-"Where have you laid him?" he asked. "Come and see, Lord," they replied.

35-Jesus wept.

A few days before this, Jesus knew Lazarus was sick, and He knew that He would be glorified because of it. Jesus knew Lazarus would die, and He knew that He would raise him from the dead. This was to prove that He had the power over death. But when He got there and He saw His friends Mary and Martha weeping over the death of their brother Lazarus, He cried with them. This is a testimony of His humanity. Jesus was fully God and fully human. In one sense there was no need for these tears; He knew what He was about to do. Why then would He cry? He was sharing the grief of Mary and Martha. It showed that Jesus was fully human. What human could see their friends weeping and in deep grief and not feel their sorrow? This is the kind of God we have. Jesus loved Mary, Martha, and Lazarus. Jesus loves us also. When you are happy, He is happy. When you are sad, Jesus is sad also. When you cry out to Him, He cries with you.

"This is a diamond (of a verse), and it cannot have another gem set with it, for it is unique. Let it stand in solitary" (Charles Spurgeon).

Spend some time today thinking about how much it means to you and me that "Jesus wept," with His friends.

God loves you.

# PRAYING WITH CHILDREN. July 24

An elderly man told D. L. Moody this story:

My wife died and left me with three motherless children. The first Sabbath after her death, my eldest girl, ten years old, said: 'Papa, may I take the children into the bedroom and pray with them as Mother used to do on the Sabbath?' I said she might.

When they came out of the room after a time I saw that my eldest daughter had been weeping. I called her to me, and said: 'Nellie, what is the trouble?' 'Oh, Father,' she said, 'after we went into the room I made the prayer that mother taught me to make.' Then, naming her little brother, he made the prayer that Mother taught him. Little Susie didn't use to pray when Mother, when she took us in there because Mother thought she was too young. But when we got through she made a prayer of her own. I could not but weep when I heard her pray. She put her little hands together and closed her eyes and said: 'O God, you have taken away my dear mamma, and I have no mamma now to pray for me. Won't you bless me and make me good just as Mamma was, for Jesus Christ's sake, Amen.' Little Susie gave evidence of having given her young heart to God before she was four years old. For sixteen years she has been at work as a missionary among the heathen."

Moms and dads, are you teaching your children and grandchildren how to pray? Are you telling them all about Jesus?

Remember what Jesus said; "Suffer the little children to come unto Me and forbid them not, for of such is the kingdom of heaven."

God loves you.

# WHAT ARE YOU DOING HERE? July 25

Elijah was hiding out in a cave because Jezebel was hunting him to kill him. Then God said to him:

> What are you doing here? 10He replied, "I have been very zealous for the Lord God Almighty. The Israelites have rejected your covenant, torn down your altars, and put your prophets to death with the sword. I am the only one left, and now they are trying to kill me too." (1 Kings 19)

Listen to what Elijah said, "Lord every one of us has been killed and I, little old me, am the only one left. What will you do when they kill me, too? I am ready, Lord. Take me home. These awful people are not worth the trouble." Now listen to how God answered him:

> 15Then the LORD told him, "Go back the same way you came, and travel to the wilderness of Damascus. When you arrive there, anoint Hazael to be king of Aram. 16Then anoint Jehu grandson of Nimshi to be king of Israel, and anoint Elisha son of Shaphat from the town of Abel-meholah to replace you as my prophet. 17Anyone who escapes from Hazael will be killed by Jehu, and those who escape Jehu will be killed by Elisha! 18Yet I will preserve 7,000 others in Israel who have never bowed down to Baal or kissed him!"

God is always able! He has people everywhere to do his work. But having said that, God has a job for you to do. So, don't miss out on your blessing; get busy doing what God has for you to do.

The blessing is yours for the taking—get busy!

God loves you.

# WHERE IS YOUR STRENGTH? July 26

Paul writes in 1 Corinthians 1:26–29:

> 26 Remember, dear brothers and sisters, that few of you were wise in the world's eyes or powerful or wealthy when God called you. 27 Instead, God chose things the world considers foolish in order to shame those who think they are wise. And he chose things that are powerless to shame those who are powerful. 28 God chose things despised by the world, things counted as nothing at all, and used them to bring to nothing what the world considers important. 29 As a result, no one can ever boast in the presence of God."

You notice there are five things mentioned that God uses: foolish things, weak things, powerless things, despised things, and things which are counted as nothing.

You might ask, "What for?" It is so that no flesh should glory in his presence. When we are weak, then we are strong in Him. People often think they do not have enough strength to carry on, but the fact is we have too much strength. It is when we feel we have no strength of our own that we are willing to let God use us and work through us. If we are leaning on God's strength, we have more than all the strength of the world. The world is not going to be reached by mere human intellectual power. When we realize that we have no strength, then all the fullness of God will flow in upon us. *

I think John the Baptist said it well, when He told His disciples to follow Jesus, for "He must increase and I must decrease."

If that is your prayer, that He will increase in you and you will decrease, then it will be amazing what He will do through you! Try it and see for yourself.

God loves you.

*Dwight L. Moody

# WHAT IS YOUR POTENTIAL? July 27

Psalm chapter one, 1Blessed is the one who does not walk in step with the wicked

Or stand in the way that sinners take, or sit in the company of mockers, 2but whose delight is in the law of the Lord, and who meditates on his law, day and night. 3That person is like a tree planted by streams of water, which yields its fruit in season and whose leaf does not wither—

Whatever they do prospers.

Kids, moms, and dads, what is possible for you? Have you set yourself up for success or failure, or have you decided to accept mediocrity? Do you realize it is all up to you and the choices you make?

Kids for you, it is the choices you make early on in your life, even before you get out of school, choices you make in high school or before. Moms and dads, you can change your future with choices you make now. Pat told me that after a great experience in church last Sunday, Parker said he wanted to go to church every Sunday from now on, now *that* would be a great choice to make that would affect his future in a successful way.

Every life is full of potential. Alert parents will help their kids develop their potential to get the very most out of their lives. This could be in the area of academics, performing arts, or athletics.

It is sad to see that many times people short-circuit their lives by making bad choices. Young people with exceptional academic acumen never really apply themselves. These young people compromise their potential by making unwise choices or allowing distractions to dominate their lives at the wrong time.

Please ask God to help you with the choices you make that affect your future!

God loves you.

# GOD HAS GIVEN US MANY OPPORTUNITIES TO SERVE HIM. July 28

The expectation is that we use them.

There was a preacher sitting beside the bed of a dying old military man who had fought in a war, and the preacher asked the man was he afraid to die. The man said "I am not!" When asked why, he said, "I have never done any harm." The preacher said, if you were going to be tried for a military court-martial, I suppose you would expect an honorable acquittal. The man looked up and said, "That I would, sir."

Then the preacher said, "But you are not going to a court-martial; you are going to Christ, and when He asks you, 'What have you done for me?' what will you say?"

The old man's gaze changed, and he appeared to look back in time, and he finally said, "Nothing. I have never done anything for Christ."

The preacher pointed out to him the awful mistake of forgetting our relationship to Christ and to God as we live our lives "doing no harm," or "doing good things," supposing that it would substitute for a relationship with Jesus.

Later after a few days went by, the preacher came to visit the old man again, and he asked the old man what he thought about it now. The dying old man said, "I am but a poor sinner." The preacher then pointed him to the Savior of poor sinners, and he left this life a repentant sinner, resting in Christ. *

Think about what an awful end that would have come to the old man if he would have died thinking he was "*okay*" because he had "done good things."

John 14:6 says, "Jesus answered, I am the way and the truth and the life No one comes to the Father accept through me."

Pray about it!

God loves you.

*DL Moody

# A CONTRAST IN SERVANTS. July 29

Jesus in Matthew chapter 24, talks about what the people will be doing when He comes back:

> Matthew 24:45–51, A faithful, sensible servant is one to whom the master can give the responsibility of managing his other household servants and feeding them.46If the master returns and finds that the servant has done a good job, there will be a reward. 47I tell you the truth, the master will put that servant in charge of all he owns. 48But what if the servant is evil and thinks, 'My master won't be back for a while,' 49and he begins beating the other servants, partying, and getting drunk? 50The master will return unannounced and unexpected, 51and he will cut the servant to pieces and assign him a place with the hypocrites. In that place there will be weeping and gnashing of teeth.

How many folks think there is no hurry because people have been talking about Jesus coming back all the way back to the disciples 2,000 years ago.

Jesus has said no one will know the time of His return, but you can know the season. We know that the Church age has to end someday, and we know that the prophecies have been fulfilled. The only thing left is for the Rapture to happen and then the clock starts, and seven years later Jesus comes to judge the people at the end of time.

This scripture speaks of two servants; one is a faithful servant of the Lord Jesus who works right up until Jesus comes back, but the other thinks, "While He is gone, I will party, and when He gets close, I will look busy and act like a good servant." One problem though, Jesus knows the heart, and there will be no wool pulled over His eyes. He knows all and sees all. He will easily separate the sheep from the goats.

Listen, I am not an alarmist, but I believe we are in the season of His return. What I don't know is how long His seasons are. One day, God will say to Jesus, "Go and get your Church." And that will be that. There will only be the worst seven years you can imagine left and then the Judgment. If you are reading this, you cannot say, "I didn't know!" Pray about which kind of servant you are today, please.

God loves you.

# A CHILD OF GOD. July 30

Before a child is born, it is in total darkness in its mom's womb. And a child of God, before he is born again, is living in total darkness of sin; he sees and knows nothing of the kingdom of God. When he is born again, the soul that had one kind of love now has a different godly kind of love. That is why it is called a new birth.

Also, when the child is born, he or she is going to cry and cry a lot.

You, who are born of God and are Christians, if you are not criers, (crying out about your love for Jesus in one way or another), your spiritual life is lacking. If you don't cry out about your Lord Jesus to your fellow man and do that which we were commanded in the Great Commission in Matthew 28:18–20, then do you really love Jesus?

> Jesus said in John 14:15 If you love me, keep my commands. 21Whoever has my commands and keeps them is the one who loves me. The one who loves me will be loved by my Father, and I too will love them and show myself to them." 23Jesus replied, "Anyone who loves me will obey my teaching. My Father will love them, and we will come to them and make our home with them. 24Anyone who does not love me will not obey my teaching. These words you hear are not my own; they belong to the Father who sent me.

If you are born again of God and do not cry it out to the world, you are missing the mark; you cannot help but tell it to someone. If you love Jesus, then keep His commands. If you have been born again, then "cry it out" so that someone may here you and come to know the Lord.

James McDonald said, "Faith and salvation in God is personal, *but it is NOT private!*"

Pray about it!

God loves you.

# PRAY FOR WISDOM AND DISCERNMENT. July 31

This is Paul's prayer to the Philippians, but it can be everyone's prayer also.

> Philippians chapter one,
> 9-And this is my prayer: that your love may abound more and more in knowledge and depth of insight, 10-so that you may be able to discern what is best and may be pure and blameless for the day of Christ, 11-filled with the fruit of righteousness that comes through Jesus Christ—to the glory and praise of God.

It is an encouragement to know that our friends are praying for us and to know that people have an interest in our walk with God. Kids, when moms and dads pray for you, it should encourage you into action to be all you can be for the Lord.

Don't you think when they pray for you, they are expecting good things for you? Like Paul said, they are praying that your love for Jesus will grow and grow for all eternity. I would think moms and dads are praying for wisdom for you so that you can discern what is best for you and what is not good for you. I know this has been Pat's and my prayer for our kids and grandkids.

Kids, discernment is so very important in today's world, just as it was in Paul's day.

As we pray for you, please pray for yourselves, asking God for wisdom and discernment. There are many wicked people out there, and you need to be able to discern who is of the world and who is of God!

God loves you.

# EVERY KNEE SHALL BOW. August 1

> Philippians 2:5 In your relationships with one another, have the same mindset as Christ Jesus: 6Who, being in very nature God, did not consider equality with God something to be used to his own advantage; 7rather, he made himself nothing by taking the very nature of a servant, being made in human likeness. 8And being found in appearance as a man, he humbled himself by becoming obedient to death—even death on a cross!

Jesus was God and Man. He came as a man to do the will of His Father. That is humility personified. He was God, and yet He suffered as a man.

We must not forget that He created man out of the dust of the ground. He healed many people. He was very capable of destroying the Roman army, the city of Rome, or the world for that matter. He could do anything. But He humbled Himself for us because He loves us and because He obeyed His Father in heaven.

> 9Therefore God exalted him to the highest place and gave him the name that is above every name, 10that at the name of Jesus every knee should bow, in heaven and on earth and under the earth, 11and every tongue acknowledge that Jesus Christ is Lord, to the glory of God the Father.

Everyone will bow before Him, either in wonderful anticipation of the future to come, or in dreadful fear of what's to come.

Thank you, Lord Jesus!

God loves you.

# PUT ON THE ARMOR OF GOD. August 2

Ephesians 6:12, New Living Bible, says, "12-For we are not fighting against flesh-and-blood enemies, but against evil rulers and authorities of the unseen world, against mighty powers in this dark world, and against evil spirits in the heavenly places."

Folks, that is a mouthful, but what does it mean? How do I "put on" the armor? And when do I put it on? When do I take it off—or do I take it off?

Let's answer the last question first. When you "put on" your armor, you should never take it off. You have to keep your full armor on all the time. The devil is always looking for weak spots. The armor is not like a hat you put on and take off. It is permanent! Once you are a saved child of God, you put on your armor and never take it off! You might ask, do I have to sleep in it? Absolutely! Remember these are darkness lovers; when the light goes off, they come out, like bugs. Your armor is permanent.

Anyway, how would you take it off?

Truth, righteousness, peace, faith, salvation, the word of God, and prayer are all things that changed your life, permanently. These things are with you now forever.

But what happens if I do take something off? Satan will slip in and cause you much pain. He will help you do things that deep down you don't want to do. He will key in on your weakness; he will always hit you where you are the weakest. You cannot live the life you have chosen to live without your protection. The battle is won, but Satan does not accept it. He is still trying to hurt us, and he will if we give him an opening. Pray it on and keep it on!

And enjoy your Christian life! Because God loves you.

# IN THE WORST OF TIMES, THERE IS OPPORTUNITY TO WITNESS. August 3

Philippians chapter one, 12-Now I want you to know, brothers and sisters that what has happened to me has actually served to advance the gospel. 13-As a result, it has become clear throughout the whole palace guard and to everyone else that I am in chains for Christ. 14-And because of my chains, most of the brothers and sisters have become confident in the Lord and dare all the more to proclaim the gospel without fear.

Listen to this, when Paul was arrested and imprisoned in Rome, he had to be chained to a Roman soldier all the time. So, the soldiers rotated in out being chained to Paul, a sold-out slave for Christ. As you can imagine, every new Roman who got chained to him heard all about Jesus. He became a captive audience for Paul. To the point that Paul led many to Christ. He looked at his captivity as an opportunity to witness to the whole Roman guard. He never stopped talking about Jesus and advancing the Kingdom, no matter his situation.

So, what about you? Are you talking about Jesus in the worst of your situations as well as the best of your situations? Are you looking for opportunities to witness in any situation? Are you crying out about Jesus?

Pray about it.

God will help you with this, you know, because He loves you.

# DANIEL IN THE LIONS' DEN. August 4

The king really liked Daniel, because he had proven himself very wise, and the king decided to put him over the empire. But others on the Kings court did not like him because he was a Jew. So, they talked the king in to making a decree that they knew Daniel could not keep. They knew Daniel would have no other gods before him but God almighty, but he was supposed to bow down to the king as if he were a God. Daniel continued doing what he always did and prayed to his God and ours. The bad guys saw him and reported it to the king, and the king had to throw Daniel into the lion's den.

But believe it or not, the king actually said a prayer to Jehovah, listen to it in,

> Daniel 6:16: "So the king gave the order, and they brought Daniel and threw him into the lions' den. The king said to Daniel, 'May your God, whom you serve continually, rescue you!'"

And God did just what the king prayed:

> 19-At the first light of dawn, the king got up and hurried to the lions' den. 20-When he came near the den, he called to Daniel in an anguished voice, "Daniel, servant of the living God, has your God, whom you serve continually, been able to rescue you from the lions?"

> 21-Daniel answered, "May the king live forever! 22-My God sent his angel, and he shut the mouths of the lions. They have not hurt me, because I was found innocent in his sight. Nor have I ever done any wrong before you, Your Majesty."

God shut the mouths of the lions, and they did not hurt Daniel. God can keep you out of danger, He can heal your sickness, He can do anything if you are "found innocent in his sight." Daniel was not worried; he got on his knees and prayed, and along came the angels, to protect him.

We all need callouses on our knees right now from praying. God loves you.

# THE DISCIPLES THOUGHT JESUS WAS A GHOST! August 5

Matthew 14:22–27, 22-Immediately Jesus made the disciples get into the boat and go on ahead of him to the other side, while he dismissed the crowd. 23-After he had dismissed them, he went up on a mountainside by himself to pray. Later that night, he was there alone, 24-and the boat was already a considerable distance from land, buffeted by the waves because the wind was against it. 25-Shortly before dawn Jesus went out to them, walking on the lake. 26-When the disciples saw him walking on the lake, they were terrified. "It's a ghost," they said, and cried out in fear.

27-But Jesus immediately said to them: "Take courage! It is I." don't be afraid."

It seems that the evil spirits were very active when Jesus was walking on the earth, possessing folks, and creating fear and havoc in many people's lives. Jesus battled them daily, healing people and setting them free from evil. We don't always understand what they are capable of, even though they are very active in these, the last days, as they were in the time Jesus walked on the earth. But for sure they are scary like a ghost. So, when the disciples saw Him walking on water, they said, "Look a ghost," and they were very scared! Jesus just said, "Be not afraid, it is I."

What are you afraid of? If you could see Jesus, think what the expression on His face would be like when He tells you, "It is I, be not afraid!"

*"It is I. I AM is here. Be not afraid!"*

Can you feel how relaxing it is to know in your heart of hearts, that *He has it*?

Be not afraid! He loves you.

# EVERYONE HAS A CALLING. August 6

God has a job for all of us. You may not have been called to preach or sing or teach Sunday school, but God has something He wants you to do. Remember we have said that you cannot keep your salvation to yourself; it is personal but not private. God told us to go and tell and teach. This, in your case, may mean be prepared to tell your story when God sends that person in your path for you to talk to. We know He does this. All of us have experienced it. We may not know God sent that person until we look back and realize that God had to be involved; it wouldn't have happened by chance. These people that He sends your way do not need a preacher or a theologian; they need to hear your personal story.

God uses you where you are. Think about it: you have a wonderful story in that once you were lost and now you are saved! Once you were damned to hell, and now you are on your way to paradise. What story could be better? Someone that you will cross paths with (by God's design), will need to hear your story. Don't hesitate; tell your story!

1 Peter 3:15 says, "But in your hearts revere Christ as Lord. Always be prepared to give an answer to everyone who asks you to give the reason for the hope that you have. But do this with gentleness and respect." Peter says always be ready.

God loves you.

# MADE ALIVE WITH CHRIST. August 7

Ephesians 2, New Living Bible.
1Once you were dead because of your disobedience and your many sins. 2You used to live in sin, just like the rest of the world, obeying the devil—the commander of the powers in the unseen world. He is the spirit at work in the hearts of those who refuse to obey God. 3All of us used to live that way, following the passionate desires and inclinations of our sinful nature. By our very nature we were subject to God's anger, just like everyone else.

4But God is so rich in mercy, and he loved us so much, 5that even though we were dead because of our sins, he gave us life when he raised Christ from the dead. (It is only by God's grace that you have been saved!) 6For he raised us from the dead along with Christ and seated us with him in the heavenly realms because we are united with Christ Jesus. 7So God can point to us in all future ages as examples of the incredible wealth of his grace and kindness toward us, as shown in all he has done for us who are united with Christ Jesus.

8God saved you by his grace when you believed. And you can't take credit for this; it is a gift from God. 9Salvation is not a reward for the good things we have done, so none of us can boast about it. 10For we are God's masterpiece. He has created us anew in Christ Jesus, so we can do the good things he planned for us long ago.

We all have something to do!
Pray that God will show you what He has for you to do today.
God loves you.

# LIVING BY THE SPIRIT'S POWER. August 8

Ephesians 5:15–20,

15So be careful how you live. Don't live like fools, but like those who are wise. 16Make the most of every opportunity in these evil days. 17Don't act thoughtlessly, but understand what the Lord wants you to do. 18Don't be drunk with wine, because that will ruin your life. Instead, be filled with the Holy Spirit, 19singing psalms and hymns and spiritual songs among yourselves, and making music to the Lord in your hearts. 20And give thanks for everything to God the Father in the name of our Lord Jesus Christ.

Paul says to make the most of every opportunity. Someone said, though I can't remember who, that you should have a plan or a strategy to lead unbelievers to Christ. So, do you know someone who needs to know the Lord?

What is your plan? The time we are here on this earth is very valuable; we cannot waste it by turning our heads to look the other way, when clearly, we need to meet the issue head on. We have said before, we are here only for a moment, compared to eternity. You may be the only Christian a lost soul knows, and if you don't lead them down the narrow road, who will?

It is a life-and-death issue. Can you seriously look at a friend who does not have the Lord in their life and not have compassion for their eternal future?

I think not!

Devise a plan, put together a strategy, pray about it, and put action to your prayers. Also love them as Jesus would, down the narrow road.

God loves you.

# PRAISE TO GOD FOR A LIVING HOPE! August 9

1 Peter 1:3–5,

3Praise be to the God and Father of our Lord Jesus Christ! In his great mercy he has given us new birth into a living hope through the resurrection of Jesus Christ from the dead, 4and into an inheritance that can never perish, spoil or fade. This inheritance is kept in heaven for you, 5who through faith are shielded by God's power until the coming of the salvation that is ready to be revealed in the last time.

Look at verse 3; it plainly says that in His great mercy, "He has given us" this new birth.

It is not a new birth that you earn like wages on a job. It does not matter how hard you work; you can never earn this "new birth," our living hope, our inheritance as children of the living God.

It is a gift of mercy. Because He loves us, He gave us "a living hope."

Ephesians 2:8–9 says, "8For it is by grace you have been saved, through faith—and this is not from yourselves, it is the gift of God—9not by works, so that no one can boast."

The hope of our salvation is a "living" hope because it will never spoil or fade or perish.

It is being kept for you by our Savior Jesus Christ, the Creator of this world, and all the rest, through your faith by God's power until the end of time.

Praise God! He loves you.

3Praise be to the God and Father of our Lord
Jesus Christ! In his great mercy he has given us
new birth into a living hope through the resur
rection of Jesus Christ from the dead.

8Though you have not seen him, you love him;
and even though you do not see him now, you
believe in him and are filled with an inexpressible
and glorious joy, 9for you are receiving the end
result of your faith, the salvation of your souls.

Though we cannot see Him, we feel Him through the joy
of our salvation. He gave us the Holy Spirit with our salvation.
And though we can't see Him, we love Him and believe in Him.
This is a supernatural thing. If you have received His gift to you,
you can understand the love you have in an unseen Savior. But
to others who have not received the gift, they may think it foolishness that we could love an unseen God. But they will never
understand unless they bow down to our Lord and stick out their
hands and accept the free gift into their hearts that He freely
gives through his mercy. It is a living hope, of a great eternal
life with the living God and Savior, Jesus Christ. This living
hope will be waiting for you until the end of time as we know it.

In John 24:3, Jesus said, "And if I go and prepare
a place for you, I will come back and take you
to be with me that you also may be where I am."

Praise God for the living hope! He loves you.

# THE MESSIAH. August 11

In Abrahamic religions, the Messiah, the Christ, is the one chosen to lead the world and thereby save it from oppression. The concepts of the Messianic Age grew from Isaiah's writings during the latter half of the 8th century BCE. The Jewish idea of Messiah is for a king, like King David, not necessarily a Savior, like Jesus.

The reason the Jewish leaders did not accept Jesus was because He did not come as the king, and rid Israel of the Romans. But God knew we needed a Savior first; then when He comes back, He will come as King to rule the world.

The term *Messiah* literally means "the anointed one" and refers to the ancient practice of anointing kings with oil when they took the throne as Samuel anointed David.

The word *Messiah* does not mean Savior. The Savior is a Christian concept that has no basis in Jewish thought.

Jesus fulfilled all the prophecies but coming back as King after the tribulation.

As Christians, Jesus is our Messiah, our King, and our Savior for all eternity! We are part of His Kingdom of heaven today. Praise God for sending His son as the Messiah, the Christ, to save us of all our sins and to be our King forever because God loves us.

# THE MESSIAH, continued. August 12

There are a wide variety of opinions on the subject of when the Messiah will come. Some of Judaism's greatest minds have cursed those who try to predict the time of the Messiah's coming because errors in such predictions could cause people to lose faith in the messianic idea or in Judaism itself. This has also happened in Christianity. Through the ages, false prophets have claimed to be the Christ, and when their lies were found out, many people were turned off.

The Bible clearly teaches that no one will know the date and time of Jesus' return. So, if anyone tells you He has come back and you did not hear the trumpet, you can know it is a lie, unless of course, the Rapture has happened and you were left behind.

When Jesus returns to rule, every knee will bow. It will not be a rumor passed around. Every soul that has ever been born on this earth will know when Jesus returns to rule because they will have to bow before him to answer for what they did about Jesus while they were alive and well. They will either be sheep or goats.

> From Matthew 25:31–46: "But when the Son of Man comes in his glory, and all the holy angels with him, then he will sit on the throne of his glory. Before him all the nations will be gathered, and he will separate them one from another, as a shepherd separates the sheep from the goats. (The believers in Christ Jesus and the unbelievers).

What have you done about Jesus? Are you a sheep or a goat? God loves you.

# A CONFIDENT HOPE. August 13

This is Paul's prayer from Ephesians 1 to all Christians:

> 18-I pray that your hearts will be flooded with light so that you can understand the confident hope he has given to those he called—his holy people who are His rich and glorious inheritance.

> 19-I also pray that you will understand the incredible greatness of God's power for us who believe him. This is the same mighty power 20-that raised Christ from the dead and seated him in the place of honor at God's right hand in the heavenly realms. 21-Now he is far above any ruler or authority or power or leader or anything else—not only in this world but also in the world to come. 22-God has put all things under the authority of Christ and has made him head over all things for the benefit of the church. 23-And the church is His body; it is made full and complete by Christ, who fills all things everywhere with himself.

Do you have a "confident hope"? Do you know for sure where your eternal future will be? You can be confident about where you will be!

So many religions do not give their folks confidence; to them it is a maybe, if I am good enough or if I do enough, but not Christianity. With Jesus Christ, you can be sure!

You can lay your head on the pillow at night and say, "Lord come tonight"! It is well with my soul.

God loves you.

# PETER DECLARED THAT JESUS WAS THE MESSIAH. August 14

Matthew 16:13-When Jesus came to the region of Caesarea Philippi, he asked his disciples, "Who do people say the Son of Man is?"

14-They replied, "Some say John the Baptist; others say Elijah; and still others, Jeremiah or one of the prophets."

15- "But what about you?" he asked. "Who sir do you say I am?"

16-Simon Peter answered, "You are the Messiah, the Son of the living God."

The Jews were looking for a King to come riding up on a white horse and wipe out the Romans, who were ruling over them. They were not looking for a suffering servant; they were not looking for the Son of God to lay down his life to save them from their sins. They expected the Son of God, to destroy their oppressors with His angels (and He will later), but not at that time.

They conveniently looked over the scripture that predicted Jesus as a Savior.

The Father revealed it to Peter, and Peter announced it to Jesus and the other disciples. "You are the Messiah, the Son of the Living God"!

What will you say when Jesus asks you, "who do *you* say, that I am"? He will ask you! We all will stand before Him, and we will have to answer the questions, "Who do you say I am? and, what have you done about Me?

Please don't ignore Him as if He were not the Son of God. God loves you.

# WHO DO MEN SAY THAT THE SON OF MAN IS? August 15

This was a question that Jesus asked the disciples, and it is recorded in Matthew 16:13. Then after that question, He got really personal with them and asked, "Who do you say I am?"

The world has many opinions. They say Christ was a myth, a good teacher, a prophet like Isaiah or Jeremiah, or even a reincarnation of John the Baptist. But Jesus also wants to know what individuals think about Him. And He expects each man and woman to decide who they think He is. The decision has to be made. It cannot be ignored. And it should not be put off until a later date. I knew a man who said many times to me, "Not now. I will deal with that later, and I am busy living my life right now."

Men and woman cannot ignore the question by being silent about it and pretend they have not made a decision yet, but that is nothing but a denial. Besides, how do you know you will have a later date? We are not promised tomorrow.

Jesus is waiting for your answer—patiently, I might add.

You have to make a choice between the wide road that most men walk on or the narrow road that leads to salvation. Every soul that is living and that has ever lived must choose: every Jew, every Muslim, every Hindu, every Buddhist, and everyone that worships any other God that has a way to heaven other than Jesus Christ must decide! Who do you say that Jesus Christ is? Remember, Peter got it.

Peter had the correct answer, when he said, "Thou art the Christ, the Son of the Living God."

He is the Savior of the world, and He loves you.

# RIGHT NOW, COUNTS FOREVER. August 16

Matthew 16:24–25 (The Message by Eugene Peterson)
Then Jesus went to work on his disciples. "Anyone who intends to come with me has to let me lead. You're not in the driver's seat; I am. Don't run from suffering; embrace it. Follow me and I'll show you how. Self-help is no help at all. Self-sacrifice is the way, my way, to finding yourself, your true self. What kind of deal is it to get everything you want but lose yourself? What could you ever trade your soul for"?

Jesus had just confirmed that he was the Son of God. And He begin to tell them that he would be sacrificed for all sins.

Peter said, "No, Lord, that will not happen," but Jesus rebuked him. Then He told them, "If anyone will follow me, he must deny himself." That is interesting, but what does it mean — how can we deny ourselves?

In the translation above, it says you have to let Jesus do the leading in your life.

We have heard it said: you don't need a co-pilot, but you need a pilot. Well, that would be, Jesus, so give Him the control stick. Let Him lead your life. Give up trying to run your life and follow Jesus. If He is your God, your Lord and Savior, and your King, then summit to His ways and His rule over you. As a born-again Christian, He is your King now! *And right now, counts forever.*

So, turn it loose, quit trying to gain the world's acceptance, follow His lead, and find out what true success is!

Right now, this moment, counts forever!
Pray about it.
God loves you.

# THE TRANSFIGURATION. August 17

Matthew 17:1–8

1-After six days Jesus took with him Peter, James and John the brother of James, and led them up a high mountain by themselves. 2-There he was transfigured before them. His face shone like the sun, and his clothes became as white as the light. 3-Just then there appeared before them Moses and Elijah, talking with Jesus. 4-Peter said to Jesus, "Lord, it is good for us to be here. If you wish, I will put up three shelters—one for you, one for Moses and one for Elijah."

5-While he was still speaking, a bright cloud covered them, and a voice from the cloud said, "This is my Son, whom I love; with him I am well pleased. Listen to him!"

6-When the disciples heard this, they fell face-down to the ground, terrified. 7-But Jesus came and touched them. "Get up," he said. "Don't be afraid." 8-When they looked up, they saw no one accept Jesus.

The Lord was transfigured, meaning He was changed (He changed form or appearance. His face shined like the sun, and His clothes became as white as a light) in an instant so that the glorious magnificence of His perfect sinless holy life as a human would be displayed. God spoke to Peter, John, and James, saying, "This is My Son, whom I love; with Him I am well pleased, listen to Him!"

He was man, as God intended man to be, perfectly sinless in thought, word, and deed.

We know nothing of that glory, for there is sin in us.

But one day, yes one day, when we are changed in a twinkling of an eye, we will be glorified also. We will have a glorious body, perfect and immortal, with no pain, no tears, and no sorrow.

As Christians, in God's sight we are sinless; all of our sins were paid for by the blood of Christ, the perfect sinless sacrifice!

Praise God today for the Transfiguration, showing Peter, John, and James that Jesus was the Christ, the God/Man our Savior!

God loves you.

# ABOUT FORGIVENESS. August 18

Matthew 18:21-Then Peter came to Jesus and asked, "Lord, how many times shall I forgive my brother or sister who sins against me? Up to seven times?"

22-Jesus answered, "I tell you, not seven times, but seventy-seven times.

I am sure Peter was surprised to hear Jesus tell him, no, seventy times seven.

That is a lot of forgiving your brother or sister, how could anyone do that? That means we have to continue to forgive our brother and sisters for the same thing they do over and over.

Is that what we do? Do we humble ourselves and forgive over and over? Not very often, I think. I think we say enough is enough; get lost. We have a hard time forgiving the first time, let alone over and over.

But think about it, how many times have we asked God to forgive us for the same things over and over? We want forgiveness, but we are stingy with our forgiveness. Don't you think this is what Jesus was saying, "You want it but you cannot give it!"

So how can we begin to forgive like Jesus asked us to? We can only do it through Him. We need Jesus to help us. We need Him to guide us and lead us to a forgiving heart. I think it is an expectation for a Christian. We must work on achieving a forgiving heart.

Jesus can do it through us if we allow Him to.

32- "Then the master called the servant in. 'You wicked servant,' he said, 'I canceled all that debt of yours because you begged me to. 33-Shouldn't you have had mercy on your fellow servant just as I had on you?' 34-In anger his master handed him over to the jailers to be tortured, until he should pay back all he owed.

35- "This is how my heavenly Father will treat each of you unless you forgive your brother or sister from your heart."

Who needs forgiving today?
Pray about it. God loves you.

# TO ENTER GOD'S KINGDOM. August 19

> Matthew 19:16-17a says, "A man stopped Jesus and asked, "Teacher, what good thing must I do to get eternal life? Jesus said, why do you question me about what's good? God is the one who is good."

If you want eternal life, just do what God tells you.

The man asked what he should do in particular or what specifically he needed to do. Jesus read his heart, and then Jesus said, "Do not murder, do not commit adultery, do not steal, do not give false testimony, honor your father and mother and love your neighbor as yourself."

The young man said "Oh, I have done all of that!"

Do you think he was perfect? I don't think so! Love your neighbors, hmm.

Listen to what A. P. Gibbs says about the fact that we do not love our neighbors like ourselves:

You are coming home from town, and you see smoke ahead, near where you live. A house is on fire. The fire engines roar past, with sirens howling. You speed up and round the corner. The fire is on your street. You break and run. Then you have a sigh of relief. You say, I am so glad! It's my house! I am so glad it is not my neighbors!

Yep! He loved his neighbor as himself! Who, other than Jesus, would ever say such a thing?

True he may not have killed anyone, and he may not have stolen anything. He may not have committed adultery. He may not have destroyed anyone with false testimony, and he may have honored his father and mother every day. He may have kept the letter of these laws. But Jesus confidently left a few out. I wonder why?

Jesus knew his heart—that is for sure—just as he knows our hearts. The man was not perfect; he thought all he needed was just a little something more to get him in heaven, so he decided to ask the good teacher, what exactly that is because he had been pretty good already.

Many people think they have been pretty good and deserve heaven, but remember the road is narrow.

God loves you.

# TO ENTER GOD'S KINGDOM,
## continued. August 20

Continuing in Matthew 19, the young man said, "I've done all that." In essence, he said, "I have kept all of those commandments."

That's right! He had kept these commandments without exception! He was perfect. I don't think so! Jesus knew his heart and knew he was rich so He told him to do something that He knew he would not do—sell everything and give it all to the poor—then He told him to "Follow me"!

The question is what did the young man really want? He really wanted to keep his luxurious life here on earth, and then when he died, he wanted the same kind of life in heaven.

Think about it. What was his problem? Does the word *greed* come to mind?

Now before you run him down, what is it that you are willing to give up to follow Jesus? Everything? Are you willing to sell all you have and give it to the poor?

I am not sure that we have to take this passage to read, "We all must sell what we have and give it all to the poor to follow Jesus."

But I do believe we are to give up everything that is keeping us from following Jesus. If there are things in your life that are preventing you from following Jesus, then get rid of them today. Do not wait!

In Revelation 3:20, Jesus says, "Here I am! I stand at the door and knock. If anyone hears my voice and opens the door, I will come in and eat with that person, and they with me."

If Christ is knocking at the door of your life, please let Him in! God loves you.

# GREED AT THE TEMPLE. August 21

Matthew 21,
12-Jesus entered the temple courts and drove out all who were buying and selling there. He overturned the tables of the money changers and the benches of those selling doves. 13- "It is written," He said to them, "'My house will be called a house of prayer,' but you are making it 'a den of robbers.'"

These men, the money changers and the dove sellers, were at the house of God, probably doing what they thought was a meaningful thing to do. The people needed to exchange their money from their kind of money to what was acceptable in the temple. And the folks wanting to buy a dove to sacrifice needed to buy one, so what was the problem?

The problem was greed! The money changers used the wrong weights on the scales to their favor, cheating the poor folks. People turned something necessary into something awful; they were getting rich off of the poor, and Jesus was angry about it.

Greed always has a way of changing the good things into something ugly. Greed is from Satan.

Be kind to your neighbor today! Look at Proverbs 14:31: "Whoever oppresses the poor shows contempt for their Maker, but whoever is kind to the needy honors God."

God loves you.

# LOVE YOUR NEIGHBOR AS YOURSELF. August 22

Romans 13,
8-Owe nothing to anyone—accept for your obligation to love one another. If you love your neighbor, you will fulfill the requirements of God's law. 9-For the commandments say, "You must not commit adultery. You must not murder. You must not steal. You must not covet." These— and other such commandments—are summed up in this one commandment: "Love your neighbor as yourself." 10-Love does no wrong to others, so love fulfills the requirements of God's law.

11-This is all the more urgent, for you know how late it is; time is running out. Wake up, for our salvation is nearer now than when we first believed. 12-The night is almost gone; the day of salvation will soon be here. So, remove your dark deeds like dirty clothes, and put on the shining armor of right living.

Paul said these things to the Romans about 2000 years ago. He said, then, that our salvation is nearer than we think. He said the night, meaning darkness, is almost gone, and the day of the Lord will be here.

Matthew 24
30-And then at last, the sign that the Son of Man is coming will appear in the heavens, and there will be deep mourning among all the peoples of the earth. And they will see the Son of Man coming on the clouds of heaven with power and great glory. 31-And he will send out his angels with the mighty blast of a trumpet, and they will

gather his chosen ones from all over the world,
from the farthest ends of the earth and heaven.

What a great day that will be, and it will be sooner
than we think.
Be looking up!
God loves you!

# MY NAME IS WHOEVER. August 23

1The Lord is my shepherd, I lack nothing. 2 He makes me lie down in green pastures, he leads me beside quiet waters, 3 he refreshes my soul. He guides me along the right paths for his name's sake. 4Even though I walk through the darkest valley, I will fear no evil, for you are with me;

(And You so loved the world that You gave Your one and only Son, that *whoever* believes in Him shall not perish but have eternal life,).

Because your rod and your staff, they comfort me.

5You prepare a banquet before me in the presence of my enemies.

You anoint my head with oil; my cup overflows.

6Surely your goodness and love will follow me all the days of my life, and I will dwell in the house of the Lord, forever.

I woke up this morning with Psalms 23 and John 3:16 in my head, kind of scrambled up. I kept thinking my name is "Whoever." Is that your name also?
God loves you!

# GOD WILL CHANGE HIS MIND. August 24

God spoke to Jeremiah in Jeremiah 26:3–6:

> 3-Perhaps they will listen and each will turn from their evil ways. Then I will relent (change my mind) and not inflict on them the disaster I was planning because of the evil they have done. 4-Say to them, 'This is what the Lord says: If you do not listen to me and follow my law, which I have set before you, 5-and if you do not listen to the words of my servants the prophets, whom I have sent to you again and again (though you have not listened), 6-then I will make this house like Shiloh and this city a curse among all the nations of the earth.' "

God was telling the Israelites, through Jeremiah, if you just listen to me and follow my ways, I will change my mind and not inflict the judgment against them.

God's mind can be changed, but *He* does not change His personality or His standards or His Love or His justice, but like a loving Father, He will listen to His children and if He so desires, He may change His mind.

It is not too late yet!

There will come a day when He has had enough, and that day He will send His one and only Son to come back as the King to judge this earth. But while He is waiting, He is listening to His children's prayers. Maybe today He will change His mind about you. If you have something you need to say to Him, He is listening.

His plan is for all the people who have rejected His Son to perish. But He also provided you a way out. If you don't know Him, today is the day.

God loves you so much that He gave His Son as the only way out.

Pray about it.

2 Corinthians 5,

1-For we know that if the earthly tent (our body) which is our house is torn down, we have a building from God, a house not made with hands, eternal in the heavens. 2-For indeed in this house (body) we groan, longing to be clothed with our dwelling from heaven,3-inasmuch as we, having put it on, will not be found naked. 4-For indeed while we are in this tent, we groan, being burdened, because we do not want to be unclothed but to be clothed, so that what is mortal will be swallowed up by life. 5-Now He who prepared us for this very purpose is God, who gave to us the Spirit as a pledge.

6-Therefore, being always of good courage, and knowing that while we are at home in the body we are absent from the Lord—7-for we walk by faith, not by sight—8-we are of good courage, I say, and prefer rather to be *absent from the body and to be present with the Lord*.

Listen to what Paul said in Philippians 1:23–24, "I am torn between the two: I desire to depart and be with Christ, which is better by far; 24-but it is more necessary for you that I remain in the body."

Paul wanted to go and be with Christ.

Rhonda has now realized this great promise. She is present with her Savior!

This is our *living hope*, to be absent from the body and present with the Lord. It is the ultimate goal in life—to be in heaven with God and our Lord Jesus.

Paul said in verse 17, "Therefore if any man be in Christ, he is a new creature: old things are passed away; behold, all things are become new."

She is a very happy girl today, I am sure!

God loves her and God loves you!

# DOES IT MATTER IF I PRAY? August 26

Many have said, if God is all knowing and has a plan and is in charge, what difference would my little prayer make? Does God answer prayer? Will He answer my prayer?

This is a very challenging subject for us to understand.

Someone has said there are three answers to prayer: yes, no, and wait.

Two of the three we can deal with, but what about the answer, no? How do we deal with it? When the answer is no, we conjure up all kinds of reasons why God said no, such as not enough faith, sin in your life, you are not worthy, bla-bla-bla. But what if it is not always about you? What if God's plan is much bigger than you? What if your problem is part of something much bigger that God is working on, and the answer no means, no for you but yes for others.

There could be a larger issue, that your *no* may affect many yeses for others. What if others come to know the Lord because of your no answer? How would you feel about that?

So, can you pray with confidence, even if your answer is no? Can we know in this life what our Lord Jesus is doing, unless we see the result we ask for? And more, are we willing to accept His will when it is not in tune with ours? How strong is our faith? Are we willing to drink from the cup like Jesus did when He prayed, "Father if it be possible let this cup of suffering pass, but not my will, but Your will be done!"

Jesus did drink from the cup of suffering for the greater good of all humanity. Can we say in our prayers with a strong faith, not my will, but your will be done?

Rhonda's *no* was a yes for many souls who have not only been saved for all eternity, but many more have grown much closer to the Lord in their relationship.

There will be people standing before Jesus because of her that she will not even know. Praise God!

Pray about it. Not my will, but Your will be done. Give Jesus your life, and He will do much more with it than you could.

God loves you.

# GOLD AND SILVER, WOOD AND STRAW. August 27

1 Corinthians 3,
11For no one can lay any foundation other than the one already laid, which is Jesus Christ. 12If anyone builds on this foundation using gold, silver, costly stones, wood, hay or straw, 13their work will be shown for what it is, because the Day will bring it to light. It will be revealed with fire, and the fire will test the quality of each person's work. 14If what has been built survives, the builder will receive a reward. 15If it is burned up; the builder will suffer loss but yet will be saved—even though only as one escaping through the flames.

So, what is the difference in gold and silver and wood and straw when it comes to works for the Lord? Gold and silver is the truth of Jesus Christ with no additions and nothing taken away, pure truth from the heart, with Jesus at the center of all thought, and Him as the cornerstone on everything you build.

Wood and straw is where we interject our ways and not His. We deviate from the mind of Christ and build on our own fancies and inventions of how Christianity should be, such as when we do something we think is required. That is like the Pharisees, who added 613 laws that no one can keep.

There will be a day when every man's work will be laid open for Christ to view, and it will be tested by the fire. If it makes it through the fire, it will be as gold and silver; if not, it will be burned up as useless. If what you do for the Lord is pure and out of a heart of love and gratification for what He has done for us; then you will be rewarded as a father rewards his son for doing what is good and right.

Again, as John the Baptist said, he must increase and I must decrease.

Get yourself out of the way and let Jesus work through you, and you will be golden!

God loves you.

# WHAT IS REQUIRED OF ME FOR MY SALVATION? August 28

There really are two questions here. One is directed to the unbeliever, and one is directed to the believer in Christ.

The first question is: what must I do to be eternally saved? And the answer is surprisingly simple. You must believe in Jesus Christ with all your heart as your Savior and ask Him to be the Lord of your life. Pretty simple, right? That's it. Paul says in Romans 10:9, "because if you confess with your lips that Jesus is Lord and believe in your heart that God raised him from the dead you will be saved."

Now the second question is a little harder; what must I do to *stay* saved?

What are the requirements? Should I list them all so that everyone can get it right? Okay, here it is: you must have faith in your Savior that whatever has to be done will be done through you by Him. Nothing we can do on our own.

So, there are no requirements of me? *That's right*! It is God's gift of eternal life with Him! There is nothing you can do to earn it or keep it!

It can only be received by faith; you can never earn it by doing anything! There are zero requirements to a gift. Ephesians 2:8 says, "for by faith you are saved through faith; and this is not your own doing. It is a gift of God."

God will do everything that He requires through you, but without Him, you can do nothing.

What does God require of me to be saved? The acceptance of His gift, plus nothing! What does God require of me to stay saved? It is a gift! It was given for all eternity, Jesus is keeping it for you. But? But nothing!

Don't confuse what you have to do with what you want to do. You will want to do as much as you can for your Lord and Savior, the King of your life. But don't do anything because you think you have a requirement to do it. If it does not come from your heart out of gratitude for your salvation, it is useless. That is just work for work's sake, and that is worth nothing, wood and straw that will get burned up as needless stubble. Your deeds should be out of love for Jesus and what He has done for us.

Then they will be golden.

God loves you.

# HOW GREAT YOUR REWARD. August 29

"For we must all appear before the judgment seat of Christ, so that each one may be recompensed for his deeds in the body, according to what he has done, whether good or bad" (2 Corinthians 5:10).

All Christians must appear before the judgment seat of Christ!

Each of us will discover the real verdict on his or her ministry, service, and motives. All hypocrisy and pretense will be stripped away; all temporal matters with no eternal significance will vanish like wood, hay, and stubble, and only what is to be rewarded as eternally valuable will be left.

First Samuel 16:7 declares that "God sees not as man sees, for man looks at the outward appearance, but the Lord looks at the heart." "There is no creature hidden from His sight," the writer of Hebrews adds, "but all things are open and laid bare to the eyes of Him with whom we have to do" (Hebrews 4:13).

The true assessment of the work God has done in and through believers will be disclosed on that day.

Believers will not be judged for sin at the judgment seat of Christ. Every sin of every believer went to the cross with Jesus Christ; sin is not what we will be responsible for, for it is covered by the blood. What we will be held accountable for are the deeds done with the right motive and deeds from the heart versus deeds done with the wrong motive, deeds done out of a work-for-salvation mentality. Remember, we said that Jesus will run all our deeds through the fire; silver and gold will survive the fire, but wood and hay will get burned up. Again, nothing required for you to do for salvation, but there will be much that you want to do. I promise you will want to share the love that God has for you with many other people; this will be gold and silver.

God loves you.

# HOW GREAT YOUR REWARD,
## continued? August 30

It is significant that among the last few verses in Revelation,

> Jesus tells us this, from 22:12, "Behold, I am coming quickly, and My reward is with Me, to render to every man according to what he has done."

While salvation is a gift, there are rewards given for faithful service in our Christian walk. We should look forward to these rewards. In sports, there is a reward, a trophy of some sort, given to whoever does his best.

But we need to understand the nature of these rewards to understand the nature of the motivation. These are not merit-based rewards like a trophy in a sporting event; these are grace-based. Rewards will be given for love-based service, service done out of love and gratification for what Jesus did for all of us. Service should be done because you wanted to do it, not because you felt that you had a requirement to fulfill. He does the service through us, (not us, but Him); then He gives us the reward. We open our hearts and wills to Him and let Him lead us in service for Him. Then He rewards us. So, realistically, who deserves the reward? You got it! He does!

Guess what we will do with our crowns that He gives us for service done out of love? Give them back to Him! We will lay them at His feet; after all, He is the one who did the service through us. The act of being open to His will for our lives, the love and the gratitude for His love, makes the service earn the reward. This is a hard teaching, I know, but we need to know the motive for service. We will want to serve Him, but we should do it for the right reasons.

God loves you.

# WHAT DO YOU WANT JESUS TO DO FOR YOU? August 31

29-As Jesus and his disciples were leaving Jericho, a large crowd followed him. 30-Two blind men were sitting by the roadside, and when they heard that Jesus was going by, they shouted, "Lord, Son of David, have mercy on us!"

31-The crowd rebuked them and told them to be quiet, but they shouted all the louder, "Lord, Son of David, have mercy on us!" 32-Jesus stopped and called them.

"What do you want me to do for you?" he asked.

33- "Lord," they answered, "We want our sight."

34-Jesus had compassion on them and touched their eyes. Immediately they received their sight and *followed Him*.

The healing power of Jesus will make you eternally whole if you know what you want Him to do for you!

These two blind men knew exactly what they wanted; they wanted to see, but when they could see, then they wanted Jesus. So, they followed Him.

What is keeping you from following Jesus? Jesus wants you to give up anything that is keeping you from following Him. He will make you whole if you let Him, not just for now, but forever!

Colossians 2:10 says, "and in Christ you have been brought to fullness. He is the head over every power and authority."

God loves you!

# NINEVEH CHANGED GOD'S MIND.
## September 1

Nineveh was an evil place, and Jonah was told by God to go and preach to the Ninevites that God would bring destruction on them in forty days if they did not repent from their evil ways.

Jonah chapter 3,
When Jonah found out (the hard way) what God wanted Him to do, Jonah began by going a day's journey into the city, proclaiming, "Forty more days and Nineveh will be overthrown." 5-The Ninevites listened and believed God. A fast was proclaimed, and all of them, from the greatest to the least, put on sackcloth.

6-When Jonah's warning reached the king of Nineveh, he rose from his throne, took off his royal robes, covered himself with sackcloth and sat down in the dust. 7-This is the proclamation he issued in Nineveh: "By the decree of the king and his nobles: Do not let people or animals, herds or flocks, taste anything; do not let them eat or drink. 8-But let people and animals be covered with sackcloth. Let everyone call urgently on God. Let them give up their evil ways and their violence. 9-Who knows? God may yet change His mind, and with compassion turn from his fierce anger so that we will not perish."

10-When God saw what they did and how they turned from their evil ways, he relented, (or changed His mind) and did not bring on them the destruction he had threatened.

The Ninevites changed their evil ways; they prayed and repented and God changed His mind about their destruction.

Here is a great example of God changing His mind and not bringing destruction on them like He said He would do. But look at what they did: they prayed and they fasted; they even made their animals and children fast. The king said, "If it is in His will, and you do as He says, who knows He may change His mind," and God listened and changed His mind when He saw that they repented.

Romans 6:23 states, "For the wages of sin is death, but the gift of God is eternal life in Christ Jesus our Lord."

God loves everyone and does not wish for anyone to perish. God will change His mind about you also. It doesn't matter what you have done; it only matters what you do about it. Nineveh repented!

God loves you very much!

# EVERYTHING NEW AND BEAUTIFUL.
## September 2

Think of a new bride getting ready for her wedding. Everything must be perfect. Some of my girls recently were getting ready for a prom dance—what excitement, and anticipation. But there is so much more preparation that has to be done for a wedding, much more than a one-night dance.

> Did you know that the Church is described as the bride of Christ in the Bible? And God is preparing a new home for His Church. Listen to what John says in,

> Revelation 21:21-27 (The Message), the main street of the city was pure gold, translucent as glass. There was no sign of a Temple, for the Lord God—the Sovereign Strong—and the Lamb are the Temple. The city doesn't need sun or moon for light. God's glory is its light, the Lamb its lamp! The nations will walk in its light, and earth's kings bring in their splendor. Its gates will never be shut by day, and there won't be any night. They'll bring the glory and honor of the nations into the city. Nothing dirty or defiled will get into the city, and no one who defiles or deceives. Only those whose names are written in the Lamb's Book of Life will get in.

This is just a taste of what our new dwelling place that is being prepared for us by our great God and Savior looks like. John had a hard time even describing it. Can you just imagine the excitement and anticipation that is going on in heaven, getting ready for the bride, the Church, to show up?

Only those whose names are written in the Lamb's Book of Life will get in!

Something to think about today!

God loves you.

# THE PHARISEES HAD JESUS IN A BOX!
## September 3

On Jesus' last trip to Jerusalem, it was the time of the Passover. The high priest and religious leaders were planning on how to get rid of Jesus, the troublemaker, at least that is what they thought He was.

I guess it is true that He was disrupting everything that they held as important. And it is true that He called them a brood of vipers,

> Matthew 23:33, he said to them, "You snakes! You brood of vipers! How will you escape being condemned to hell?" And again, in Matthew 12:34, "You brood of vipers, how can you who are evil say anything good? For the mouth speaks what the heart is full of."

So, they did not like Him very much. Now during this time Satan entered Judas Iscariot, one of the twelve disciples, and he conferred with the high priest about betraying Jesus.

Now we have the picture: all of the religious leaders conferring with Judas about how they would kill Jesus, the one and only Son of God!

They denied that Jesus was the Messiah. They would not believe it, no matter what he did. Why? Because He was not who they wanted Him to be. They wanted a king to ride up on a great white stallion and over throw the Romans. They did not want this king, riding on a donkey; they wanted a king of their own making. They had the Messiah in a box.

What about you? What does your king look like? Is He exactly like you want Him? Is He taking care of all of your wish list like a genie in a bottle? How big of a box designed by your subconscious mind does your king fit in? Satan would love for you to keep Jesus in a nice secure box of your own choosing.

Get God out of the box and worship the all-knowing, all-present God, your King and your Savior.

He loves you.

# UNCOMPREHENDING LOVE! September 4

Isaiah 53:3–4,

He was despised and rejected by mankind, a man of suffering, and familiar with pain. Like one from whom people hide their faces he was despised, and we held him in low esteem. Surely, he took up our pain and bore our suffering, yet we considered him punished by God, stricken by him, and afflicted.

This is what happened to our Lord and Savior when He came to save us; this is what they did to Him, and Isaiah told that it would happen hundreds of years before it happened. So how many Messiahs did God send to save us? There was and is only One!

When He came, they treated Him with disrespect! They rejected their Lord and Savior! They looked away and turned their nose up at him! Those awful people rejected Jesus. But doesn't this sound familiar? It sounds a lot like today, don't you think? Christians in His name are being persecuted all over the world, even right on your street where you live. Jesus is being rejected today just like He was then. The world might not put Him on a cross if He came today, but they might try to cut His head off.

Why on earth or in heaven would God care if we were saved or not?

Only He knows why; He loves us.

I sure don't know; to me it does not make since. But I believe it. I believe with all my heart that in spite of our wicked selves, He loves us enough to send Jesus, His one and only Son to be our sacrifice. Uncomprehending love!

God's grace to an awful people.

He loves you.

# UNCOMPREHENDING LOVE,
## continued September 5

Isaiah 53:3–4, "He was despised and rejected by mankind, a man of suffering, and familiar with pain. Like one from whom people hide their faces he was despised, and we held him in low esteem. Surely, he took up our pain and bore our suffering, yet we considered him punished by God, stricken by him, and afflicted."

Yesterday we looked at the love God has for us, the uncomprehending love, and the grace He shows us. What an amazing God! In spite of the rejection, He continues to reach out to humanity — what wonderful love.

But there is also the judgment He shows those who reject His Son. Would it really be love if those who rejected Jesus were not punished? What will He do to cruel persecutors? They must be held accountable! They have their day now, but we know that His day is coming when there will be weeping and gnashing of teeth! In Luke 13:28 Jesus tells them, "There will be weeping there, and gnashing of teeth, when you see Abraham, Isaac and Jacob and all the prophets in the kingdom of God, but you yourselves thrown out."

They have their day now, but it will only be a moment, compared to eternity. All will stand before the King at Judgment Day.

Everyone has a choice!

Our King that loves everyone, but will be forced to judge those who reject Him.

Matthew Henry says, "The hottest place in hell will be the portion for hypocrites and persecutors."

He loves you very much and does not wish for any to perish!

# THE HEAVENLY WARRIOR KING RIDES!
## September 6

We read in Matthew 21:10–11 "10-When Jesus
entered Jerusalem, the whole city was stirred and
asked, 'Who is this?' 11-The crowds answered,
'This is Jesus, the prophet from Nazareth in
Galilee.'" Why do you think they called Him a
prophet, and not the Son of God?

In their minds, the Messiah would not ride in on a donkey,
remember we said He would come in on a donkey first and later
on a white stallion.

When God tells His Son, Jesus Christ, to go and set up our
new home in Jerusalem, He will come as a warrior King and
defeat Satan and his demons along with all nations that oppose
Israel. Look at Revelation19:11–16, where John tells us:

> 11-I saw heaven standing open and there before
> me was a white horse, whose rider is called
> Faithful and True. With justice he judges and
> wages war. 12-His eyes are like blazing fire, and
> on his head are many crowns. He has a name
> written on him that no one knows but he, him-
> self. 13-He is dressed in a robe dipped in blood,
> and his name is the word of God. 14-The armies
> of heaven were following him, riding on white
> horses and dressed in fine linen, white and clean.
> 15-Coming out of his mouth is a sharp sword
> with which to strike down the nations. "He
> will rule them with an iron scepter." He treads
> the winepress of the fury of the wrath of God
> Almighty. 16-On his robe and on his thigh, he
> has this name written:
>
> KING OF KINGS AND LORD OF LORDS.

This will all happen sometime in the near future!
Praise God! He loves you.

# HOW MANY "THINK" THEY ARE SAVED?
## September 7

This is a question that a lot of folks are asking: how can I be sure I am saved? Some will say, "I think I am."

But I believe that God wants us to know for sure if we are saved or not. And if you are, you should be able to say, "Praise God, I know I am saved!"

Do you think for one minute that a loving God would want His children to walk around in doubt or to be uncertain if they are saved or not? I sure do not! Wondering and worrying—I don't think so!

Someone once said; if you could have it and not know it, you could lose it and not miss it. The truth is if you are saved, you know it, and if you have it and know it, you can never lose it!

Some will say, "No one can know for sure that they are saved," but I don't see how this can be true when John tells us different.

> Look at 1 John 5:13: "I write these things to you who believe in the name of the Son of God so that you may *know* that you have eternal life."

Your eternal life starts the day you are saved!

John says, "so that you may *know* that you have eternal life." Eternal life *is* Salvation and Salvation *is* eternal life!

The only other option is eternal death for those who are not saved.

So, if you *know* something to be true, then you can rest assured that it is true because you *know* it. The word *know* means absolute assurance.

John did not say, so you can think you are; he did not say, so you can guess you are; but He said that you can *know* you are saved!

So, if you don't know you are saved, then you may not be, and if that is so, it is easy to fix. Pray to your God and Savior about it!

God loves you. This I know!

# DO YOU KNOW YOU ARE SAVED? part two
## September 8

This is a story from Adrian Rogers:

One night while out soul winning, I asked a man if he wanted to receive Christ as his personal Lord and Savior. After we prayed together, and he accepted Jesus, I said, "Now sir, I want to give you your spiritual birth certificate." And I turned to John 5:24 and read, "Very truly I tell you, whoever hears my word and believes him who sent me has eternal life and will not be judged but has crossed over from death to life."

I said to him, "This is Jesus speaking. Do you believe that?" "Yes," he said. "He that hears my word. . .. Have you heard my words?"

"Yes," he said. "And believes on Him that sent me. . .. Have you believed on the God that sent Jesus?" "Yes," he said. ". . . has eternal life? Do you have eternal life?" He said, "Well, I hope so!"

I said, "Let's read it again." And we did, and again he answered, "I hope so." So, a third time we read it, and I asked, ". . . eternal life?" And he finally saw it and said, "Why yes, yes I do." I said, "Who says so?" And he said, "God said so! God says so!"

It took this man three times reading this passage to understand that when you accept God's gift of salvation, Jesus Christ, you have eternal life because God says so!

Isn't it better to have God's word on the subject of eternal life, rather than your neighbor's or your pastor or your opinions, emotions, wishes, or dreams?

God said it and that's final! Salvation *is* eternal life!

Now, do you have eternal life? Do you need to read it again? Then praise God for it, and quit doubting your salvation. He loves you!

# SOME THINK THEY CAN BE GOOD ENOUGH. September 9

A resent Christian survey asked some really good questions and came up with some interesting facts about born-again Christians. Only three out of ten adults currently qualify as "born again," and this represents a significant drop in the last twenty years, where five out of ten said they were born again. Also, less than 50 percent believe that the Bible contains absolute moral truths.

Here is the shocker, six out of ten, professed born-again Christians believe if you are good enough and do enough good deeds, you can earn your salvation.

I guess people just do not want to believe you can be saved only through God's Son!

Jesus is the only way! No one can work their way in to heaven; it is impossible!

You know what I think the problem really is? These people are not reading the word of God. They may have life insurance, but they haven't read their policy.

You must read God's word, the Bible, to know what you believe!

> Ephesians 4:14–15, Then we will no longer be infants, tossed back and forth by the waves, and blown here and there by every wind of teaching and by the cunning and craftiness of people in their deceitful scheming. 15-Instead, speaking the truth in love, we will grow to become in every respect the mature body of him who is the head, that is, Christ.

They may say they believe, but what is it that they believe? It is important to know what you believe, so get the Bible off the shelf and find a comfortable place and start reading.

Just for grins and giggles, what if when you get to heaven, Moses walks up to you and introduces himself to you, and you don't have a clue who he is or what he did or maybe you'll see Ezekiel or maybe Habakkuk! It may be embarrassing, just saying.

God loves you and wants you to know how much, so read His letter to you, the Holy Bible.

# THE ANGEL ROLLED AWAY THE STONE!
## September 10

Do you think the angel was happy the day he was chosen to roll the stone away? I do! I believe he was probably one of the happiest of all angels that day.

Even though he did not roll the stone away for Jesus to come out, he rolled it away so people could go in and see that Jesus was already gone, it still was a big assignment. He was the one that told Mary and the other ladies that Jesus had risen as He said He would. Out of tens of thousands of angels, he was chosen to do it. What an honor.

> Matthew 28:2–7, 2-There was a violent earthquake, for an angel of the Lord came down from heaven and, going to the tomb, rolled back the stone and sat on it. 3-His appearance was like lightning, and his clothes were white as snow. 4-The guards were so afraid of him that they shook and became like dead men. 5-The angel said to the women, "Do not be afraid, for I know that you are looking for Jesus, who was crucified. 6-He is not here; he has risen, just as he said. Come and see the place where he lay. 7-Then go quickly and tell his disciples: 'He has risen from the dead and is going ahead of you into Galilee. There you will see him.'
>
> Now I have told you."

Listen, Jesus defeated death and was resurrected so that we would not experience what we deserve for our sinful lives. This angel, whoever he was, was part of the team that announced to the world that Jesus had risen. What a glorious day for all of the angels! Jesus job was complete, His suffering was over, He had His new glorified body, and the angels rejoiced!

God loves you.

# THE WEDDING CRASHER! September 11

Jesus told another parable about a king who invited people to a wedding banquet, but none would come for various reasons. They injured some of the king's servants when they went out to summon those invited and killed others. The king sent other servants, but they mistreated them also. The king was enraged and sent out his troops to punish the murderers. Then he sent more servants to gather anyone they could find to come to the banquet.

Read the parable in Matthew 22, but this is the part that I wanted to talk about. It is recorded in Matthew 22:11-14,

> But when the King came in to see the guests, he noticed a man there who was not wearing wedding clothes. 12-He asked, how did you get in here without wedding clothes, friend? *

> The man was speechless.

> 13- "Then the king told the attendants, 'Tie him hand and foot, and throw him outside, into the darkness, where there will be weeping and gnashing of teeth.'

> 14- "For many are invited, but few are chosen."

This character represents people who say they are believers but have never repented of their sins and accepted Jesus as their Savior. They want the benefits of the Kingdom without the responsibilities. This man's behavior was an insult to the king.

*The wedding clothes were provided for those who had none.

Just as the wedding crasher was speechless before the king, so too will many people have no answer or excuse when standing before the heavenly Judgment seat without having received Christ as Savior.

God loves you.

# BIBLICALLY LITERATE? September 12

While many Americans assume that born-again Christians are biblically literate, Bible-believing people, the reality is different. Less than half of all born-again Christians (46%) read the Bible at least once a week. *

This once a week may be on Sunday. You know the routine; you leave church, grab something to eat, go home, put the Bible "in its place," and then go on about your business until Sunday comes back around and you take it out of "its place" again and go to church again.

Where is your Bible's "place"?

And what about the other (54%), who don't even read it at least once a week?

How will you ever know what God's kingdom is really like if you don't read about it?

Do you know that Satan loves these statistics? Why? Because he can use nonbelievers to say any religious stuff (most of the time made up) to sway you into believing anything!

Do you know how many born-again Christians believe being good enough is good enough to get you in heaven? Are you ready for this? Sixty percent! I wonder what they think the cross was all about.

Listen, folks, there are many false teachers and false religions in the world today. Satan is hard at work, trying to steal the joy of your salvation and your mission for Jesus, and he loves it when your Bible collects dust because he knows he can lead you down a crazy road.

Where did you say your Bible's "place" is? Why not make your Bible's place within arm's length? Will it fit in your purse? What about a pocket-sized Bible?

In spite of what some people believe, it is okay to make notes or underline verses in your Bible.

Who would you like to please? Jesus, who loves it when you read about Him, or Satan, who loves it when you don't?

God loves you.

# THE GOOD SHEPHERD. September 13

John 10, Translation, "The Message" (MSG)

10 1–5 "Let me set this before you as plainly as I can. If a person climbs over or through the fence of a sheep pen instead of going through the gate, you know he's up to no good—a sheep rustler! The shepherd walks right up to the gate. The gatekeeper opens the gate to him and the sheep recognize his voice. He calls his own sheep by name and leads them out. When he gets them all out, he leads them and they follow because they are familiar with his voice. They won't follow a stranger's voice but will scatter because they aren't used to the sound of it."

This is what I was talking about Friday, being biblically literate.

How will you know the sound of His voice if you are not in His word? From Genesis to Revelation, the complete book is about Jesus.

How will you know if He came through the gate or over the fence? The one who comes over the fence will lead you astray to a place you do not want to be.

Satan comes to steal and rob you of your joy with the Lord. He will come over the fence.

Jesus is your Shepherd. He will walk through the gate and lead you to green pastures and cool waters—all you could ever ask for.

You must get familiar with your Shepherd so that you can know His voice!

Read His word!

He loves you so much!

# THE GATE FOR THE SHEEP. September 14

Translation "The Message"

> John 10:6–10 Jesus told this simple story, but they had no idea what he was talking about. So, he tried again. "I'll be explicit, then. I am the Gate for the sheep. All those others are up to no good—sheep stealers, every one of them. But the sheep didn't listen to them. I am the Gate. Anyone who goes through me will be cared for, will freely go in and out, and find pasture. A thief is only there to steal and kill and destroy. I came so they can have real and eternal life, more and better life than they ever dreamed of."

Did you get that? Jesus is the gate to heaven. No one gets in heaven unless they go through Him. No one will ever see the Father unless they go through Jesus. No one will ever have eternal life unless they go through the gate, Jesus. He made the way for us; He sacrificed His life so that we can see the Father in heaven. He gave His life as a gift of salvation.

Accept the gift and live forever.

All the other ways to heaven are there to kill and destroy, to take you to eternal death; they will rob you of your eternal life that Jesus has provided.

Read John chapter 10. If you have not been reading His word, start today in the book of John!

Jesus is the word, Jesus is the only gate to heaven, and Jesus is your Savior, your God, and your King forever

And He loves you.

# I KNOW MY OWN SHEEP. September 15

14–18 I am the Good Shepherd. I know my own sheep and my own sheep know me. In the same way, the Father knows me and I know the Father. I put the sheep before myself, sacrificing myself if necessary. You need to know that I have other sheep in addition to those in this pen. I need to gather and bring them, too. They'll also recognize my voice. Then it will be one flock, one Shepherd. This is why the Father loves me: because I freely lay down my life. And so, I am free to take it up again. No one takes it from me. I lay it down of my own free will. I have the right to lay it down; I also have the right to take it up again. I received this authority personally from my Father.

Jesus did exactly what He said He would do: He laid down His life for us, and in three days He came back to life. Our sins were forgiven because of it.

Think of it, Jesus has the power over life and death. He breathed life into Adam, and He freely died for us so that we will have eternal life after death—abundant life. Think about a sheep: what could be better for a sheep than lush green pastures and a cool water stream? It's all a sheep could dream of.

What do you dream heaven could be for you? Have you ever thought about heaven? In the Bible, Jesus talked a lot about it! Why don't you see just what heaven is all about; read the Bible!

If He would provide lush green pastures and cool water for a sheep, what do you think He will provide for the people He went to the cross for? He has been there 2000 years, preparing it for you and me. Read about it in Revelation 22.

He loves you!

# THE SHEEP ARE PROTECTED! September 16

John 10:24b–30 (NIV)

"How long will you keep us in suspense? If you are the Messiah, tell us plainly."

> 25Jesus answered, "I did tell you, but you do not believe. The works I do in my Father's name testify about me, 26but you do not believe because you are not my sheep. 27My sheep listen to my voice; I know them, and they follow me. 28I give them eternal life, and they shall never perish; no one will snatch them out of my hand. 29My Father, who has given them to me, is greater than all; no one can snatch them out of my Father's hand. 30I and the Father are one."

How could Jesus explain eternal life any better? He says no one could ever get them away from His Father or Him.

This is why we say that eternal life starts the moment you accept Jesus into your heart. If you are His, no one can take you away from Him! "If God, the Creator of everything, is with you, who could be against you?

The devil and his demons can steal your joy on this earth if you let them, but that will end when Jesus comes to get us. However, the devil will flee from you if you continue to resist him.

Rick Warren said, "If you praise the Father for being able to resist temptation, then the devil will leave you alone; the last thing he wants from you is for you to sing praises to the Father. That would give him an ear-ache!"

God loves you. Praise His Holy Name.

# WHAT ABOUT THE CROSS? September 17

In a pagan world before Christ, the cross meant a very slow and painful death. To Christians, the cross is where love and justice meet—God's love for His people and the justice deserved for their sins.

It is also what the message of the Bible is about, God's redeeming love.

Jesus was the perfect Lamb for the sacrifice for the sins of all men and woman.

When John the Baptist, saw Jesus, he called Him the Lamb of God, as recorded in,

> John 1:29, "The next day John saw Jesus coming toward him and said, 'Look, the Lamb of God, who takes away the sin of the world!'"

You see, there was always a penalty for sin! Adam and Eve was kicked out of the Garden of Eden when they sinned against God, but you don't hear much about the fact that there was blood spilled so that they had something to cover themselves with.

Israel used a perfect little lamb for the sacrifice, and there was blood.

Our Triune God, the Father, the Son and the Holy Spirit, gave of Himself to be our sacrifice and the penalty for our sins.

> Romans 8:32 says, "He who did not spare his own Son, but gave him up for us all—how will he not also, along with him, graciously give us all things?"

The song writer penned, "Were you there when they crucified my Lord? Sometimes, it causes me to tremble, tremble, tremble"! We were not there but our sins were!

> 1 Peter 2:24, He himself bore our sins" in his body on the cross, so that we might die to sins

and live for righteousness; "by his wounds you have been healed." 25For "you were like sheep going astray," but now you have returned to the Shepherd and Overseer of your souls.

Without the cross, we would be doomed to hell for the penalty of our sinful lives.
But God loves you instead.

# IS YOUR RELATIONSHIP WITH JESUS GOING STRONG, OR SLIGHTLY WEAK?
## September 18

Yes, I am a Christian, and my relationship is strong! Or, is your answer no, not so much?

You probably know that I am talking about—your one-on-one relationship with your Lord.

We all know what happens when a relationship is broken; there is either something said or done that causes a break in the relationship. And then, of course, time is the worst enemy to repairing the broken relationship. And in this case the time delay comes from pride and or Satan. Satan does not want you to maintain good relations with each other or Jesus.

Okay, so you said, no, not so much. My relationship, right now with my Lord is not what it has been, and I wish it was. Ask yourself a question: when did it break down, last night, last week, last month, or you don't remember? Next question, what was it that I did or was doing right before I realized it's broken? This, you will remember!

Are you with me so far?

Once you figure out what your sin was, then get on your knees and get it cleared up.

Stop condemning yourself. That's what we do, you know, with Satan's help. Satan is the one who condemns. Jesus came to save the world, not to condemn it. Remember what He said to the woman caught in sin and the men were going to stone her?

John 8:10
"Jesus straightened up and asked her, "Woman, where are they? Has no one condemned you?"

11- "No one, sir," she said.

"Then neither do I condemn you," Jesus declared.
"Go now and leave your life of sin."

He wants a strong relationship with you because He loves you!

# ARE YOU COMFORTABLE PRAYING?
## September 19

Think about it, you are speaking to *God*, the Creator of the universe! Think about it that way, and it can be uncomfortable. He *is* the Creator, so we have to think of Him that way.

But, *He knows you by name*! He knows all about you! He laughs with you, and He weeps with you. He walked in the garden with Adam, and He walks with you every day! He is always there. God is in your heart, if you have accepted Him in your heart!

A born-again Christian has the living God in their heart, guiding you and teaching you and loving you. And speaking to you in many different ways. Listen to John 17:

> 25 "Righteous Father, though the world does not know you, I know you, and they know that you have sent me. 26 I have made you known to them, and will continue to make you known in order that the love you have for me may be in them and *that I myself may be in them*."

He is in your heart!

Can you speak to a neighbor, a friend, a relative, or a parent? They are not living *in* your heart; they are just with you! How much easier could it be to speak to the living God, living in you?

It is as simple as a silent, good morning, Lord, or a thank You, Jesus, or I love You, Lord, or forgive me, Jesus!

Ponder on the fact that God is in you today!

And what that means for your prayer to Him because He loves you very much!

# SHINE LIKE THE STARS! September 20

Paul and Timothy were together when Paul wrote to the Philippians. Paul was teaching them how to live a good Christian life and maintain a good witness for our Lord Jesus. Listen to this:

> Philippians 2,
> 14 Do everything without grumbling or arguing,
> 15so that you may become blameless and pure,
> "children of God without fault in a warped and crooked generation." Then you will shine among them like stars in the sky.

Paul was speaking directly to the church for the Philippians, but the Holy Spirit was using Paul to speak to all of us also. Do we really do everything without grumbling and arguing so that we can have a witness in this warped world? The world was warped then, and it is still warped. And if the truth be known, it will only get worse as we get closer to the end times.

It will get better when Jesus comes back to rule over it, as our King. But in the time between now and then, we are to be *shining like the stars* for Jesus so that a lost soul may see Christ in you and want what you have, eternal life. Even in bad times as well as the good times, *we need to shine*!

Chuck Swindoll says:

> Paul knew, as did the Philippians, that true joy comes only through humble faith in the saving work of Jesus Christ, joining ourselves in harmony with His followers, and serving others in the name of Christ. This was the life experienced by the Philippian believers, and it is a life available to us today. Allow the joy you find in Christ to keep you from useless quarrels and divisions and to instead guide you into harmonious relationships with God's people.

God loves you.

*A Father's Love* | 364

# WHERE ARE YOU GOING? September 21

What is your plan; where are you going? If you don't know where you are going, any road will get you there! Did you get that? If you don't know where you are going, you can get there anyway you go!

In eternal matters, this would most likely be the broad road (Matthew 7:15–20).

Most Christians know where they are going. They are going to heaven. They are going down the narrow road.

But the folks that are just living their life as it comes along, and they have no regard for their final destination, are the folks on the broad road. Listen to what Matthew Henry says about it:

> There are but two ways; right and wrong, good and evil; the way to heaven and the way to hell; in the one or other of these, all are walking: there is no middle place hereafter, no middle way now. All people are saints or sinners, godly or ungodly.
>
> You see, concerning the way of sin and sinners that the gate is wide, and stands open. You may go in at this gate with all your lusts about you; it gives no check to appetites or passions.
>
> It is a broad way; there are many trails going this way.
>
> But what profit is there in being willing to go to hell with others, because they will not go to heaven with us? The way to eternal life is narrow. And yet this way should invite us all; it leads to life.
>
> This plain declaration of Christ has been disregarded by many who have taken pains to explain it away; but in all ages the real disciple of Christ

has been looked on as a singular, unfashion-
able character; and all that have sided with the
greater number, have gone on in the broad road
to destruction.

If we are to serve God, we must be firm in our religion. We may get singled out by doing it; this road is narrow for those who will walk with God.

Picture in your mind a cliff with a crowd of people walking over the edge just because the person next to them does it, (the broad road). Are we cattle or humans?

Think about it!

God loves you and wants you on the narrow road.

# WHO IS YOUR NEIGHBOR? September 22

With Pat in the hospital, I have been walking the halls quite a bit. This is a busy hospital. So naturally, you pass many people. People are interesting. I try to greet every person I pass.

Most have their head down, busily watching where they are going. When you greet them, they will look your way to see who spoke to them. Some will act like I am an interruption to their thoughts, but most are friendly.

Some of them will look at me and smile and greet me back, and some will just nod and look away. This has me thinking: do we really *see people* we walk by? Do we see the people around us, wherever we are? Do we see people as an interruption or a chance meeting arranged by God?

Are we looking for the people that God is sending our way? He is, you know? As a Christian, God will use you to witness to the lost.

A ruler of the law asked Jesus, in Mark 12, of all the commandments, which is the most important?"

> 29- "The most important one," answered Jesus, "is this: 'Hear, O Israel: The Lord our God, the Lord is one. 30-Love the Lord your God with all your heart and with all your soul and with all your mind and with all your strength.' 31-The second is this: 'Love your neighbor as yourself.' There is no commandment greater than these."

So, who is your neighbor that you are to love? When the expert in the law asked Jesus this, he wanted clarification so that he would not have to worry about loving more than necessary in Luke 10:25–37.

I hope that is not what we think as Christians—that we need clarification when the question comes up: who is my neighbor? How much does a little love shared to a stranger cost you? Many of the people I greet look at me, like "Were you really greeting me," as if it is strange to be greeted by a stranger.

Is it possible to change a person's life with a little love showed to them?

Of course, it is. How will you know who is in need or who has been sent your way by God if you don't talk to folks? I am not even one-tenth as good at this as my wife is, as most of you know already if you know her. This is something we all need to work on: love your neighbor as yourself!

Who is your neighbor? Everyone—everyone you come in contact with!

Be alert, God will send someone your way, and you do not want to miss the blessing of witnessing to one God has sent to you!

God loves you.

# BIRTH PAINS, YOU THINK? September 23

Matthew 24,
When Jesus sat down on the Mt. Of Olives, the disciples asked him what will be the sign of your coming at the end times.

4Jesus answered: "Watch out that no one deceives you. 5For many will come in my name, claiming, 'I am the Messiah,' and will deceive many. 6You will hear of wars and rumors of wars, but see to it that you are not alarmed. Such things must happen, but the end is still to come. 7Nation will rise against nation, and kingdom against kingdom. There will be famines and earthquakes in various places. 8All these are the "beginning of birth pains."

Look at these signs of the coming of the Lord. We will not know the time but He said like we can see the seasons change, we will see the things happening that are building up to a climax.

Since World War II, there has not been very many years go by without a war or a rumor of a war in the world. In 1967, the Jews took over Jerusalem. There are many, many people dying of famines around the world. And we have had plenty of earthquakes. There are false religions all around us. With technology improving every day, people are hearing about Jesus now who never could have before.

Only one thing left to happen before the seven-year count down to the end, and that is the Rapture.

So, if Jesus came today to get His Church, it would be seven years to the day, and then the end!

He could, you know! He could come tonight; how would you like that? A loud shout and you are with Him!

*If* you are ready, what a glorious day that will be.

But that is a very important *if*—if you are ready.

God loves you!

# THE DITCH BESIDE THE NARROW ROAD.
## September 24

Matthew 7:13–14 says, "Enter through the narrow gate. For wide is the gate and broad is the road that leads to destruction, and many enter through it. 14-But small is the gate and narrow the road that leads to life, and only a few find it."

We have been talking about the narrow gate and narrow road that Christians walk on, moving toward heaven, and how important it is to find this road. Jesus said "few find it."

Jesus was just telling it like it was and like it is now. Compared to the billions of people that have and are living on this Earth, few have found the narrow gate that leads to the narrow road. Only a few people are willing to accept Jesus as their Savior and Lord. All the others would rather follow the crowd down the road to destruction.

Now, metaphorically speaking, there is a ditch on the side of the narrow road, and it is filled with mud that hard to stay out of. Satan lives in the ditch and loves for Christians to join him in the ditch. Because we listen to others, sometimes we wind up in the ditch, and then we get mud all over us. But a miracle happens every time you ask for forgiveness and get out of the ditch—when you look at yourself, you are squeaky clean again. When you walk in the middle of the road, the mud disappears.

Listen, Kids, the closer you get to Jesus, the less time you will spend in the ditch. So, stay in God's word and grow in the Lord because He loves you very much.

# WAS THERE EVER A TIME. September 25

That you loved Jesus more than today? Let me rephrase that question; I know you love Jesus, but was there ever a time that your witness showed more love of Jesus than it does today? Was there ever a time that you read the Bible more than you do today? Was there ever a time that you worshiped the Lord more than you do today? Was there ever a time that the fire for Jesus that burns in your heart burned hotter than it does today? *

If the answer to any of these questions is yes, then the next question has to be, have you drifted away from your Lord?

Listen to what Jesus says about it to some of the churches in Revelation

> Yet I hold this against you: You have forsaken the love you had at first. 5-Consider how far you have fallen! Repent and do the things you did at first. If you do not repent, I will come to you and remove your lampstand from its place.

> And again, to the Church in Sardis, 2-Wake up! Strengthen what remains and is about to die, for I have found your deeds unfinished in the sight of my God. 3-Remember, therefore, what you have received and heard; hold it fast, and repent. But if you do not wake up, I will come like a thief, and you will not know at what time I will come to you.

> And again, to the church in Laodicea 15-I know your deeds, that you are neither cold nor hot. I wish you were either one or the other! 16-So, because you are lukewarm—neither hot nor cold—I am about to spit you out of my mouth.

All of these are warnings to the Christians from Jesus to keep your first love, don't be lukewarm, and hold fast to your walk with the Lord. In other words, get back on the narrow road and get out of the ditch! If your relationship with Jesus is not going forward, then you are backing up, and sitting still is not a good option.

God loves you and wants you to grow closer to Him!

*Questions from J. Harold Smith's sermon "God's Three Deadlines"

# WHAT SHALL I DO WITH JESUS?
## September 26

Pilate asked in Matthew 27:22, "What shall I do, then, with Jesus who is called the Messiah?"

You know, Pilate really did not want to crucify Jesus because he did not think He had committed a wrong, but he was weak and he went along with the crowd down the broad road. But the question is a good one!

What shall I do with Jesus?

Here are three questions to think about:

1. What have I done with Jesus in the past? Have I ignored Him or put Him off? Or did I make Him my King and the Lord of my life?

2. What will I do with Jesus today? The Bible says today is the day of salvation. A friend of my daughters sat in church last Sunday and fought off Satan all through the sermon, and finally when the preacher was done, she walked the aisle received Jesus in her heart and got baptized! Today was the day of salvation for her! Satan lost her to Jesus.

3. What will I do with Jesus tomorrow? Many people while sitting in the church fight off the nudge from the Holy Spirit and say not today, but I will do it later. Over and over, Sunday after Sunday, they say; "Not today," never thinking what a gamble that is; who ever said we were promised a tomorrow? So, the gamble is, eternal death tomorrow or eternal life today.

I am not sure about you but I would choose eternal life and not gamble that I would wake up tomorrow. What if you had fought off the Holy Spirit's nudges so many times that He turned you over to the devil? What a scary thought!

Not the fact that you may not have a tomorrow, but that He turned you over to the devil!

Think about this today, Paul was speaking to the Corinthians:

2 Corinthians 6:1 as God's co-workers we urge you not to receive God's grace in vain. 2 For he says, "In the time of my favor I heard you, and in the day of salvation I helped you." I tell you, now is the time of God's favor, NOW is the day of salvation.

God loves you.

Psalm 103

1-Praise the Lord, O my soul; all my inmost being, praise his holy name.

2-Praise the Lord, O my soul, and forget not all his benefits, 3-who forgives all your sins and heals all your diseases, 4-who redeems your life from the pit, and crowns you with love and compassion, 5-who satisfies your desires with good things so that your youth is renewed like the eagle's.

6-The Lord works righteousness and justice for all the oppressed.

7-He made known his ways to Moses, his deeds to the people of Israel:

8-The Lord is compassionate and gracious, slow to anger, abounding in love.

9-He will not always accuse, nor will he harbor his anger forever;

10-He does not treat us as our sins deserve or repay us according to our iniquities.

11-For as high as the heavens are above the earth, so great is his love for those who fear him;

12as far as the east is from the west, so far has he removed our transgressions from us.

13-As a father has compassion on his children, so the Lord has compassion on those who fear him;

14-for he knows how we are formed, he remembers that we are dust.

15-The life of mortals is like grass, they flourish like a flower of the field; 16-the wind blows over it and it is gone, and its place remembers it no more.

17-But from everlasting to everlasting, the Lord's love is with those who fear him, and his righteousness with their children's children — 18-with those who keep his covenant and remember to obey his precepts.

19-The Lord has established his throne in heaven, and his kingdom rules over all.

20-Praise the Lord, you his angels, you mighty ones who do his bidding, who obey his word.

21-Praise the Lord, all his heavenly hosts, you his servants who do his will.

22-Praise the Lord, all his works, everywhere in his dominion.

Praise the Lord, O my soul.

God loves you.

# GO AND MAKE DISCIPLES! September 28

Matthew 28,
The Great Commission

18-Then Jesus came to them and said, "All authority in heaven and on earth has been given to me. 19-Therefore go and make disciples of all nations, baptizing them in the name of the Father and of the Son and of the Holy Spirit, 20-and teaching them to obey everything I have commanded you. And surely, I am with you always, to the very end of the age."

So here is the question: is sharing the gospel a privilege or burden?

If you believe that Jesus is God and Savior and if it is true, and if you believe it to be true, then are you doing what Jesus commanded you to do? He says therefore go and make disciples!

Suppose you speak to ten people about Jesus, and you only find one out of the ten interested? Is it worth your time? If you said, "Yes, it is worth it", (and I believe with all my heart that saving one person out of ten from a dreadful eternity is more than worth it), then don't get discouraged at the nine who are not interested.

Don't forget the road is broad to destruction and the road to life is narrow for a reason. More will say no than will say yes to Jesus. By the way, Jesus did not say, "Hey, when you think it is a good time, share Me with others," and He did not say, "If someone bumps into you and asks you about me, share Me with them." No, No, He said to go and make disciples, using His power that God gave Him.

Now, how would you like to up the odds? Yes, okay, then pray that God will send folks who need Jesus your way! That way you could influence ten out of ten into choosing Jesus over eternal destruction! If the Holy Spirit sends a person your way, they are ready to be talked to about Jesus. Folks, I think that each one of us needs to pray about this; time is running out!

Jesus loves you, now go and tell!

# TRIALS AND AFFLICTIONS. September 29

2 Corinthians chapter 1, Paul writing to the church at Corinth,

3 "Blessed be the God and Father of our Lord Jesus Christ, the Father of mercies and God of all comfort; 4 who comforteth us in all our affliction, that we may be able to comfort them that are in any affliction, through the comfort wherewith we ourselves are comforted of God. 5 For as the sufferings of Christ abound unto us, even so our comfort also aboundeth through Christ."

It has been said we are either going into a trial, we are in a trial, or we are coming out of a trial, and in my experience that is just about right. It seems we are always needing comfort from our trials.

What would we do, if not for Jesus in those times when we are hurting or just not sure what to do?

Jesus will sustain you and give you peace; He loves you very much!

# JESUS HAS AUTHORITY TO JUDGE.
## September 30

John 5

24- "Very truly I tell you, whoever hears my word and believes him who sent me has eternal life and will not be judged but has crossed over from death to life. 25-Very truly I tell you, a time is coming and has now come when the dead will hear the voice of the Son of God and those who hear will live. 26-For as the Father has life in himself, so he has granted the Son also to have life in himself. 27-And He has given "Him authority to judge" because he is the Son of Man.

All men and women who have lived will one day hear Jesus' voice and will rise out of their graves to be judged with those who are still alive on the earth at the great Judgment Day. This will happen at the end of time.

Matthew speaks about Jesus separating the sheep from the goats in chapter 25; the sheep will have eternal life, and the goats will have eternal death, along with Satan and his demons.

At the end of Matthew, Jesus says that the Father has given Him all authority, He has the authority to rule and to judge. He is King!

Please do not allow your friends and family and neighbors and co-workers, or any one you come in contact with, to wake up one day and find out that they have died without Jesus and to find out that they have to face Jesus, and explain to Him why they rejected Him. What a miserable day that will be for them!

You are responsible for all of those folk's eternal well-being because of what you know about Jesus.

God loves you.

# BE PREPARED TO TELL. October 1

Isaiah 6, 1 In the year that King Uzziah died, I saw the Lord, high and exalted, seated on a throne; and the train of his robe filled the temple. 2 Above him were seraphim, each with six wings: With two wings they covered their faces, with two they covered their feet, and with two they were flying. 3 And they were calling to one another:

"Holy, holy, holy is the Lord Almighty; the whole earth is full of his glory."

4 At the sound of their voices the doorposts and thresholds shook and the temple was filled with smoke. 5 "Woe to me!" I cried. "I am ruined! For I am a man of unclean lips, and I live among a people of unclean lips, and my eyes have seen the King, the Lord Almighty."

6 Then one of the seraphim flew to me with a live coal in his hand, which he had taken with tongs from the altar. 7 With it he touched my mouth and said, "See, this has touched your lips; your guilt is taken away and your sin atoned for."

8 Then I heard the voice of the Lord saying, "Whom shall I send? And who will go for us?"

And I said, "Here am I. Send me!"

9 He said, "Go and tell this people:

This was God speaking to Isaiah the prophet; He then went on to tell him what He wanted him to tell His people.

If we look at this passage and assume God is calling us, what will we say to the Lord?

Send the missionaries. It is the pastor's job. I was called to sing. Well, I keep the children. How many different things could we say, besides, Send Me!

God does not call everyone to be a missionary in China or Bangladesh. He calls some, but God knows exactly who to send to those places. But God does call all Christians to go and tell!

When you "go," you are to tell about Him! Okay, where am I supposed to go? When you are going, tell! When you are going *anywhere*, tell about Jesus! You can be a missionary in Walmart or the grocery store or the shoe store; when you go, tell about Jesus!

Go and tell, that is the command! So, wherever you go, be prepared to tell about your Lord, Jesus!

Because God loves you.

# GOD WILL HELP YOU SPEAK! October 2

Exodus 3,

10 Moses said to the Lord, "Pardon your servant,
Lord. I have never been eloquent, neither in the
past nor since you have spoken to your servant.
I am slow of speech and tongue."

11 The Lord said to him, "Who gave human
beings their mouths? Who makes them deaf or
mute? Who gives them sight or makes them
blind? Is it not I, the Lord? 12 Now go; "I will
help you speak" and will teach you what to say."

13 Moses said to God, "Suppose I go to the
Israelites and say to them, 'The God of your
fathers has sent me to you,' and if they ask me,
'What is his name?' Then what shall I tell them?"
14 God said to Moses, "I AM who I AM. This is
what you are to say to the Israelites: 'I AM" has
sent me to you.'"

God told Moses to go and tell the people of Israel that He
had heard their prayers, and Moses was afraid they would not
listen to him.

God said, "I gave you a mouth and I can tell you what to say,
so what's your problem? (My paraphrase).

Moses was afraid and thought he couldn't speak to folks;
does this sound like anyone you know? Many people would
say, I am afraid to talk about Jesus because I may not have the
answers to their questions if they ask me a "spiritual question"!
So, who made your mouth?

The same God that said to Moses tell them, "I AM sent you"
is the same today as He was 4,000 years ago. If He tells you to
go, He will help you speak, and He will teach you what to say!

What more could we ask for?

God loves you.

# DAVID HAD CONSEQUENCES! October 3

2 Samuel 12,

7 Then Nathan said to David, "You are the man! This is what the Lord, the God of Israel, says: 'I anointed you king over Israel, and I delivered you from the hand of Saul. 8 I gave your master's house to you, and your master's wives into your arms. I gave you all Israel and Judah. And if all this had been too little, I would have given you even more. 9 Why did you despise the word of the Lord by doing what is evil in his eyes? You struck down Uriah the Hittite with the sword and took his wife to be your own. You killed him with the sword of the Ammonites. 10 Now, therefore, the sword will never depart from your house, because you despised me and took the wife of Uriah the Hittite to be your own.'

13 Then David said to Nathan, "I have sinned against the Lord."

Nathan replied, "The Lord has taken away your sin. You are not going to die. 14 But because by doing this you have shown utter contempt for the Lord, the son born to you will die."

David committed terrible sins, adultery and murder, just to name a few, but God forgave David and washed his sins away because He loved David. But you know what? The consequences of those sins did not go away, David's son died, and the sword did not leave David's house. God loved David, but He hated his sin.

We can be forgiven for our sins, with our relationship with God reinstated, because God loves us, but the results of the sin will still remain. In David's case, the result of the sin was a baby. Just because David was forgiven did not change the fact that there was still a baby caused by the sin. The consequences of the sin was still there.

Do not think when you are forgiven for your sin, that the consequences of that sin goes away also; in most cases it does not.

The best policy is not to violate God's laws; then you don't have consequences to deal with.

Pray about it.

God loves you.

# JESUS IS PREPARING A PLACE FOR YOU! October 4

What will your place be like in heaven? After all, we will be there infinitely longer than we will be here. Jesus said in John 14:1–3 (NLT)

> 1"Don't let your hearts be troubled. Trust in God, and trust also in me. 2-There is more than enough room in my Father's home. If this were not so, would I have told you that I am going to prepare a place for you? 3-When everything is ready, I will come and get you, so that you will always be with me where I am."

Some might say, "Man, as long as I can get there, I would take a closet!" Is that what you think? I understand just getting there is important, but a closet? I remember a lady telling me one time, "I will gladly be the cleaning lady. Just give me a broom and I would sweep all of heaven." Do you think Jesus wants us, His heirs, His children, to expect to live in a closet?

Jesus says "in my Father's house," there are many rooms. Jesus is going to prepare a place for *you*—especially just for you—in His Father's house.

Maybe, according to your faith, a closet will be what you should expect. But I personally think God will do you one better than that. Maybe a walk in—just kidding!

As Christians we will be judged by our works here on earth, not saved by them, but judged by them. We will put the crowns we earn after becoming a Christian, at Jesus feet. We will give them back to Jesus because He earned them through us! You may say, "I don't think I have earned many, if any, crowns!"

If your lifestyle depicts poor faith, then change your lifestyle. Surely an attitude of just getting your foot in the door of heaven so that I may live like I want here has to be stinking thinking.

Jesus is all about second chances; you can start over anytime. So, don't sell yourself short. You have no idea today what God will call you to do tomorrow!

Listen, kids, study the Bible, pray in earnest, and be willing to obey the call of your Creator!

There can be nothing more valuable than the location Jesus is preparing for you! He knows exactly what you need in heaven! But personally, I think when you see Jesus and the scars He took for you, where you live will not enter your mind.

Whatever it is, the *only* important thing is you will be with God in His house. Trust Him!

God loves you.

# IT IS FINISHED! PAID IN FULL! October 5

John 19:30 (NIV) says, "When he had received
the drink, Jesus said, "It is finished." With that,
he bowed his head and gave up his spirit."

Found only In the Gospel of John, the Greek word translated
"it is finished" is *tetelestai*, an accounting term that means "paid
in full." When Jesus uttered those words, He was declaring the
debt owed to His Father was wiped away completely and forever.

Not Jesus' debt, He had none; rather, Jesus eliminated the
debt owed by all men and woman, the debt of sin. He declared
the debt for sin cancelled, with nothing else required! Not
good deeds, not generous donations, nothing, nada, zip, nutin-
honey! The penalty for sin was death, and we were all born into
sin and debt.

But Jesus paid our debt in full, *tetelestai*, paid in full!

Whose place did He take on the cross? It was your place
and my place.

John 3:16 says, "For God so loved the world that he gave
his one and only Son, that whoever believes in him shall not
perish but have eternal life." Have you believed in Him; if not,
why not? If so, then your debt was *paid in full*? *Tetelestai* means
paid in full.

But what about yesterday's sins? *Tetelestai*!

But what about today's sins? *Tetelestai*!

But what about tomorrow's sins? *Tetelestai*!

IT IS FINISHED!

God loves you. Do you hear me, *God loves you*!

# ELI, ELI, LEMA SABACHTHANI! October 6

Matthew 27,
45-From noon until three in the afternoon darkness came over all the land. 46About three in the
afternoon Jesus cried out in a loud voice, "Eli,
Eli, lema sabachthani?" (Which means "My God,
my God, why have you forsaken me?").

Why would God forsake Jesus? He had completed the job
He was sent to do. He had no sin. Could it be, He thought His
Father had looked away from Him, if only for a moment because
of our sin? We know He took them to the cross with Him. Just
think of the total loneliness of a lost soul when they realize that
God is not there and that hell will be their home for an eternity.

Jesus may have felt that, only for a moment or two, and was
in total disparity. Can you imagine what an eternity without
God's presence would be like? You can't really say, "Lord help
them" because He won't be there. Total darkness! Complete
loneliness, forever! That really is the hell of it, eternity without
God. Everything that is good is not there—only the terror of
eternal death. Eternal fire. Eternal damnation!

We deserved it, but Jesus took our debt to the cross and cried
out in despair when he felt the weight of it, "My God, My God
why have You forsaken Me?"

How could anyone in their right mind reject the love of the
Son of the living God and choose to go to hell? Don't let this
happen to someone you know!

God loves you.

# THE SCAPEGOAT. October 7

Leviticus 16, God speaking to Moses,
5-From the Israelite community Aaron is to take two male goats for a sin offering and a ram for a burnt offering. 6- "Aaron is to offer the bull for his own sin offering to make atonement for himself and his household. 7-Then he is to take the two goats and present them before the Lord at the entrance to the tent of meeting. 8-He is to cast lots for the two goats—one lot for the Lord and the other for the scapegoat. 9-Aaron shall bring the goat whose lot falls to the Lord and sacrifice it for a sin offering. 10-But the goat chosen by lot as the scapegoat shall be presented alive before the Lord to be used for making atonement by sending it into the wilderness as a scapegoat.

22-The goat will carry on itself all their sins to a remote place; and the man shall release it in the wilderness.

The priest figuratively laid all of Israel's sins on the scapegoat, and a fit man led him away to the absolute wilderness. The man left the goat there by himself with no water, no grass, and no companions, totally alone in the ultimate wilderness. There far from any humans or any of his kind, it was abandoned in the desolation. When it hollered out, "baaa," it was answered by total silence. It called and called, but there was no answer.

The lost souls will cry out how bad it is in hell, but there will be no answer, only silence.

"It's bad," they will say, but no one will hear them speak.

However, the good news in Romans 6:23 tells us, "For the wages of sin is death, but the gift of God is eternal life in Christ Jesus our Lord." Jesus is our Savior; he took the sins of the believers into the wilderness, and when He cried out, there was total silence! Then after He died, He woke up and again He is the King of kings, the Ruler of the universe, our Lord and Savior.

Is Jesus your Savior?

God loves you.

# FATHER, FORGIVE THEM FOR THEY KNOW NOT WHAT THEY DO. October 8

> Luke 23,
> 33-When they came to the place called the Skull, they crucified him there, along with the criminals—one on his right, the other on his left. 34-Jesus said, "Father, forgive them, for they do not know what they are doing." And they divided up his clothes by casting lots.

They knew they were killing an innocent man, but they were barbaric and it did not matter to them who they killed. The Romans were killers. They perfected the art of killing a man to inflict the most pain. But they did *not* know what they were doing. They did not know that they crucified the Creator of the universe.

Jesus could have called down legions of angels to snuff out the Romans, but not at this time; that would come much later. This time when He cried out, it was for others, He cried out for the soldiers because He loved everyone. At this time, Jesus ask God the Father to forgive these evil men. What love—He knew they were only pawns, doing what they were told to do. Listen to what Jesus said earlier:

> Matthew 5, 44-" But I tell you, love your enemies and pray for those who persecute you, 45-that you may be children of your Father in heaven. He causes his sun to rise on the evil and the good, and sends rain on the righteous and the unrighteous. 46-If you love those who love you, what reward will you get? Are not even the tax collectors doing that? 47-And if you greet only your own people, what are you doing more than others? Do not even pagans do that? 48-Be perfect, therefore, as your heavenly Father is perfect."

God loves you.

# TODAY YOU WILL BE WITH ME IN PARADISE! October 9

Luke 23,
39-One of the criminals who hung there hurled insults at him: "Aren't you the Messiah? Save yourself and us!"

40-But the other criminal rebuked him. "Don't you fear God," he said, "since you are under the same sentence? 41-We are punished justly, for we are getting what our deeds deserve. But this man has done nothing wrong."

42-Then he said, "Jesus, remember me when you come into your kingdom."

43-Jesus answered him, "Truly I tell you, today you will be with me in paradise."

Two men were crucified on either side of Jesus. One mocked Him, and one asked for forgiveness. With his insults, one sealed his fate and went to hell, and one went to heaven. The soul of the crook who asked Jesus for forgiveness went straight to heaven when he died! That day, he went to be with Jesus in paradise. He was the first of many that would come after him. Just as Jesus said, "Today you will be with Me!"

One chose life, and one chose death; everyone has a choice.

All men will choose one or the other, either life or death, paradise or hell. At some point in every man or woman's life, they will choose. Even if they choose not to make a choice, they are choosing death. No one can avoid the choice. It is Jesus and life or Satan and death.

Deuteronomy 30:19, "Today I have given you the choice between life and death, between blessings and curses. Now I call on heaven and earth to witness the choice you make. Oh, that you would choose life, so that you and your descendants might live! 20-You can make this choice by loving the LORD your God, obeying him, and committing yourself firmly to him.

Choose Jesus because He loves you.

# WOMAN, HERE IS YOUR SON! October 10

25Near the cross of Jesus stood his mother, his mother's sister, Mary the wife of Clopas, and Mary Magdalene. 26When Jesus saw his mother there, and the disciple whom he loved standing nearby, he said to her, "Woman, here is your son," 27and to the disciple, "Here is your mother." From that time on, this disciple took her into his home.

Why do you think Jesus assigned John to be the son of Mary? She had other sons, but they were not followers of Christ, yet. Maybe Jesus did not want her to go back home where she might be mocked by unbelievers. John loved Jesus, and she would be safe with him. She would be with believers instead of doubters. She would also be with the disciples. A woman without a husband and now her son would need someone like John to take care of her. Jesus, even dying on the cross, had love and compassion for Mary and made arrangements for her well-being.

Think of all the people Jesus took care of while on the cross.

The thief beside Him, His mother, me, and you, plus untold millions of other people—all the believers who would love Him and follow Him from the time He started His earthly ministry until the day He comes back to get them. He died for all of those people. He died a miserable death so that all of them could have eternal life with Him in heaven.

Aren't you glad you are a follower of Jesus Christ?

Jesus loves you very much!

# I AM THIRSTY! October 11

John 19,

28-Later, knowing that everything had now been finished, and so that Scripture would be fulfilled, Jesus said, "I am thirsty." 29-A jar of wine vinegar was there, so they soaked a sponge in it, put the sponge on a stalk of the hyssop plant, and lifted it to Jesus' lips.

The Lord deliberately let the Roman put the sponge of wine to His lips. This was one of the last prophecies that was yet unfulfilled.

Jesus knew all the rest, everything that the psalmist had said, the mocking, word for word, the soldiers gambling for His clothes, and how most of His followers had abandoned Him, and He watched as each one unfolded. At the end, there was one thing left for Him to do. He said "I'm thirsty." Psalm 69:21b says, "and in my thirst, they gave me vinegar to drink."

Jesus was human and He was God, but on the cross, He experienced a human's death. He went through a horrendous tortuous death, and of course, after all of the blood loss, He would have been very thirsty. Then when He received the drink, He said, "It is finished," and He died! It was all complete! Every single thing, every word said about Him in scripture, was all complete! Only God the Creator could have foreseen and fulfilled every word spoken about Him for thousands of years before Him.

Our Creator provided a way for us, a sinful lot of folks, to be with Him for all eternity!

God loves us, guys!

# FATHER, INTO YOUR HANDS I COMMIT MY SPIRIT. October 12

> Luke 23,
> 44-It was now about noon, and darkness came over the whole land until three in the afternoon, 45-for the sun stopped shining. And the curtain of the temple was torn in two. 46-Jesus called out with a loud voice, "Father, into your hands I commit my spirit." When he had said this, he breathed his last.

Before this, Jesus had addressed God as "My God, My God, why has thou forsaken me," but now at His death, all of that, the job He was sent to do, was all done. Now He addresses God as *Father* again. He turns His spirit over to the Father for His loving care.

His body was buried by His friends, and His soul went to hades to proclaim His triumph over death.

> Revelation 1, John speaking, 17-When I saw him, I fell at his feet as though dead. Then he placed his right hand on me and said: "Do not be afraid. I am the First and the Last. 18-I am the Living One; I was dead, and now look, I am alive for ever and ever! And I hold the keys of death and Hades.

Have you put your soul in the faithful hands of Jesus? He is the only one who has the keys to life and death.

Jesus loves you!

*I used John Phillips commentary on this series.

# TEACH THE CHILDREN. October 13

Psalm 78,

5 God decreed statutes for Jacob and established the law in Israel, which he commanded our ancestors to teach their children, 6-so the next generation would know them, even the children yet to be born, and they in turn would tell their children. 7-Then they would put their trust in God and would not forget his deeds but would keep his commands.

God's plan was always for the parents to teach their children God's laws and His commands.

But listen to what Satan has sold to so many parents: "I am not going to force religion on my children. I will let them make up their own minds when they are old enough." Have you ever heard that? This is nothing more than a bunch of hogwash! And this is one of the reasons the road to destruction is so broad. With no guidance, the kids choose wrong. They do not really have a choice, they follow their peers! When they are not taught the right way, all they have to choose from is the wrong way!

So, in the all-important years of learning, all they have is what the world can offer, and what the worldly teachers* and professors are bloviating, (speaking at length about worldly things and not really saying anything useful, empty words). Is this who you want to mold and shape your child's mind? Folks that bloviate or Sunday school teachers and yourself?

God says that parents should teach your children about Me, children teach the grandchildren, grandchildren teach the great-grandchildren, and so on and so on, so that all will know that I AM is your God!

God wants a spiritual chain reaction of the truth.

God loves you and your kids and their kids!

*John Phillips commentary

# TEACH THE CHILDREN, part two. October 16

Psalm 78,
Listen to what happens when you teach your children the ways of the Lord; 7-Then they would put their trust in God and would not forget his deeds but would keep his commands.

But what happens when you fail to teach them God's ways, listen to this; 10-they did not keep God's covenant and refused to live by his law. 11-They forgot what he had done, the wonders he had shown them.

32-In spite of all this, they kept on sinning; in spite of his wonders, they did not believe.

36-But then they would flatter him with their mouths, lying to him with their tongues; 37-their hearts were not loyal to him, they were not faithful to his covenant.

56-But they put God to the test and rebelled against the Most High; they did not keep his statutes.

Several places in this psalm, Asaph tells us of how the children of the Israelites were not taught about God and what they did in rebellion toward Him.

So here we have another choice in life, we can teach them His ways and how much He loves us, or we can let them do as they want and learn about life from the TV or video games or their peers at school. What will you choose? Keep in mind, we will answer for how we raised our children to God who gave them to us and who loves us very much.

## HAPPY IS THE FORGIVEN. October 14

Psalm 32:1–2 says "Blessed is the one whose transgressions are forgiven, whose sins are covered. Blessed is the one whose sin the Lord does not count against them and in whose spirit is no deceit."

*Blessed* is another word for happy. The psalmist says you are happy when your sins have been forgiven, and the Lord does not hold them against you. But how does this happen? Many will say, "How can I be happy inside?

You can be happy. Listen to the rest of the Psalm 32:

3-When I kept silent, my bones wasted away through my groaning all day long. 4-For day and night your hand was heavy on me; my strength was sapped as in the heat of summer.

5-Then I acknowledged my sin to you and did not cover up my iniquity. I said, "I will confess my transgressions to the Lord."

And you forgave the guilt of my sin.

This is the way to have inner peace. To be happy inside, you must have an unbroken relationship with your Lord and Savior. All it takes is the inner strength to get on your knees and simply ask Him to forgive you. When you ask and even while you are asking, He is forgiving you! Jesus never holds a grudge against you or anyone else; once you are forgiven, the sin disappears, never to be looked at again. You can't even say, "It's history" because history is remembered.

For the believer, Jesus died for all sins. Your Lord will never think of your sin again because He loves you.

# LIGHT EXPOSES EVIL. October 15

Ephesians 5,
10-Carefully determine what pleases the Lord.
11-Take no part in the worthless deeds of evil and
darkness; instead, expose them. 12-It is shameful
even to talk about the things that ungodly people
do in secret. 13-But their evil intentions will be
exposed when the light shines on them, 14-for
the light makes everything visible. This is why it
is said, "Awake, O sleeper, rise up from the dead,
and Christ will give you light."

We all know what happens when you turn a light on in the
kitchen in the middle of the night, you might see things of the
darkness running to get out of sight. They hate the light because
it exposes them.

Why do they run in the light? Because with the light,
everyone sees what they are doing.

The things that people do in the darkness and are ashamed
to do in the light are destructive.

Jesus is the light of the world, and you cannot hide from
His light. Listen to what Matthew Henry says about it: "A good
man will be ashamed to speak of what many wicked men are
not ashamed to do."

Sin is a breach of God's holy law. So, watch your step. Use
your head. These are desperate times. Many will try to lead
you astray.

Ephesians 6:13 says, "Therefore, put on every
piece of God's armor so you will be able to resist
the enemy in the time of evil. Then after the
battle you will still be standing firm."

God loves you.

# GOD'S ABOUNDING LOVE. October 17

Psalm 103,
8-The Lord is compassionate and gracious, slow
to anger, abounding in love.

9-He will not always accuse, nor will he harbor
his anger forever;

10-he does not treat us as our sins deserve or
repay us according to our iniquities.

11-For as high as the heavens are above the earth,
so great is his love for those who fear him; 12-as
far as the east is from the west, so far has he
removed our transgressions from us.

13-As a father has compassion on his children, so
the Lord has compassion on those who fear him.

So, if you are standing on top of the world, and you point
one arm to the east and one arm to the west, just how far is the
east from the west. As far as the universe is concerned, do they
ever meet? No, I don't think they do.

So, if God throws our sins as far away as the east is from
the west, they must just disappear, as far as we are concerned!
Wouldn't you agree?

How much more gracious and compassionate could God
be than that? When we violate His laws and then we realize it
and we ask Him for forgiveness, He dumps them off to the east,
never to be heard from again.

That my friend is *abounding love*.

It is much more than we can understand!

God loves us abundantly!

# LOVE THAT NEVER DIES! October 18

1 Corinthians 13, translation, "The Message,"
8–10 Love never dies. Inspired speech will be
over some day; praying in tongues will end;
understanding, will reach its limit. We know only
a portion of the truth, and what we say about God
is always incomplete. But when the Complete
arrives, our incompletes will be canceled.

11 When I was an infant at my mother's breast, I
gurgled and cooed like any infant. When I grew
up, I left those infant ways for good.

12 We don't yet see things clearly. We're
squinting in a fog, peering through a mist. But it
won't be long before the weather clears and the
sun shines bright! We'll see it all then, see it all
as clearly as God sees us, knowing him directly
just as he knows us!

13 But for right now, until that completeness,
we have three things to do to lead us toward
that consummation: Trust steadily in God, hope
unswervingly, love extravagantly. And the best
of the three is love.

Paul says one day time will run out, the created universe will
collapse, and the sun and moon will be unnecessary because
of the Light of the world, but love will never fail us. It will
be forever.

When the Lord comes back, all of this will be over! But until
then, we have to continue to live our everyday lives.

Paul says there are somethings we need to keep in mind: trust
in God, keep the hope alive within you, and love your neighbor
and God extravagantly because He loves you very much!

# LOVE IS THE GREATEST. October 19

1 Corinthians 13,

1-If I could speak all the languages of earth and of angels, but didn't love others, I would only be a noisy gong or a clanging cymbal. 2-If I had the gift of prophecy, and if I understood all of God's secret plans and possessed all knowledge, and if I had such faith that I could move mountains, but didn't love others, I would be nothing. 3-If I gave everything I have to the poor and even sacrificed my body, I could boast about it; but if I didn't love others, I would have gained nothing.

4-Love is patient and kind. Love is not jealous or boastful or proud 5-or rude. It does not demand its own way. It is not irritable, and it keeps no record of being wronged. 6-It does not rejoice about injustice but rejoices whenever the truth wins out. 7-Love never gives up, never loses faith, is always hopeful, and endures through every circumstance.

Paul uses the word *agape* here. It is a New Testament word for love. This word is used for the love of the Father for the Son and us.

This is a perfect love that Jesus exemplified. This love is not something that we feel or an emotional thing. This is a love that we can only have and share through the Holy Spirit. With agape love, we must love and help our neighbor. Most of us do not love like this, but it is the very love required from a Christian.

Paul says without agape love, whatever we do is useless.

So, go back and review verses 4–7, and ask the Lord to help you with agape love toward your neighbor. How else but by the Holy Spirit could you love someone who mistreated you? How else but by the Holy Spirit could we go against human nature and love others more than we love ourselves?

Folks, we all need to pray about this as most of us fall short here.

God loves us more than we can imagine, with an agape love.

# WHAT DOES THE RESURRECTED BODY LOOK LIKE? October 20

1 Corinthians 15, "The Message"
35–38 Some skeptic is sure to ask, "Show me how resurrection works. Give me a diagram; draw me a picture. What does this 'resurrection body' look like?" If you look at this question closely, you realize how absurd it is. There are no diagrams for this kind of thing. We do have a parallel experience in gardening. You plant a "dead" seed; soon there is a flourishing plant. There is no visual likeness between seed and plant. You could never guess what a tomato would look like by looking at a tomato seed. What we plant in the soil and what grows out of it don't look anything alike. The dead body that we bury in the ground and the resurrection body that comes from it will be dramatically different."

Some would ask, "Why don't we have a diagram?" Because Jesus is the only one we know of that has a resurrected body, and it happened 2000 years ago. But remember, Mary stood face to face with Him and thought He must be the groundskeeper; she did not recognize Him. He also appeared in the middle of a room where all the doors were locked. When John saw Him on the isle of Patmos, he fainted as dead at the Lord's feet.

We will be different. We will never experience pain and suffering again, and we will live forever in the new body, so it must be awesome. Paul said the body will be imperishable, it is raised in power and glory, and it will be a spiritual body, which is immortal.

Wow, I can't wait. Come on, Lord Jesus; come and take us home!

God loves you.

# FREEDOM FROM RULES. October 21

Colossians 2,

6 "And now, just as you accepted Christ Jesus as your Lord, you must continue to follow him. 7 Let your roots grow down into him, and let your lives be built on him. Then your faith will grow strong in the truth you were taught, and you will overflow with thankfulness."

How do roots on a plant grow? That's right, they grow through nourishment—water and minerals in the soil.

Paul says, "Okay, you have accepted Christ; now live your life in Him." However, this will take nourishment for your soul. You need food for your soul so that your roots will grow and your Christian life will flourish. Where do you get food for your soul?

It is with a daily Bible study, but most of you know your way around the faith, so live it and enjoy.

In Christ you have freedom; live it, and enjoy your Christian walk. Let the love of God shine in you. Remember you are to be a reflection of Jesus. Jesus did not walk around looking like a religious prude. He enjoyed life, and you should also. Walking the narrow road can be very enjoyable.

Quick question: think back. Did you smile more before you were a Christian or after you became a Christian? I bet most if not all, of you said, after—because God loves you.

# HELL CRASHERS! October 22

Luke 19:10 says, "For the Son of Man came to seek and to save the lost."

Every man or woman, at some point in their lives, will have an encounter with God. He put it in our hearts to seek the God of creation. Think about that for a moment. When God created us, He gave us the ability to choose life or death, but also, He made us in His likeness, and in doing so, He put something in us that makes us want to learn about our Creator.

Everyone will have a time in their life when they want to know how they got here and what life is all about! At that point in your life, you will learn you have a choice to make. You can choose to love and accept your Creator as your Savior, or you can choose to ignore what your heart is telling you. You see, Jesus came to seek you and save you.

You and I are the reason He came to live and die on this earth. He is always seeking the lost.

Did you know that hell was not established for human beings? No, sir, it was made for the devil and his demons, and if you show up down there, you will be somewhere you were not intended to be. You were intended to be in heaven with God.

But there are so many people who do not listen to the reason that is implanted in their own hearts. Their hearts say yes, but their pride says, "I can't! Not now. Maybe later."

But later never comes for so many and they become a *"hell crasher"*; they show up in hell without a ticket.

Their ticket was to heaven, but they decided to change their destination. What a big mistake because God loves them.

# RAISED TO A NEW LIFE. October 23

Kids, three of you are now starting a new chapter in your lives. You guys have graduated from one school and starting another. But the influence around you will be very different. So, listen to what Paul says in Colossians:

> Colossians 2
> 8 Don't let anyone capture you with empty philosophies and high-sounding nonsense that come from human thinking and from the spiritual powers of this world, rather than from Christ. 9 For in Christ lives all the fullness of God in a human body. 10 So you also are complete through your union with Christ, who is the head over every ruler and authority.
>
> 12 For you were buried with Christ when you were baptized. And with him you were raised to new life because you trusted the mighty power of God, who raised Christ from the dead.

Paul says these folks who would try to sell you all this high-sounding nonsense are probably not following Christ. They are walking the broad road and want as many as possible to walk it with them.

Of course, they are of their father, the devil. You must test everything against what you have learned about Christ through the Holy Spirit who lives in you and the Bible. If you are not sure about something just pray about it, but if you listen to God within you, the Holy Spirit, you will be fine.

Love you guys, and we are praying for you.

God loves you.

# THE SUPREMACY OF THE SON OF GOD.
## October 24

Colossians 1,

15 The Son is the image of the invisible God, the firstborn over all creation. 16 For in him all things were created: things in heaven and on earth, visible and invisible, whether thrones or powers or rulers or authorities; all things have been created through him and for him. 17 He is before all things, and in him all things hold together. 18 And he is the head of the body, the church; he is the beginning and the firstborn from among the dead, so that in everything he might have the supremacy. 19 For God was pleased to have all his fullness dwell in him, 20 and through him to reconcile to himself all things, whether things on earth or things in heaven, by making peace through his blood, shed on the cross.

Matthew Henry asks, "If this is true (and I believe it with all my being) that God loves us this much, what will we do for Him?"

Will we give Him a small token of our time and an even smaller portion of our talents, which by the way, He gave to us? Or will we give Him our all—all that we are? After all, what are we without God?

If eternity with Jesus is our mindset, instead of the present world, then we must give Him everything that we are. Not just a small piece of us, but all—our whole heart, mind and soul.

God loved you first!

# TURKEYS AND EAGLES. October 25

There is a story about an American Indian who found an eagle's egg and put it into the nest of a turkey. The eaglet hatched with the brood of chicks and grew up with them.

All its life, the eagle thought it was a turkey, so it did what turkeys do. It scratched in the dirt for seeds and insects to eat. It clucked and cackled and flew in a brief thrashing of wings and flurry of feathers no more than a few feet off the ground. After all, that's how turkeys were supposed to fly.

Years passed, and the eagle grew very old. One day, it saw a magnificent bird far above in the cloudless sky, hanging with graceful majesty on the powerful wind currents, and it soared with scarcely a beat of its strong golden wings.

"What a beautiful bird!" said the eagle to its neighbor. "What is it?"

"That's an eagle—the king of the birds," the neighbor clucked. "But don't give it a second thought. You could never be like him." So, the eagle never gave it a second thought. Throughout its entire life, the eagle prided itself as being a good turkey, and it died thinking it was one. *

Think on this today; are you walking with turkeys or soaring with eagles?

God loves you.

*Melvina Harrison

# TURKEYS AND EAGLES, conclusion.
## October 26

The turkeys are considered to be "bird brained," so much so that they can drown themselves looking up in a storm.

On the other hand, eagles are considered the king of birds because of its great size and its keen vision; it never kills except to eat. It is so magnificent it is labeled as our national emblem.

People are known to flock together with people they think are like themselves. All of us have heard the saying, "birds of a feather, flock together." We have a tendency to hang out with people who make us feel good, so we can stay in our comfort zone. However, being in our comfort zone can keep us from reaching the potential that God has for us. *

The question is, have you become a turkey because of the people you hang with?

All of us can soar like an eagle if we are in God's will for our lives. If we want to follow God's plan for our lives, listen to Isaiah 40:31: "but those who hope in the Lord will renew their strength. They will soar on wings like eagles; they will run and not grow weary, they will walk and not be faint."

Conclusion, don't live your life thinking you are "bird brained" because if you follow Jesus, you can soar like an eagle!

God loves you.

*Melvina Harrison

# TEMPTATION IS NOT FROM GOD. October 27

James chapter 1,

13-" When tempted, no one should say, "God is tempting me." For God cannot be tempted by evil, nor does he tempt anyone; 14-but each person is tempted when they are dragged away by their own evil desire and enticed. 15-Then, after desire has conceived, it gives birth to sin; and sin, when it is full-grown, gives birth to death.

16-Don't be deceived, my dear brothers and sisters. 17-Every good and perfect gift is from above, coming down from the Father of the heavenly lights, who does not change like shifting shadows. 18-He chose to give us birth through the word of truth that we might be a kind of first-fruits of all he created."

James explains exactly how we get into messes. First it starts with our own evil desires. That is where it originated. Then once it is conceived, it gives birth to sin.

Many will say Satan made me do it! Not so, in all cases; most comes from our own evil thoughts. Satan will surely help you along the way if he can, but it starts with you and your own desires and thoughts. But God always provides an escape route. Temptations are those that are good to touch, it feels good, or it will make me happy! All are lies of Satan because he knows our evil desires. So, certainly don't blame God; only good things come from God.

And you might as well quit blaming Satan for everything because most of the sin is hatched out by our own desires.

Thank God for Jesus and the fact that He loves us and saved us from ourselves!

# YELL "NO" TO THE DEVIL! October 28

James 4, translation, "THE MESSAGE,"
4–6 You are cheating on God. If all you want is your own way, flirting with the world every chance you get, you end up enemies of God and his way. And do you suppose God doesn't care? The proverb has it that "he's a fiercely jealous lover." And what he gives in love is far better than anything else you'll find. Its common knowledge that "God goes against the willful proud; God gives grace to the willing humble."

7–10 So let God work his will in you. "Yell a loud no to the Devil" and watch him scamper.

Say a quiet "yes to God" and he'll be there in no time. Quit dabbling in sin. Purify your inner life. Quit playing the field. Hit bottom, and cry your eyes out. The fun and games are over. Get serious, really serious. Get down on your knees before the Master; it's the only way you'll get on your feet."

Old leather knees, (James)* tells us to say no to the devil and yes to God. Then he says get down on your knees before the Lord so that you can walk upright with Jesus.

The Bible says to resist the devil and he will flee from you. Then come near to God, and He will come near to you! Because God loves you.

*James' nickname was leather knees because he stayed on his knees praying; what a testimony in itself!

# HOLY AND BLAMELESS. October 29

Colossians 1,
*All* things were reconciled to God the Father through Jesus' death on the cross.

21 "This includes "you" who were once far away from God. You were his enemies, separated from him by your evil thoughts and actions. 22 Yet now he has reconciled you to himself through the death of Christ in his physical body. As a result, he has brought you into his own presence, and you are holy and blameless as you stand before him without a single fault."

Did you get that? When you stand before Him, you will be blameless, without a single sin counted against you, because of the blood of Christ you received when you accepted His grace for your life. You will be blameless as you stand before Him.

Everyone will stand before Him; some will be blameless and others will not. Only those who have received the gift of salvation will be blameless.

Now you will be accountable for those things you have done in His name after you were saved—or those things that you have not done.

Listen to what James 1 says:

22-Do not merely listen to the word, and so deceive yourselves. Do what it says. 23-Anyone who listens to the word but does not do what it says is like someone who looks at his face in a mirror 24-and, after looking at himself, goes away and immediately forgets what he looks like. 25-But whoever looks intently into the perfect law that gives freedom, and continues in it—not forgetting what they have heard, but doing it— they will be blessed in what they do?"

Just do what you know how to do because God loves you!

# LET US REASON TOGETHER. October 30

The Israelites in Jerusalem had once again drifted away from God. Isaiah the prophet was given a message from God to tell them. Listen to what he says, in chapter 1. It is a sad day for sure. God is speaking: "15, "When you spread out your hands in prayer, I hide my eyes from you; even when you offer many prayers, I am not listening. Your hands are full of blood."

It is very obvious that God had reached a point where He was fed up with them as He does with us sometimes.

But guess what, even when He has had enough, listen then to what He tells them:

> Isaiah 1,
> 18-Come now, and let us reason together, saith the LORD: though your sins be as scarlet, they shall be as white as snow; though they be red like crimson, they shall be as wool.
>
> 19-If ye be willing and obedient, ye shall eat the good of the land:
>
> 20-But if ye refuse and rebel, ye shall be devoured with the sword: for the mouth of the LORD hath spoken it."

God always gives us another chance. He gave the Israelites a choice to be obedient and live a good life or rebel and die by the sword.

He gives us a choice also: follow Jesus and live eternally or rebel against Jesus and die an eternal death.

He says, "Listen, let's reason together, be reasonable, these are not hard choices, live or die!"

Which do you choose?

God loves you.

# SMOOTH SAILING! October 31

Jesus walked on the water, and when Peter got out of the boat, his lack of faith made him sink in the water. Then Jesus saved him from drowning.

> Matthew 11:32 says, "and when they climbed into the boat, the wind died down. 33 Then those who were in the boat worshiped him, saying, 'Truly you are the Son of God.'"

I am looking at a very calm ocean, probably the calmest ocean I have ever seen, truly a glassy sea. When I saw it, the first thing I could think of was, the song "Smooth Sailing" by NewSong.

The ship is moving through the water effortlessly, it feels like we are just sliding through the water.

The song says:

> I thought of you, Lord, how you charted my courses, set my sails and moved me out to sea.
>
> It is smooth sailing, when we trust in the Lord, and it is smooth sailing when we rest in His word.
>
> Even when the storms may come and the dark clouds block my view of you Lord, it is still, smooth sailing Lord with you! *

This song is about a life that has been turned over to Jesus. When we let him chart our course and set our sails, we will sail on a glassy sea! Even during the storms, we will come out of them with smooth sailing! The oceans of blessing will carry us through the troubled seas!

All of the circumstances that threaten us are nothing because He loves us, and when the wind blows, there is no worry because He is the Master of the wind and the Lord of the sea.

God loves us.

"Smooth Sailing," by NewSong

# JOHN THE BAPTIST WAS THE GREATEST OF THEM ALL. November 1

Matthew 11, Jesus speaking,

10 This is the one about whom it is written: "I will send my messenger ahead of you, who will prepare your way before you.' 11-Truly I tell you, among those born of women there has not risen anyone greater than John the Baptist; yet whoever is least in the kingdom of heaven is greater than he.

14-And if you are willing to accept it, he is the Elijah who was to come."

What made John the greatest of all prophets? He had the great honor of announcing that the Christ was here. He was not only a prophet but he was part of the prophesy.

Jesus did not need to be baptized because He had no sin, but he told John to baptize Him. John even said, "Lord, you should baptize me."

John knew that his mission was over now that Jesus had started His ministry. Listen to what John says about it in chapter 3. John the Baptist was speaking:

28-You yourselves can testify that I said, 'I am not the Messiah but am sent ahead of him.' 29-The bride belongs to the bridegroom. The friend who attends the bridegroom waits and listens for him, and is full of joy when he hears the bridegroom's voice. That joy is mine, and it is now complete. 30-He must become greater; I must become less.

John says, "He must increase and I must decease." The days of the prophets were over now. Jesus has come; the Messiah is here!

We should all say, "I want more of Jesus in me and less of me! Lord, fill me up!"

John was baptizing in the wilderness, and thousands came to him to listen to his preaching about Jesus coming, but now Jesus had come and John's ministry was complete. It was time for him to bow out. He said the Messiah was coming, and He did.

Soon He will come again to get His Church.

God loves you.

# FOREIGNERS IN THIS WORLD. November 2

1 Peter 1,

17-Since you call on a Father who judges each person's work impartially, live out your time as foreigners here in reverent fear. 18-For you know that it was not with perishable things such as silver or gold that you were redeemed from the empty way of life handed down to you from your ancestors, 19-but with the precious blood of Christ, a lamb without blemish or defect. 20-He was chosen before the creation of the world, but was revealed in these last times for your sake. 21-Through him you believe in God, who raised him from the dead and glorified him, and so your faith and hope are in God.

Are you a foreigner in this world? Are you living your life as if this dark sinful world is not your home? Do you live every day with an *eternity in heaven* on your mind?

This is what Peter is saying! If you are a Christian, you are not of this world. Your residence has already been prepared for you by your Savior in heaven. You are a foreigner here! You are living in this world now, but you are not to be part of it.

Your citizenship in heaven was paid for by the blood of your Savior, Jesus Christ! Are you living your life as if you were grateful for what He did for you?

Think about it today!

God loves you.

# BE PATIENT AND STAND FIRM. November 3

James 5,

7-Be patient, then, brothers and sisters, until the Lord's coming. See how the farmer waits for the land to yield its valuable crop, patiently waiting for the autumn and spring rains. 8-You too, be patient and stand firm, because the Lord's coming is near. 9-Don't grumble against one another, brothers and sisters, or you will be judged. The Judge is standing at the door!

How patient are you? If you are like me, not so much! We run out of patience very easily, especially when we can't see the end in sight. We know we are near the end, but as we live day to day, it just seems life goes on as before. But God always keeps His promises. Think of Abraham; God promised him a nation when he was very old and his wife Sara was barren. But God fulfilled His promise.

Look at Joseph: his brothers threw him in a pit, but God fulfilled His promise, and he became a high-ranking official that people bowed down to.

Jesus is coming back. He always keeps His promises!

Listen to what Paul says in 1 Thessalonians 5:

4-But you, brothers and sisters, are not in darkness so that this day should surprise you like a thief. 5-You are all children of the light and children of the day. We do not belong to the night or to the darkness. 6-So then, let us not be like others, who are asleep, but let us be awake and sober. 7-For those who sleep, sleep at night, and those who get drunk, get drunk at night. 8-But since we belong to the day, let us be sober, putting on faith and love as a breastplate, and the hope of salvation as a helmet. 9-For God did not appoint us to suffer wrath but to receive salvation

*A Father's Love* | 421

through our Lord Jesus Christ. 10-He died for us so that, whether we are awake or asleep, we may live together with him. 11-Therefore encourage one another and build each other up, just as in fact you are doing.

God loves you.

# THE SHEPHERD OF YOUR SOUL. November 4

1 Peter 2,

11-Dear friends, I urge you, as foreigners and exiles, to abstain from sinful desires, which wage war against your soul. 12-Live such good lives among the pagans that, though they accuse you of doing wrong, they may see your good deeds and glorify God on the day he visits us.

24- "He himself bore our sins" in his body on the cross, so that we might die to sins and live for righteousness; "by his wounds you have been healed." 25-For "you were like sheep going astray," but now you have returned to the Shepherd and Overseer of your soul.

It is a battle every day. Satan wants your soul, but he does not always get what he wants! If you belong to Christ, he will never get it. But it is not just Satan you are at war with; you also have to battle your fleshly side of the old you, your sinful desires.

Peter says "by His wounds you have been healed," and the Shepherd of your soul will protect you! You just have to keep your eyes on Him. Say no to the old you and yes to the new you!

You can win the battle because you have a God who loves you and will help you abstain from evil desires.

# TODAY IS THE DAY TO ADORE HIM!
## November 5

Psalm 95,
3 "For the Lord is the great God, the great King above all gods. 4-In his hand are the depths of the earth, and the mountain peaks belong to him. 5-The sea is his, for he made it, and his hands formed the dry land. 6-Come, let us bow down in worship, let us kneel before the Lord our Maker; 7-for he is our God and we are the people of his pasture, the flock under his care. 8-Today, if only you would hear his voice!

The psalmist David says today is the day, this instant. It is imperative that you hear him today, right now!

Do not put it off. There is nothing more important. This is life's highest duty, life's supreme moment for you in all time! If you let even one moment of time go by, then the mundane will set in and the time will fade away. So many people miss their time by making the wrong choice and letting their time slip away.

Listen to what Paul says about it, 2 Corinthians 6:1–2,

1-As God's co-workers we urge you not to receive God's grace in vain. 2-For God says,

"In the time of my favor I heard you, and in the day of salvation I helped you."

"I tell you, now is the time of God's favor, now is the day of salvation."

Paul said the same thing David said, today is the time!

The only preparation for tomorrow is the right use of today. God has never promised us tomorrow. Boast not thyself of tomorrow; now is the day of salvation!

God loves you.

*A Father's Love* | 424

# HOW TO GET INTO THE KINGDOM OF GOD!
## November 6

John 3:1–2 after dark one night a Jewish religious leader named Nicodemus, a member of
the sect of the Pharisees, came for an interview
with Jesus. "Sir," he said, "we all know that God
has sent you to teach us. Your miracles are proof
enough of this."

3 Jesus replied, "With all the earnestness I possess I tell you this: Unless you are born again,
you can never get into the Kingdom of God."

Jesus took control of the conversation. Did you hear
what He said?

Jesus said, "With all the earnestness I possess." He could not
be any clearer. He was sincere! He was truthful! He was serious!
He meant what He said with all the earnestness that the God/man
possessed! He told Nicodemus, "There is no way I could mean
it any more than I do right now; there is no way anyone will get
in the Kingdom, at all, no one, will get in, unless they are 'born
again'"! You must become a Christian. He said, "You must be
born again! You must receive my grace! You must become a new
person! Put off the old and put on the new. You must receive the
good news" (My paraphrase). He said it with "all earnestness"!

The phrase *born again* literally means "born from above."
Nicodemus had a real need. He needed a change of his heart—a
spiritual transformation. New birth, being born again, is an act of
God whereby eternal life is imparted to the person who believes
in Christ.

"For God so loved the world that he gave his one and only
Son, that who so ever believes in him shall not perish but have
eternal life" (John 3:16).

Nicodemus was a seeker; he was looking for the Messiah,
and according to other historical writings, Nicodemus became
a Christian. He came with Joseph of Arimathea to take Jesus

down off the cross and apply the embalming spices to His body. Later, he was baptized by Peter and John. Nicodemus got the message; he understood the sincerity of what Jesus said to him!

God loves you.

# I AM THE BREAD OF LIFE. November 7

JOHN 6,

31-Our ancestors ate the manna in the wilderness; as it is written: 'He gave them bread from heaven to eat.'

32-Jesus said to them, "Very truly I tell you, it is not Moses who has given you the bread from heaven, but it is my Father who gives you the true bread from heaven. 33-For the bread of God is the bread that comes down from heaven and gives life to the world."

34- "Sir," they said, "Always give us this bread."

35-Then Jesus declared, "I am the bread of life. Whoever comes to me will never go hungry, and whoever believes in me will never be thirsty."

God the Father who gave the Israelites the manna from heaven for physical existence, now gives the bread of life, Jesus Christ, for our souls' spiritual existence.

Jesus is to the soul what bread is to the body. Jesus is the bread of God! If you accept him, you will never need bread again. You will never hunger again!

John 6:40 says, "for my Father's will is that everyone who looks to the Son and believes in him shall have eternal life, and I will raise them up at the last day."

Jesus is our everything; we will need nothing more than Him to sustain us for an eternity.

This is one of the seven I AM statements made by Jesus in John. Over the next several days we will look at each one.

God loves you.

# I AM THE LIGHT OF THE WORLD!
## November 8

"When Jesus spoke again to the people, he said,
'I am the light of the world. Whoever follows me
will never walk in darkness, but will have the
light of life'" (John 8).

Christ is the light of the world. God is light, and Christ is
the image of the invisible God. Those who follow Christ shall
not walk in darkness. *

When we take a lit candle into a dark room, the light from
the candle eliminates the darkness, just as the light of Jesus will
eliminate the evil darkness.

Light exposes evil.

Just as the moon has no light of its own, only reflecting the
light of the sun, so are believers to reflect the light of Christ so
that all can see it in us. The light is evident to others by the good
deeds we do in faith and through the power of the Holy Spirit.
Walking in the light means following Jesus. Jesus said to His
disciples, "Follow me!"

Are you a follower of Jesus?

God loves you.

*got question.org

# I AM THE GATE FOR THE SHEEP!
## November 9

John 10,

1- "Very truly I tell you Pharisees, anyone who does not enter the sheep pen by the gate, but climbs in by some other way, is a thief and a robber. 2-The one who enters by the gate is the shepherd of the sheep. 3-The gatekeeper opens the gate for him, and the sheep listen to his voice. He calls his own sheep by name and leads them out. 4-When he has brought out all his own, he goes on ahead of them, and his sheep follow him because they know his voice.

7-Therefore Jesus said again, "Very truly I tell you, "I am the gate for the sheep."8-All who have come before me are thieves and robbers, but the sheep have not listened to them. 9-I am the gate; whoever enters through me will be saved. They will come in and go out, and find pasture."

Jesus is the door to heaven. No one who does not belong to Him passes through the door, only those who follow Him. The Door keeps the demons out and lets the born again pass through.

We as men and woman depend on our Creator, just as sheep depend on their shepherd. Sheep are the only animals that require a human to take care of them. They are much like us, don't you think? We are doomed to hell without our Shepherd to lead us down the narrow road to our green pastures in heaven. The devil and his demons are the ones who try to climb over the fence and steal your soul, but don't listen to them because we know our Shepherd's voice.

Always remember, God loves you!

# I AM THE GOOD SHEPHERD! November 10

John 10,
11- "I am the good shepherd. The good shepherd lays down his life for the sheep.

14- "I am the good shepherd; I know my sheep and my sheep know me—15-just as the Father knows me and I know the Father—and I lay down my life for the sheep. 16-I have other sheep that are not of this sheep pen. I must bring them also. They too will listen to my voice, and there shall be one flock and one shepherd."

If a shepherd did not protect his sheep, many sheep would get hurt.

David killed lions and bears, among other predators, while protecting his sheep; this is the reason he was not afraid of Goliath.

Jesus, however, laid down His life freely as a sacrifice for the eternal protection of all sheep, those who were, those who are, and those who will be His sheep. Jesus says He knows His sheep, and they know Him. He knows you better than you know yourself, and yet, He still was willing to die for you. That is a love that we sometimes can't comprehend. How could He know me and know how rotten I am and still love me? I am a sinner, and He still loves me. You are a sinner, and He still loves you!

The Good Shepherd knows everything about each one of His sheep. The next verses say that He is not just a hired hand that is just watching over the sheep. Nope, He is the owner of the sheep. He cares deeply about each sheep. Remember Jesus told a parable about the lost sheep, how He would leave the ninety-nine to find the one who was lost. He will not lose any of His sheep. He is the Good Shepherd forever because He loves you.

# I AM THE RESURRECTION AND THE LIFE!
## November 11

John 11,
21- "Lord," Martha said to Jesus, "if you had been here, my brother would not have died. 22-But I know that even now God will give you whatever you ask."

23-Jesus said to her, "Your brother will rise again." 24-Martha answered, "I know he will rise again in the resurrection at the last day."

25-Jesus said to her, "I am the resurrection and the life. The one who believes in me will live, even though they die; 26-and whoever lives by believing in me will never die. Do you believe this?"

After this, Jesus brought Lazarus back to life after he had been dead for four days. He called in a loud voice, "Lazarus come out," and he came out, wrapped in burial clothes. Commentators say if he had not been specific on the name He called out, many might have come out of the graves, but I am sure Jesus and the Father knew what they were doing.

Look at what Paul says in 1 Thessalonians 4,

16-For the Lord himself will come down from heaven, with a "loud command," with the voice of the archangel and with the trumpet call of God, and the dead in Christ will rise first. 17-After that, we who are still alive and are left will be caught up together with them in the clouds to meet the Lord in the air. And so, we will be with the Lord forever. 18-Therefore encourage one another with these words."

One day, sooner than we think, the Lord will call all of His followers, the dead in Christ first, and then those Christians that are still living next, and all of us will be raised to meet Him in the air! Each and every one of us will be "snatched out" of the ground or if we are living, we will be snatched up from wherever we are to meet with Jesus and live forever with Him in heaven. What a glorious day that will be!

Jesus is the resurrection and the life—eternal life!

Here is the thing, everyone will be resurrected in the end times, whether Christian or non-Christian. Earlier, some will go on to heaven at the Rapture. Followers of Jesus will be received in heaven, and all the rest will stand before Him and be judged at Judgment Day and separated between sheep and goats for either eternal life or eternal death.

It is good to be a sheep of the Good Shepherd.

Jesus is the resurrection and the life!

God loves you.

# I AM THE WAY, THE TRUTH, AND THE LIFE!
## November 12

John 14:6–7 says, "Jesus answered, "I am the way and the truth and the life. No one comes to the Father accept through me. 7-If you really know me, you will know my Father as well. From now on, you do know him and have seen him." Jesus said this the night before He was crucified.

He told His disciples that He was the Way! As we learned when He said, "I AM the gate," Jesus is the only way to the Father in heaven! When He said this two thousand years ago, it was very controversial. The Jews accused Him of blasphemy, which was punishable by death.

But I think it is just as controversial today or maybe even more so in the world. To tell all the people of all the religions in the world that Jesus Christ is the only way to the Father in heaven, well, some people might stone you, even today. People love darkness more than the light.

We have also talked about Him being "the life." With Jesus, you have eternal life, but without Him, you have eternal death. That is also a very controversial statement in the world.

But then He says I AM the truth, and if He is truth (and He is), then everything else He says is true also, controversial or not!

So, to summarize, Jesus is the only way to eternal life, and that's the truth because Jesus said it!

There, is the comfort that we have in Jesus. He tells us the absolute truth. We know this because He and the Father are one, and we know the Father cannot even look at a lie. So, Jesus is the only way to eternal life.

God loves you.

# I AM THE TRUE VINE! November 13

John 15, Jesus speaking,
1- "I am the true vine, and my Father is the gardener. 2-He cuts off every branch in me that bears no fruit, while every branch that does bear fruit he prunes so that it will be even more fruitful. 3-You are already clean because of the word I have spoken to you. 4-Remain in me, as I also remain in you. No branch can bear fruit by itself; it must remain in the vine. Neither can you bear fruit unless you remain in me. 5- "I am the vine; you are the branches. If you remain in me and I in you, you will bear much fruit; apart from me you can do nothing."

Anyone ever see a branch withered on the vine? It was probably from lack of water, or it was broken off. The water comes through the vine to the branches. The water is the life blood of the plant. The branch will not survive away from the vine, as it cannot get water anyplace else. If it is attached to the vine and healthy, it will bear fruit. A disciple of Jesus depends on being connected to the Lord for their spiritual life and the ability to serve Him as we should. The fruit of the Spirit—love, joy, peace, goodness and kindness, self-control, and faithfulness—is produced in us by the Holy Spirit. This fruit is not in us except through the Holy Spirit. You cannot achieve anything of value to the Lord without His guidance. Without Him, you are nothing but a cut-off branch, ready for the burn pile!

He also mentions those branches that are not bearing fruit. These are those who claim to be Christians, but God sees through them and knows they are not truly His because they are not bearing any fruit. They will get cut off and thrown into the burn pile.

At the end time, many will say to Him, "Lord, Lord, didn't we go to church some?

Lord, remember that dollar I gave to the guy at the interstate highway?

Lord, remember my mom and dad went to church all the time.

Lord, I thought about you while I was at the lake.

Lord, I meant to receive You in my heart. I was planning on doing that in a week or two.

He will say, "Cut those branches and throw them in the burn pile; there is no fruit!"

Jesus says, "By their fruit, you will know them"!

He is the true vine, and we are the branches. We are to bear much fruit! Because God loves you.

# THE INWARD AND OUTWARD YOU!
## November 14

2 Corinthians 4,
16-Therefore we do not lose heart. Though outwardly we are wasting away, yet inwardly we are being renewed day by day. 17-For our light and momentary troubles are achieving for us an eternal glory that far outweighs them all. 18-So we fix our eyes not on what is seen, but on what is unseen, since what is seen is temporary, but what is unseen is eternal."

Every day when I look in the mirror I realize that what Paul is saying is very true. My outward man is wasting away, and that is all the more reason I must be renewing my inward man.

We have an eternal promise that our inward self will come together with a much better glorified outward self. God is going to give us (our inward self) a much better body, a perfect you, a body to last an eternity. This is great, and we can never say enough good things about our new outward glorified body; but what about your inward self? Are you renewing it daily?

When you get to heaven, will you know anything about it?

Look at Revelation 4 and 5, at what John saw going on in heaven. John got a glimpse of a heavenly worship service. Do you know what he saw?

People shy away from Revelation by saying it's too hard to understand, and rightly so; it is difficult, but not too hard for your inward self to understand. Does it not communicate with the Holy Spirit? Didn't He give the words to John to write? He helps you to understand what He inspired John to write. Paul said our inward self is being renewed every day. What about you? Are you allowing your inward self to grow in the Lord?

The things you learn today may come in handy a few thousand years from now! Don't waste the little bit of time we are here!

God loves you.

# ARE YOU SALTY? November 15

Matthew 5:1–2 state, "Now when Jesus saw the crowds, he went up on a mountainside and sat down. His disciples came to him, and he began to teach them."

This was the Sermon on the Mount!

First Jesus taught them the beatitudes. After the beatitudes, He told them about how salt is like Christianity. This is found in,

Matthew 5:13: "You are the salt of the earth. But if the salt loses its saltiness, how can it be made salty again? It is no longer good for anything, accept to be thrown out and trampled underfoot."

Let's look at the difference in salt and sugar. Salt comes in smaller packages than sugar because a little salt will go a long way, whereas, I have seen people put four or five packages of sugar in a cup of coffee. Before we were saved, we were like sugar, too numerous to make a difference.

So why did Jesus say we are to be the salt of the earth?

Look at what Matthew Henry says about it:

Mankind, lying in ignorance and wickedness, were as a vast heap, ready to rot; but Christ sent forth his disciples, by their lives and doctrines to "season it" with knowledge and grace. (People used to use salt to preserve foods). If the salt was not salty the food would rot!

So, if Christians do not walk the talk, they are as salt that has lost its saltiness. If a man can profess to be a Christian and yet remain graceless, no other doctrine, no other means, can make him profitable. Once you lose your witness how will you ever get it back? Your witness is what makes the way you live your life, desire-able to a lost world. God sprinkled us among the people of the world to show them that God loves them and He wants them to live eternally, under grace. He does not want them to rot away damned to hell.

So, are you still salty? Are you making a difference for Jesus? He loves you, you know.

# EMPTY PROMISES; HAVING IT YOUR WAY!
## November 16

From The Message, Matthew 5,
33–37 "And don't say anything you don't mean.
This counsel is embedded deep in our traditions.
You only make things worse when you lay down
a smoke screen of pious talk, saying, 'I'll pray
for you,' and never doing it, or saying, 'God be
with you,' and not meaning it. You don't make
your words true by embellishing them with religious lace. In making your speech sound more
religious, it becomes less true. Just say 'yes' and
'no.' When you manipulate words to get your
own way, you go wrong."

I don't suppose any one reading this has ever manipulated
their words to get your own way, have you? Well, of course not,
I know. But some people live their lives trying to manipulate
whoever they come in contact with. Smile right now, if you
know someone like that.

Jesus says in Matthew 5:37 that all you need to say is simply
yes or no; anything beyond this comes from the evil one.

I think this is all about your character and your integrity. If
you are trying to manipulate someone for personal gain, how
does that fit with the golden rule as recorded in Matthew 7:12
that says,

"So, in everything, do to others what you would
have them do to you, for this sums up the Law
and the Prophets."

And what about loving your neighbor as yourself? Do you
think you would try to manipulate Jesus? I know one that tried
to, and he ran off licking his wounds in the wilderness.

If you do good or bad to the least of His people, you are
doing it to Him also!

So, picture Jesus, standing in front of you before you try to pull something over someone. You might change your mind, especially knowing that Jesus said in Mark 12:30–31 to: "Love the Lord your God with all your heart and with all your soul and with all your mind and with all your strength. 31 The second is this: 'Love your neighbor as yourself.' There is no commandment greater than these."

God loves you.

# THE DEAD ZONE! November 17

Think about a beautiful ocean and pretty white sand—the beach at its best—but even in all of God's beautiful creation, there were dead fish washing up on the beach today with the waves. When we asked what happened to them, we found that there is a dead zone in the Gulf caused by bad things floating down the Mississippi River into the Gulf. The zone creates a lack of oxygen, and when large schools of fish swim into the zones, the large number of fish suck up what little air there is and they suffocate.

This got me thinking about the broad road to destruction.

> Matthew 7:13–14 says: "You can enter God's Kingdom only through the narrow gate. The highway to hell is broad, and its gate is wide for the many who choose that way. 14-But the gateway to life is very narrow and the road is difficult, and only a few ever find it."

So, do you think if a few fish decided to go a different way than the whole school, like the narrow road, could they have been saved? Yes of course they could, but they would have to make a conscious decision to break away from the large group, and that is dangerous for them because there is safety in numbers.

As Christians, we are called to go a different way than most of the people on the broad road.

Like Jesus said, the road to heaven is narrow and the road is difficult, but the reward is great because God loves you.

# THE THIRD HEAVEN. November 18

We are looking at all the stars and God's beautiful creation, the Big Dipper and the Little Dipper, Venus, and the North Star from the beach at night—what an awesome God we serve. We see the two heavens: the immediate heaven where birds fly and the clouds are and the stars and the galaxies, most of which we can't even see with the naked eye.

So where is the heaven that Jesus is preparing our place for eternity, the third heaven? Look at what Paul says about it;

> 2 Corinthians 12,
> 2-" I know a man in Christ who fourteen years ago was caught up to the third heaven. Whether it was in the body or out of the body I do not know—God knows. 3-And I know that this man—whether in the body or apart from the body I do not know, but God knows—4-was caught up to paradise and heard inexpressible things, things that no one is permitted to tell."

The third heaven appears to be north. Isaiah 14:13 (KJV) says that Satan thought he could rise above God in the north. So, we don't know exactly where it is, but some think because of this verse, it is north from earth, maybe beyond the North Star.

Paul said the man who was taken to the third heaven saw and heard things so marvelous that he could not talk about it; can you imagine what he saw? Read Revelation 4:1–6, and you will see what John saw.

I think heaven may be very far, but it is very close also. If you accepted Jesus is in your heart and the Holy Spirit is with you, then your eternal life has started and you are experiencing the love of the Father every day. This is a taste of what is to come. Always view things with heaven in mind, and it will be closer to you than you can imagine.

God loves you.

# MADE ALIVE IN CHRIST! November 19

Ephesians 1,

1-As for you, you were dead in your transgressions and sins, 2-in which you used to live when you followed the ways of this world and of the ruler of the kingdom of the air, the spirit who is now at work in those who are disobedient. 3-All of us also lived among them at one time, gratifying the cravings of our flesh and following its desires and thoughts. Like the rest, we were by nature deserving of wrath. 4-But because of his great love for us, God, who is rich in mercy, 5made us alive with Christ even when we were dead in our transgressions—it is by grace you have been saved.

I heard a preacher on the radio say that studying the Bible is as easy as asking yourself a few questions about the scripture you are reading. Let us ask a few basic questions about these verses:

*Who*? Paul says as for you, Christian, if you are a Christian this means you!

*What*? God's grace that He gave us, even while we were sinners!

*When*? (This is getting good), get this, while you were dead in your sins and headed straight to hell to an eternal death, that's when He saved you.

*Where*? Exactly where you were! You did not have to go anywhere; He came to you with more love than you can understand!

*How*? Nothing but God's pure grace. Not anything you did, just God's grace, Jesus Christ's sacrifice!

*Why*? Because God loves you!

# GOD'S HANDIWORK. November 20

Ephesians 2,

6And God raised us up with Christ and seated us with him in the heavenly realms in Christ Jesus, 7in order that in the coming ages he might show the incomparable riches of his grace, expressed in his kindness to us in Christ Jesus. 8For it is by grace you have been saved, through faith—and this is not from yourselves, it is the gift of God—9not by works, so that no one can boast. 10For we are "God's handiwork," created in Christ Jesus to do good works, which God prepared in advance for us to do.

Okay let's try the questions again;

*Who*? Once again, *you*, a Christian. God the Creator. Jesus Christ the Savior.

*What*? God's handiwork is us, to do good works that God has for us to do. He created and saved us to do His will; are you doing it?

*When*? The day you were saved. God prepared in advance what He wants us to do. Think about it: God knew you before time started. He knew you would be saved, so he prepared something important for you to do. Are you doing it?

*Where*? The answer to this question is between you and God; you have to determine what God's will is and where He wants you to do it!

*How*? When you know what God's will for you is and what He wants you to do, He will show you how; there will be doors open wide for the right way and closed doors for the wrong way.

*Why*? Again, because He loves you and wants the very best for you. Remember you are His handiwork!

# WHO IS THE CLOUD OF WITNESSES?
## November 21

> Hebrews 12:1 states, "Therefore, since we are
> surrounded by such a great cloud of witnesses,
> let us throw off everything that hinders and the
> sin that so easily entangles. And let us run with
> perseverance the race marked out for us."

When we read this verse it starts with the word *therefore*, so
we have to ask what's it there for? To get the answer we have
to go back to chapter 11. This is the famous faith chapter. We
have Abraham and Sarah, Isaac, Jacob, Noah, Joseph, Moses,
Samuel, and all the rest of the greats in the Old Testament. But
then the writer of Hebrews wrote this in the first century, 2,000
years ago, since then there have been untold millions of saints
that received Jesus by faith and have passed on from this earth.

Do you know some? A mom or dad an uncle or niece or
grandparent a child maybe? Someone who made it into the great
cloud of witnesses?

Look at the next witness, in verses 2–3:

> Fixing our eyes on Jesus, the pioneer and per-
> fecter of faith. For the joy set before him he
> endured the cross, scorning its shame, and sat
> down at the right hand of the throne of God.
> 3Consider him who endured such opposition
> from sinners, so that you will not grow weary
> and lose heart.

These are all our witnesses. What are they witnessing from
you and me in today's world?

Like the writer says, don't grow weary and lose heart, keep
the faith, and grow closer to the Lord because He loved you first!

# THANKSGIVING DAY. November 22

We have much to be thankful for. I am thankful for my Father God, for His love, for His Son, Jesus Christ, for His sacrifice for salvation, and for the Holy Spirit that guides my days and my words and for living inside me (and loving me anyway).

I am thankful for my wife Pat who is the greatest partner a man could ask for, given to me by God a long time ago. God gave her an unbelievable power to put up with me for so long. I am thankful for Paige and Nena, my kids who have listened to the Spirit and are growing in their love for the Lord and my grandkids, who need to read my messages.

I am thankful that God has extended our family to so many who love the Lord. I am thankful that God is in charge, and we have no worries. There are many things I am sad about, but God's will shall be done. I am thankful that we are 2,000 years closer to Jesus' return.

Think about things you are thankful for, and praise the Father for His Son.

Thanks for all that read what I believe to be words of love and knowledge from the Spirit to help you grow in your walk with the Lord.

God loves all of you.

# WORLDLY APPETITES. November 23

Philippians 3,

18-For I have told you often before, and I say it again with tears in my eyes, that there are many whose conduct shows they are really enemies of the cross of Christ. 19-They are headed for destruction. Their god is their appetite, they brag about shameful things, and they think only about this life here on earth. 20-But we are citizens of heaven, where the Lord Jesus Christ lives. And we are eagerly waiting for him to return as our Savior. 21-He will take our weak mortal bodies and change them into glorious bodies like his own, using the same power with which he will bring everything under his control.

Paul knew that many of the Philippians were not living their everyday lives with eternity in mind, with heaven as their goal. He says their God was their appetite. I think he means their appetite for the things the world has to offer. We are in a constant battle with our appetites because Satan has planned it that way. Everywhere we look there is something or someone ready to take us down the wrong path. We are so afraid we might miss something.

Paul says that Christians are citizens of heaven, not of the world! Very soon, you will be transformed into your glorious eternal body, and you will be with Jesus forever!

You might ask, how do you know it will be very soon?

What is time when you are living with a mind of eternity? It will be soon!

What worldly things do you have an appetite for? Are they controlling you? Are they leading you down the wrong path? Put away foolish things and get your mind on Jesus because He loves you very much!

# WHAT PICTURE ARE YOU PAINTING?
## November 24

> First Timothy 1:12 tells us, "I thank Christ Jesus our Lord, who has given me strength, that he considered me trustworthy, appointing me to his service."

Suppose you were painting a picture of your life that you were to present to God. What would your picture look like? How do you see yourself at the end of time when you are standing before your Savior?

I know you are thinking, I won't be standing. My face will be in the dirt, yes, but at some point, you will look Him in the eyes, and He will look you in the eyes. What will the painting of your life look like to Him? Will He be pleased or sad for all the missed opportunities to serve Him? Maybe because you were so focused on yourself you couldn't see all the opportunities to serve around you!

> Matthew 6:24, 24"No one can serve two masters. Either you will hate the one and love the other, or you will be devoted to the one and despise the other. You cannot serve both God and money.

> Joshua 24,
> 15" But if serving the Lord seems undesirable to you, then choose for yourselves this day whom you will serve, But as for me and my household, we will serve the Lord."

> John, 12: 26 whoever serves me must follow me; and where I am, my servant also will be. My Father will honor the one who serves me.

> Jeremiah 29, 11-For I know the plans I have for you," declares the Lord, "plans to prosper you

and not to harm you, plans to give you hope and a future.

I know when we get to heaven, under grace, we will be washed clean by the blood of Christ, but every opportunity we miss is a crown we won't have to give to our Lord. Paint your picture daily of you walking with Jesus because He loves you!

# THE DAY AND HOUR UNKNOWN.
## November 25

Mark 13,
32"But about that day or hour no one knows, not even the angels in heaven, nor the Son, but only the Father. 33Be on guard! Be alert! You do not know when that time will come. 34It's like a man going away: He leaves his house and puts his servants in charge, each with their assigned task, and tells the one at the door to keep watch.

35"Therefore keep watch because you do not know when the owner of the house will come back—whether in the evening, or at midnight, or when the rooster crows, or at dawn. 36If he comes suddenly, do not let him find you sleeping. 37What I say to you, I say to everyone: 'Watch!'"

We have said that we know it will be soon, but like Jesus said, no one but the Father knows exactly when. We do know it has been a long time since Jesus spoke these words, so we are a lot closer to the end times than Mark was. So, it is all guesswork at this point. We do have clues, though, from Jesus. And these clues of wars and rumors of wars and earthquakes and famines are all around us. Jesus said to be on alert! The owner of this earth can come home to get His people at any moment. He also says it will be sudden, and in another place, He says in a twinkling of the eye, and that, my friend, is quick!

So, we should always be ready to receive our Lord at any moment.

Where will you be when He returns? What will you be doing?

Hopefully we will be working on His business and looking forward to His return.

He loves us very much!

## ABBA FATHER. November 26

"Going a little farther, he fell to the ground and prayed that if possible the hour might pass from him. 'Abba, Father,' he said, 'Everything is possible for you. Take this cup from me. Yet not what I will, but what you will'" (Mark 14:35–36).

The word *Abba* is an Aramaic word that would most closely be translated as "Daddy." It was a common term that young children would use to address their fathers. It signifies the close, intimate relationship of a father to his child, as well as the childlike trust that a young child puts in his daddy.

Jesus is praying in the garden before He was arrested; it was a very stressful time for Jesus, and He was talking to His "Daddy" about the horrible beating and death He was facing. As you know, Jesus went on and became the supreme sacrifice for all of His children.

Do you think just anyone can call God the Father, Abba, or do you need to be an adopted child of God to call the Father, Abba (Daddy)? Don't you think common sense would tell us that if you are not one of His children, He may not answer to Daddy from a person that has not been adopted into His family, unless you are asking Him for forgiveness and want Him to except you as one of His children?

So, how do you get adopted? How do we become children of God?

John 1:12–13 gives us the answer: "Yet to all who did receive him, to those who believed in his name, he gave the right to become children of God—children born not of natural descent, nor of human decision or a husband's will, but born of God."

Born-again Christians are children of the living God— God the Father, God the Son, and God the Holy Spirit—children who have the right and privilege to address the Father as Abba, (Daddy)!

Why don't we all, tonight, get on our knees and pray to our "Daddy" in heaven? What a difference in intimacy, it will make!

God loves us!

# WHAT'S YOUR EXCUSE? November 27

ACTS 8,
1On that day a great persecution broke out against the church in Jerusalem, and all accept the apostles were scattered throughout Judea and Samaria. 2Godly men buried Stephen and mourned deeply for him. 3But Saul began to destroy the church. Going from house to house, he dragged off both men and women and put them in prison.

Acts 9:3 As he neared Damascus on his journey, suddenly a light from heaven flashed around him. 4 He fell to the ground and heard a voice say to him, "Saul, Saul, why do you persecute me?"5 "Who are you, Lord?" Saul asked. "I am Jesus, whom you are persecuting," he replied. 6 "Now get up and go into the city, and you will be told what you must do."

People say, "God could not love me, look at what a terrible person I am! I am rotten to the core! He would never accept me into His Kingdom because of the things I have done."

Did you ever kill a Christian, did you ever drag one out of his home and beat him until he was almost dead? Did you ever throw stones at someone until you killed them just because they loved Jesus Christ? Well, guess what? Paul did all of those things, and God saved him and used him in a mighty way. He penned a large portion of the New Testament.

Moses killed a man and tried to hide the body, but God loved him and used him in a mighty way! He wrote the first five books of the Old Testament.

David committed adultery with a soldier's wife, when he was king. Then he had the guy murdered! But God loved him and used him in a mighty way! He wrote many of the Psalms.

So now what is your excuse? Are you a worse sinner than Paul, Moses, and David? Well, even if you are, which I doubt very much, God still loves you and can use you to do mighty things for Him.

You might say, "I am too young or too old." David was a young lad when he was first anointed king, Moses was eighty, and Noah was over one hundred years old. All of these men repented of their wicked ways, and God used them.

So, what is your excuse again?

Listen, God loves you very much and wants you to love Him also, so quit giving Him lame excuses and get on your knees and ask Him what He needs you do!

God loves you.

# ARE YOU STILL SLEEPING? November 28

Mark 14,
37Then he returned to his disciples and found them sleeping. "Simon," he said to Peter, "are you asleep? Couldn't you keep watch for one hour? 38Watch and pray so that you will not fall into temptation. The spirit is willing, but the flesh is weak."

39Once more he went away and prayed the same thing. 40When he came back, he again found them sleeping, because their eyes were heavy. They did not know what to say to him.

41Returning the third time, he said to them, "Are you still sleeping and resting"?

Peter, James and John had been walking and living daily with Jesus for three years. When Jesus was stressed, He asked them to stay alert and pray for Him, so what did they do? They fell asleep!

Their attention span, much like ours, was only alert when it came to them personally. Have you ever fallen asleep while praying? Then when you wake up, you are frustrated with yourself for not being focused enough to even finish your prayers? Well, obviously Jesus knows us and knows about our attention span; He experienced it with the disciples in the garden.

Jesus knows us very well! Wouldn't it be good if we had Jesus' insight and understanding of each other?

Sometimes I think we expect too much from our friends and loved ones. When we expect them to stay focused, they fall asleep. Do you think we may all be too self-centered? Probably. Understanding the problem means we are well on our way to correcting the bad behavior.

Now is not the time to fall asleep. We are too close to the end of the race. There is too much work that needs to be done

for the kingdom. Like Jesus said, "Watch and pray so that you will not fall into temptation," so be alert. Time is running out!
  God loves you.

# A PSALM OF CONFESSION. November 29

When Nathan exposed David's sin with Bathsheba to him, David repented and was ashamed of what He did. Here is some of the psalm he wrote after that:

> Psalm 51,
> 1Have mercy on me, O God, according to your unfailing love;
>
> According to your great compassion blot out my transgressions.
>
> 2Wash away all my iniquity and cleanse me from my sin.
>
> 3For I know my transgressions, and my sin is always before me.
>
> 4Against you, you only, have I sinned and done what is evil in your sight; so, you are right in your verdict and justified when you judge.
>
> 9Hide your face from my sins and blot out all my iniquity.
>
> 10Create in me a pure heart, O God, and renew a steadfast spirit within me."

This is a great psalm that David wrote to the Lord.

David confessed, and God forgave him. Are there things you need to confess?

David then had many consequences he had to suffer because of his sins. He was forgiven and he was in right standing with God, but there were still the results of the sins that he had hanging over his head. Folks, the sins we commit can be forgiven and forgotten by God, but in many cases, consequences of those sins are left lingering around.

Jesus told the woman who was about to be stoned, "to go and sin no more." If we don't want to deal with consequences, then we need to "go and sin no more." That is easy to say and hard to do, I know, but we can live our lives trying not to sin, can't we?

Because God loves us.

# ANTICIPATING CHRIST'S RETURN.
## November 30

We need to anticipate Christ's second coming and to be aware that He could come anytime and not be fearful of what He might find us doing. We know we have but a moment or two of time to live here on this world, and no one knows the time for the judgment.

Our Lord's coming will be a happy time to those who are ready but very scary to those who are not.

> Matthew 24:21, 30
> For then there will be great distress, unequaled from the beginning of the world until now — and never to be equaled again."
>
> 30"Then will appear the sign of the Son of Man in heaven. And then all the peoples of the earth will mourn when they see the Son of Man coming on the clouds of heaven, with power and great glory."

If a person, professing to be the servant of Christ, is actually an unbeliever, he will not be glad to see the Lord's coming. Those who choose the world and the broad road will have hell in their future in the next life. That has to be the worst of the worst of all the ways a person can live!

Pretenders live a lie to themselves, the people around them, and the Lord. What a miserable way to live. These folks need to repent, be honest, and get off that awful road to hell.

May our Lord, when He comes, pronounce us blessed and present us to the Father, washed in his blood, purified by his Spirit, and fit to enter into His inheritance! Amen.

God loves you.

# LOOK AT THE FIG TREE. December 1

Jesus' disciples asked Him when the end times would be, and Jesus told them no man knew the answer to that but the Father in heaven. But we know the end of the world will not come until the Gospel has done what it was intended to do—bring all that will be saved into the kingdom.

He said you will see the signs, though, like the fig tree:

> Matthew 24,
> 32-" Now Learn this lesson from the fig tree: As soon as its twigs get tender and its leaves come out, you know that summer is near. 33Even so, when you see all these things, you know that the end is near, right at the door. 34Truly I tell you, this generation will certainly not pass away until all these things have happened.35heaven and earth will pass away, but my words will never pass away."

The elect of God at that time, as it is today, will be scattered all around the globe, but when the trumpet blows, not a single one will be left behind.

What example but the fig tree could tell us more about the coming end times. As in Noah's day, men were working, woman were having babies, and things appeared quite normal. Then the doors were shut, and it started to rain. Today men and woman are working, kids are playing ball, spring and summer activities are happening. All of a sudden, a loud shout will be heard by the Christians, and then they will be gone, resurrected to a new life, and the seven-year clock to the end will begin and then the Judgment Day! Great news for some; sad news for others.

I wish I could convey the sudden sadness that will come over all of the people who will know they should have accepted Jesus but pushed that thought further back in their mind until it was too late. They were too involved in what the world has to offer. The choice was simple: Satan's world of pleasure or eternal heaven, a moment of pleasure or an eternity of blessings.

What will it be for you?

God loves you.

# ARE YOU BLESSED TODAY? December 2

Are you happy today? Are you blessed? David says blessed is the one whose sins are forgiven. Blessed also means "happy."

That is why we asked are you happy today? Do you feel blessed? Are your sins forgiven? Do you know it to be true? If so, then you are happy! There is nothing that can make you happier than being in good standing with your Lord and Savior. It makes you want to jump and shout!

Psalm 32,
1Blessed is the one whose transgressions are forgiven, whose sins are covered.

2Blessed is the one whose sin the Lord does not count against them and in whose Spirit is no deceit.

3When I kept silent, my bones wasted away through my groaning all day long.

4For day and night your hand was heavy on me; my strength was sapped as in the heat of summer.

5Then I acknowledged my sin to you and did not cover up my iniquity.

I said, "I will confess my transgressions to the Lord."

And you forgave the guilt of my sin."

What is the opposite of being so happy, you want to jump and shout? It is being so miserable you want to bury your head in the sand. David said he was wasting away, moaning and groaning all day, because of his sin. He said it sapped his strength; there was nowhere for him to hide from an all-knowing Lord.

And then he acknowledged his sin to God. God forgave him, and then he felt blessed (happy). He could look up and did not feel he had to hide from God, which is a foolish thought anyway! His life had meaning again.

Do not try to hide from God! Lose your pride. Speak to your Savior about your sins and be happy!

David says blessed is the one whose sins are covered.

Is that you today? Are you happy?

God loves you. You should be!

# REJOICE IN THE LORD AND BE GLAD.
## December 3

Psalm 32, this portion, God is speaking,

8" I will instruct you and teach you in the way you should go;

I will counsel you with my loving eye on you.

9 Do not be like the horse or the mule, which have no understanding but must be controlled by bit and bridle or they will not come to you.

10 Many are the woes of the wicked, but the Lord's unfailing love surrounds the one who trusts in him.

11 Rejoice in the Lord and be glad, you righteous; sing, all you who are upright in heart!"

God teaches us with His word and hints and suggestions for His will. He makes His will known to us in indirect ways, including an inward impulse, the word of God, and trending circumstances. *

Without a doubt, He teaches and guides us when we are willing to learn — if we are open to His will.

David uses the stubborn mule here to show how so many of us are unwilling to follow Jesus and listen to His teachings. It takes a bridle or bit to get them to go anywhere. He goes on to say, "Many are the woes of the wicked! But His love surrounds the ones who trust Him!"

What are the woes of the wicked?

Psalm 10:7 says, "His mouth is full of cursing and deceit and fraud: under his tongue is mischief and vanity."

The meaning here is probably that those who will not submit themselves to the Lord will experience bitter sorrow. Jesus said,

"Woe to you" to scribes and Pharisees, and told them about their condemnation. But if you rejoice in the Lord and are glad in Him, you will experience heavenly things. For God did not send His Son to condemn, but to save the world.

God loves you.

*David Jeremiah

# WORSHIPING IDOLS! December 4

Romans 1,
21For although they knew God, they neither glorified him as God nor gave thanks to him, but their thinking became futile and their foolish hearts were darkened. 22Although they claimed to be wise, they became fools 23and exchanged the glory of the immortal God for images made to look like a mortal human being and birds and animals and reptiles.

You might say, come on now, we don't worship statues in the United States! And for the most part, you would be right, but there are a lot of people from other countries living among us who do worship statues. So, we should know that they are witnessing opportunities.

But let's talk about the idols that we Americans worship, for instance, collegiate sports. Does anyone disagree that this has become an idol for many people lately? And then there is professional sports and racing that mostly happens on Sunday. Yes, I know; I am really meddling, but I am just trying to call it like it is. Then of course there is the almighty dollar, fame, TV, and the Internet. Just think of all the things that Satan has convinced us are more important than the Father, Son, and Holy Spirit—our God!

So, was Paul only talking to the Romans when he said, "Although they claimed to be wise, they became fools and exchanged the glory of the immortal God for images, and idols"? Or was he talking to us also?

Exodus 20:4–5 says, "You shall not make for yourself an idol in the form of anything in heaven above or on the earth beneath or in the waters below. You shall not bow down to them or worship them; for I, the LORD your God, am a jealous God . . ."

Notice that God is jealous when someone gives to another something that rightly belongs to Him. Your worship belongs to God, only, because He loves you very much!

# ONE PLUS ONE PLUS ONE EQUAL ONE!
## December 5

How could this be? Most folks would say that it is three not one. But there are times when 1 + 1 + 1 = 1.

Let's look at the Father plus the Son plus the Holy Spirit, three persons, but one God. This is the Holy Trinity. We don't fully understand it, but with our faith we accept it. But, Kids, there is another way also.

When you find your mate and you unite in marriage, you two become one. Then when you add Jesus into the equation, it is 1 + 1 + 1 and it equals *one*. All are united to create a perfect union, and it will last forever!

I cannot tell you how much I love my wife. It is a heavenly love because I know without a shadow of a doubt that God put Pat and me together. We were absolutely meant to be married. We were in the second grade together; my mind doesn't go back that far but we were. Then we went steady in the ninth grade and got married in the last year of high school. Our marriage was put together in heaven, and when we look at all of our kids and grandkids and how perfect they are, it is the evidence of our perfect union.

The world has the wrong idea about marriage; God has the right plan.

The world says divorce is an option, and if it feels good, do it! Satan smiles at these worldly slogans because he knows it will create pain and suffering for God's children when they stray from God's plan. Satan loves to keep God's children in the ditch where it is dark and sinful.

God's plans for each one of you is for you to save yourself for the man, girls, or the woman, guys, He has picked out for you. Kids, anything other than God's plan is living in the ditch; God's plan will keep you on the road to happiness and success.

I promise you that if you will wait on God, you will have a perfect marriage that will give you eternal happiness. God does not make mistakes; only people do that. You will know without any doubts when His mate for you comes along.

God says, "When I am in it, you will know it, and it will last forever!"

$1 + 1 + God = 1$ forever. Never forget this!

Pray continuously about this please. Moms and dads, get on your knees and pray continually for your children and their future mates.

God loves you.

# A BLIND BEGGAR RECEIVES HIS SIGHT.
## December 6

Luke 18:35 As Jesus approached Jericho, a blind man was sitting by the roadside begging. 36 When he heard the crowd going by, he asked what was happening. 37 They told him, "Jesus of Nazareth is passing by."

38 He called out, "Jesus, Son of David, have mercy on me!" 39 Those who led the way rebuked him and told him to be quiet, but he shouted all the more, "Son of David, have mercy on me!"

40 Jesus stopped and ordered the man to be brought to him. When he came near, Jesus asked him, 41 "What do you want me to do for you?" "Lord, I want to see," he replied.

42 Jesus said to him, "Receive your sight; your faith has healed you." 43 Immediately he received his sight and followed Jesus, praising God. When all the people saw it, they also praised God."

Maybe if we were to do like the blind man and ask God to open our eyes, we could see exactly what He has for us to do. I heard Rick Warren say that every single person born of God has a job God wants them to do. We are part of the body of the Christ.

You might say, "Well, I have so many things going on in my life, I am sure I am an unimportant part of the body." But think about that, what part of your body is unimportant to you right now? Sure, there may be things your body can go on living without, but I doubt they would be there if it did not make your body work more efficiently. Don't you think the church needs to work as efficiently as possible?

How well does your body work if you have a bum knee, like I do right now? It is hard to do what I want and need to do for focusing on what I can't do! The Church does not need distractions.

If you are not sure what God has for you to do, ask Him to open your eyes so that you can see.

Think of all the people that God used in the Bible for a job He needed doing, but then you didn't hear anything else about them, and all of them were very important. A quick example is the man who had the donkey that Jesus used to ride into Jerusalem. Could it be that having the donkey exactly in the correct place at the right time was this man's job to advance the Kingdom?

> Romans 12:4–5 says, "Just as our bodies have many parts and each part has a special function, so it is with Christ's body. We are many parts of one body, and we all belong to each other."

What could your job be? Pray about it because, God loves you and wants you to be ready when He needs you.

# THE SON OF MAN COMING IN A CLOUD!
## December 7

Joel 2:29-32, Luke 21:25-28
29 Even on my servants, both men and women, I will pour out my Spirit in those days.

30 I will show wonders in the heavens and on the earth, blood and fire and billows of smoke.

31 The sun will be turned to darkness and the moon to blood before the coming of the great and dreadful day of the Lord."

Luke 21, Jesus speaking, 25 "There will be signs in the sun, moon and stars. On the earth, nations will be in anguish and perplexity at the roaring and tossing of the sea. 26 People will faint from terror, apprehensive of what is coming on the world, for the heavenly bodies will be shaken. 27 At that time they will see the Son of Man coming in a cloud with power and great glory. 28 When these things begin to take place, stand up and lift up your heads, because your redemption is drawing near."

Joel and Luke among others talked about the end times.

About signs and wonders that will happen in the end of days. We believe that this will happen during the great tribulation. But Jesus also said look at the fig tree, you can tell that the next season is coming.

We do not know the day but we can tell the seasons are changing!

Jesus is coming back, this we know absolutely. I believe we need to be doing everything we can to share the gospel to the lost. We also know absolutely, that time is running out! It has been a very long time since,

Jesus said in Revelation 3: 3 "Remember, there-fore, what you have received and heard; hold it fast, and repent. But if you do not wake up, I will come like a thief, and you will not know at what time I will come to you".

But Joel goes on to say, 32 And everyone who calls on the name of the Lord will be saved; for on Mount Zion and in Jerusalem there will be deliverance, as the Lord has said, even among the survivors whom the Lord calls.

God loves you
More tomorrow

# A DAY IS LIKE A THOUSAND YEARS.
## December 8

2 Peter 3:3-9,

3 Above all, you must understand that in the last days scoffers will come, scoffing and following their own evil desires. 4 They will say, "Where is this 'coming' he promised? Ever since our ancestors died, everything goes on as it has since the beginning of creation." 5 But they deliberately forget that long ago by God's word the heavens came into being and the earth was formed out of water and by water. 6 By these waters also the world of that time was deluged and destroyed. 7 By the same word the present heavens and earth are reserved for fire, being kept for the Day of Judgment and destruction of the ungodly. 8 But do not forget this one thing, dear friends: With the Lord *a day is like a thousand years*, and a thousand years are like a day.

9 The Lord is not slow in keeping his promise, as some understand slowness. Instead he is patient with you, not wanting anyone to perish, but everyone to come to repentance".

Listen to what the Nay Sayers, are saying even today; "everything goes on just it always did", God is dead.

Little do they know it is happening that way just so that everyone will come to repentance, even the Nay-Sayers. God loves everyone and wants everyone to come to Him.

Think of this, in Noah's day, how many listened to Noah? How many did he convince to get on the ark, before it started raining? How many believed in the Lord? Only a few, eight in all!

Eight people out of tens of thousands were saved. You might ask; how could that be? Why wouldn't they listen? Noah told them about the flood that was coming, why were they so hard headed?

They were busy living their lives!

In their eyes, they did not have time for such nonsense! It was nonsense to the people of Noah's day and it will be nonsense to many people in the last days, but just as (nonsense to them) drowned all the people with a flood, "nonsense" to the unbelievers in the end times, will be death to them also. And they will be standing in line behind the people that drowned in the flood, at the Great Judgement Day, waiting for their sentence.

Folks this is serious, tell them about Jesus, maybe they will listen.

Who knows, maybe each one can win one!

God loves you

# JESUS' WORDS WILL NEVER PASS AWAY!
## December 9

In Matthew 24 Jesus says, "34 Truly I tell you, this generation will certainly not pass away until all these things have happened. 35heaven and earth will pass away, but my words will never pass away."

Don't you think we are on a downhill slide, sliding right into the end days? As the radical religious population is growing leaps and bounds, how will terrorism ever be stopped? I don't see it happening, I see a gallant effort, but I can't see how it can be stopped. What makes these times look like we are getting closer to the end times? Let's see what Jesus said about that:

Luke 17, 26 "Just as it was in the days of Noah, so also will it be in the days of the Son of Man. 27 People were eating, drinking, marrying and being given in marriage up to the day Noah entered the ark. Then the flood came and destroyed them all.

28 "It was the same in the days of Lot. People were eating and drinking, buying and selling, planting and building. 29 But the day Lot left Sodom, fire and sulfur rained down from heaven and destroyed them all."

The majority of the people could care less because they are not Christians; they think it is nonsense! It is up to us to help convince the folks that the Holy Spirit sends us to talk to. We need to tell them that God loves them. Paul said, make the best of every opportunity!
Because God loves us.

# GABRIEL VISITS ZECHARIAH IN THE TEMPLE. December 10

Having children was the greatest legacy in the Jewish family in Old Testament days. Elizabeth and Zacharias' case was hopeless at this stage of their lives, or so they thought. The beginning of old age was sixty-five in the Jewish community. In his seventies, he was considered in the gray hair span, and after eighty, he was said to be well stricken in years.

Luke 1:7 says about Zacharias and Elizabeth: "And they had no child, because that Elisabeth was barren, and they both were now well stricken in years."

It sounds like they were in their eighties, but we don't know exactly how old they were. But they were well stricken in years, far from child-bearing age.

It was Zacharias' time to go into the temple, into the Holy place, and burn incense. While he was in there, the angel Gabriel appeared to Him and told him he and Elizabeth would have a son, and he would be the prophet WHO would announce the coming of the Christ. Gabriel said to him, "your prayers have been answered."

How many prayers do you think he and Elizabeth had prayed about children over the last forty or fifty years? And finally, they were answered, wow, God's timing and his thoughts are way different than ours.

But think of this, they had to wait and take abuse for years and years by their community about not having children. But God had a plan, a tremendous plan, that worked out wonderfully for the old priest and his wife. He would have not a son, but they would have *the son*, that to a priest would have been second to none. A priestly son with the spirit and power of Elijah that would announce to the world that the Messiah is come. John the Baptist was his name. What an honor God had given the old man and woman who had lived a righteous life.

God answers prayer for the Godly, but He does it in His timing, so it will fit into His plan. We serve an awesome God! God loves you.

# THIS IS THE SEASON FOR PEACE AND HOPE. December 11

Romans 5:1-Therefore, since we have been justified through faith, we have peace with God through our Lord Jesus Christ, 2-through whom we have gained access by faith into this grace in which we now stand. And we boast in the hope of the glory of God. 3-Not only so, but we also glory in our sufferings, because we know that suffering produces perseverance;

4-perseverance, character; and character, hope. 5-And hope does not put us to shame, because God's love has been poured out into our hearts through the Holy Spirit, who has been given to us. 6-You see, at just the right time, when we were still powerless, Christ died for the ungodly. 7-Very rarely will anyone die for a righteous person, though for a good person someone might possibly dare to die. 8-But God demonstrates his own love for us in this: While we were still sinners, Christ died for us.

While we were sinners, Jesus died for us, He paid the ultimate price for sinners. Why? Because He loves us much more than we could ever imagine. He died for us so that when we die, we can be with Him forever in a place He is preparing for us.

As mere humans, we cannot understand the love that God has for us, but, Lord Jesus, we thank You for it!

God loves you.

# WHAT IS THE CHRISTMAS SPIRIT?
## December 12

When you consider the lonely, those with personal struggles, and the consumers who fight over gifts and the broken relationships, they think, "Is this it; is this all there is to Christmas?? People say, "I don't have the Christmas spirit. What is it? What is the spirit of Christmas?"

When we think of the prophecies, the Baby in a manger, a virgin mother, a husband who listens to angels, why they couldn't find a room, why the King of kings would come as a baby, why the angels appeared to the shepherds, who the wise men were and what their gifts meant, why would a God come to earth as a human anyway, and why do I need to believe it? Then why would He come back after all we killed Him the first time?

We will start a series on the twelve days before Christmas, December 13th through Christmas Day and think about all these things. Just maybe we will find out if the hustle and bustle of Christmas is really worth it.

Why do we give gifts, and what is the greatest gift of all?

Who knows? Maybe we will find that out also!

God loves you.

# THE PROPHECIES OF THE MESSIAH, THE CHRIST. December 13

In the Old Testament, there are several dozen major prophecies about the coming of the Messiah, the Christ, whom God would send to redeem His people. There would only be one man, one God/Man, who matches these prophecies. Here are a few:

> Deuteronomy 18, Moses speaking, there will be one coming greater than me. 15-The Lord your God will raise up for you a prophet like Me from among you, from your fellow Israelites. You must listen to him. 19-I myself will call to account anyone who does not listen to my words that the prophet speaks in my name.

> Isaiah 7:14, 14-Therefore the Lord himself will give you a sign: The virgin will conceive and give birth to a son, and will call him Immanuel. (God is with us)

> Isaiah 53, 5But he was pierced for our transgressions, he was crushed for our iniquities; the punishment that brought us peace was on him, and by his wounds we are healed. 6-We all, like sheep, have gone astray, each of us has turned to our own way; and the Lord has laid on him the iniquity of us all. 7-He was oppressed and afflicted, yet he did not open his mouth; he was led like a lamb to the slaughter, and as a sheep before its shearers is silent, so he did not open his mouth. 9-He was assigned a grave with the wicked, and with the rich in his death, though he had done no violence, nor was any deceit in his mouth. 12b-For he bore the sin of many, and made intercession for the transgressors.

And where will this happen? Micah 5:2 has that for us: "But you, Bethlehem Ephrathah, though you are small among the clans of Judah, out of you will come for me one who will be ruler over Israel, whose origins are from of old, from ancient times."

A Ruler, a King, whose origins are from distant past can only be the Creator; He is the distant past, He is our present, and He is our Future! Jesus Christ is Lord!

God loves you.

# MARY, THE FAVORED WOMAN. December 14

Mary was a fairly typical young Jewish lady of Nazareth. She had no idea what a tremendous impact she would have on the people of the earth. Mary was betrothed to Joseph; legally they were man and wife, though they could not be together until their wedding. Most likely, Mary was a happy young lady, planning her wedding and her future life with her husband. And then her normal life was about to change by a supernatural moment. An angel stood before her, and said:

Luke 1
28-Gabriel appeared to her and said, "Greetings, favored woman! The Lord is with you!"

29-Confused and disturbed, Mary tried to think what the angel could mean. 30- "Don't be afraid, Mary," the angel told her, "for you have found favor with God! 31-You will conceive and give birth to a son, and you will name him Jesus. 32-He will be very great and will be called the Son of the Most High. The Lord God will give him the throne of his ancestor David. 33-And he will reign over Israel forever; his Kingdom will never end!"

34-Mary asked the angel, "But how can this happen? I am a virgin." 35-The angel replied, "The Holy Spirit will come upon you, and the power of the Most High will overshadow you. So, the baby to be born will be holy, and he will be called the Son of God. 36-What's more, your relative Elizabeth has become pregnant in her old age! People used to say she was barren, but she has conceived a son and is now in her sixth month. 37-For nothing is impossible with God."

Certainly, her thoughts changed from wedding planning to motherhood and angels and miracles and a baby boy.

God chose Mary to be the mother of the Savior of the world. What an honor! Talk about a life-changing encounter; she was now in the center of a spectacular miracle. Mary would deliver the Christmas package, the ultimate Gift, to all of us, eternity with God, by the one who will save us from our sins.

God loves you.

# JOSEPH, THE ADOPTED FATHER OF THE SON OF GOD. December 15

God selected Joseph and Mary, these two, out of all the people in the world at that time to raise and protect His Son. Other than the fact that Joseph was a carpenter, we know very little about him.

The Bible tells us of four supernatural dreams that he had. At his first dream, he was thinking of breaking off the engagement with Mary quietly because she was with Child, and Joseph knew it was not his.

> Matthew 1
> 20-As he considered this, an angel of the Lord appeared to him in a dream. "Joseph, son of David," the angel said, "do not be afraid to take Mary as your wife. For the child within her was conceived by the Holy Spirit. 21-And she will have a son, and you are to name him Jesus, for he will save his people from their sins."

Joseph had been visited by an angel in his dream, and the angel said the baby was the Son of God. Joseph knew the prophecies; what an honor! But there were issues to deal with, one being a pregnant Mary, and yes, he was up to the challenge. God chose him, and I am sure he thought, "I will do my best for God!"

Joseph was chosen by God to be the earthly father to teach Jesus all the things young boys have to learn. He must have been everything God wants a family man and a father to be.

All of our kids are gifts from God, so we should look at each one as a miracle and a supernatural gift, not exactly like Jesus because He is God, but a miracle for sure.

This Christmas, think of all the gifts God has given you, make a list, and be thankful that He loves you enough to die for you. I am sure as we ponder the first Christmas from day to day, it will improve our Christmas Spirit.

God loves you.

*A Father's Love* | 484

# THE KING OF KINGS AS A BABY. December 16

When you think of all the kingdoms on earth and all the beautiful palaces; that are fit for a king, how can we understand why the King of all the kings, Jesus Christ, was born in a stable with smelly animals where there was no safety or solitude?

Joseph had to go to Bethlehem at this time for the census. He feared for Mary's safety, so he took her with him, even though it was almost time to deliver. We think, *my goodness how bad could a donkey ride be during the final days of pregnancy.* I would think every stone and pothole would be uncomfortable. God asks us to do the uncomfortable sometimes, for His glory.

Imagine how panicked Joseph was when he could not find his bride a comfortable place to stay, running from place to place, banging on doors.

Jesus was to come in a manger, not a palace with kings and queens and palace guards and not lying on a silk bed. The Christ chose a stable with farm animals and hay to lie on, to be brought into this world so that he could identify with the least of us, the poor and vulnerable. He did not need the world's comforts; He created them. He came exposed to all the dangers the world could offer, even the cross! Listen to what Paul says about it in 2 Corinthians 8:9, "You know the generous grace of our Lord Jesus Christ. Though he was rich, yet for your sakes he became poor, so that by his poverty he could make you rich."

He entered by the stable so that you may dwell eternally in a palace!

God loves you.

# THEY COULD NOT FIND A ROOM!
## December 17

Bethlehem was a quiet suburb of Jerusalem, only about five or so miles from the big city. But it was an historic city. David, the king, was from Bethlehem. Jacob's beloved wife Rachel was buried there. Ruth and Boaz and Naomi lived there, generations before. So, the town had plenty of history, and it was because of David that Joseph was there with his wife, looking for a room. We think of silent night because of the great Christmas hymn, but it probably was not too quiet. The inns were filled to the brim, and if they had pubs, they were full also. It was like a huge kinfolk celebration. All of David's descendants had to be there to be counted for tax purposes, so the little town was overflowing with people.

Israel's King was being born, and all of his earthly kinfolk were too busy celebrating to care. I wonder would it be any different if they knew what we know now.

It was by God's design that He would be born in a stable and not a room at the inn. We know that the inns had room for everyone but the King. There would not even be a pillow offered; the baby was to be laid in a feeding trough in hay.

But He was known to say later to His disciples in John 14:2, "There is more than enough room in my Father's home. If this were not so, would I have told you that I am going to prepare a place for you?"

There will be plenty of room in our Father's house for all that will follow Jesus!

Is your room guaranteed?

God loves you.

# GOD CAME TO DWELL WITH US.
## December 18

"And the Word was made flesh, and dwelt among us, (and we beheld his glory, the glory as of the only begotten of the Father,) full of grace and truth" (John 1:14).

The word *dwelt* meant he would set up His tent among us. He came to live with us, but why? We are awful people.

God created everything around us. He created life, and then He created man because he wanted friendship, a man in His image who could think and make his own choices and who could choose to love God or love self. They chose wrong and disobeyed their Creator. When this happened, their perfect and just Father, the Father who loved them and wanted to walk and talk to them, had to separate from them because of their sin. The children longed for the Father's fellowship; they loved to walk and talk to Him, and they cried—and He heard them.

There had to be atonement for their sin so that there could be fellowship again. No one person, no human, could pay the price. God had to do it. It had to be a perfect sacrifice, a sinless sacrifice. Only He could live up to that; surely none of His creations could do it. They had flaws of their own doing.

He would do it because as much as they missed His fellowship, He missed them much more. They could not come to Him, so heaven would come to them.

He would become a man, a man/God, and He would pay our sin debt. He would provide a way for the fellowship to continue. And they would walk and talk again for an eternity.

Praise our magnificent Father for His love!

God loves you.

# THE ANGELS IN THE STORY. December 19

What comes to mind when you think of the angels? Why do they almost always introduce themselves with, "Do not be afraid"? Do you see them in your mind like the Renaissance painters painted them or like the soldier who stood in the way of Balaam and his donkey, with sword drawn? Or some other way, maybe like a tree topper angel. Maybe as a human, like

> Hebrews 13:2 that says, "Do not forget to show hospitality to strangers, for by so doing some people have shown hospitality to angels without knowing it."

I think we can safely say that if we saw one today, appearing as an angel, we most likely would be terrified. I read a book that said they were over seven feet tall, weighing probably four hundred or more pounds, with 0 percent fat, all muscles. The writer said he saw them, hmm. I could believe the size, though, that certainly would be scary.

In the Christmas story, they were very active. They appeared to Zechariah, Mary, Joseph (in dreams), the wise men (in a dream), and the shepherds. They are God's messengers to us; they carry out the work of the Father.

The one appearance that was a surprise was to the shepherds. The least appreciated worker of all and in those days the lowest of the low, they would have their own angelic experience. They would be invited to witness the birth of the King of kings. They would not just have one angel appear, they would see a company of them as it says in,

> Luke 2:13–14, "Suddenly a great company of the heavenly host appeared with the angel, praising God and saying, 'Glory to God in the highest heaven, and on earth peace to those on whom his favor rests.'"

I am sure there are angels all around today, doing God's work, protecting His people, and whispering messages from God. We may not see them, but they are still very useful to God, maybe like,

> Daniel 9:21, "While I was still in prayer, Gabriel, the man I had seen in the earlier vision, came to me in swift flight about the time of the evening sacrifice."

Gabriel brought the answer before he was finished praying. All of you read Hebrews 2:5–9, here is verse 9: "But we do see Jesus, who was made lower than the angels for a little while, now crowned with glory and honor because he suffered death, so that by the grace of God he might taste death for everyone."
God loves you.

# THE SHEPHERDS. December 20

Sheep herding was an undesirable job, but many did this because Israel needed the sheepherders. They did not like them; they felt that they were unclean. When they walked past one, they would look down their nose at them.

The Hebrews prized cleanliness and purity. If you know anything about sheep, you would know cleanliness is not at the top of the description list, and then there is the smell. There is always the smell. Israel had to have the perfect little lambs for the sacrifice, so sheep herders were very much needed. Even David, Israel's king, was a shepherd as a boy. He was very close to God as a shepherd; sometimes it was just David, God, and the sheep, David developed a great relationship with God during those times. David was not afraid of anything; he stood against lions and bears and other wild animals protecting his sheep and a giant, protecting Israel, God's people. It was men like David the shepherd that God would allow to be the first witnesses to His birth. The men that men favor, the kings, the rich, and even the priests were not there, but the men that God favored were invited to see Him in the manger by a company of angels. Jesus the Son of God had peasants for parents and unnamed shepherd visitors to see the most joyful event in human history.

These men took the narrow road to the Father through the Son. Imagine, if you will, one moment you are sitting by a campfire, holding a stick in your hand poking at the fire, and the next moment you are in the presence of angels who were speaking about things you have been dreaming about: a king for the people, one that would save them from the oppression and evil men who were over them, a Savior!

> Luke 2:13–14 says, "Suddenly a great company of the heavenly host appeared with the angel, praising God and saying, 14'Glory to God in the highest heaven, and on earth peace to those on whom his favor rests.'"

What did they do when the angels left them? Did they ponder, *Well, what shall we do? Let's form a committee to decide, or did they decide to sleep in today?* Nope!

They ran to the Savior, the only Son, and worshiped Him! They got off the couches, they got out of bed, they went to their place of worship, the Manger, and they *ran* to the place of worship! They took the narrow road!

Verse 16 says, "So they hurried off and found Mary and Joseph, and the baby, who was lying in the manger."

God loves you.

# WISE MEN! December 21

These were very wise men from the East. They were *seekers* of the living God, the King of all kings. They had heard the prophecies of old, and they were looking for the sign. The heavens would shout it out; there would be a special star they were always looking for because they wanted to see God!

Are you a seeker? Do you need a Savior?

Who were these men, the magi, eastern kings? We first meet them in Matthew 2, "Magi from the east came to Jerusalem 2-and asked, 'Where is the one who has been born king of the Jews? We saw his star when it rose and have come to worship him.'"

They were told, maybe by a priest, that he was to be born in Bethlehem, so when they looked that way, there it was the star that had been leading them, pointing the way for them.

By this time, Joseph and Mary and Jesus were in a house. These travelers had traveled a great distance to see this King, and they would not go home until they did. The magi had very little information, but they continued seeking, always seeking the one who could give them peace and salvation. Finally, they found Him. It had been a long journey, a lifetime, a journey for life eternal—an eternal life of love and acceptance. They found Him!

Did you know that God loves you, too? He has sent you many signs, maybe not a star in the night, but many signs of His love for you. Look around; they are everywhere. The wise men, the very wise men, were looking for the One who could set them free. What about you? Are you looking? Are you a wise man or woman? Can you see the signs? Open your eyes this Christmas and see the signs of His love for you; it will make this Christmas for you!

God loves you.

# THE WISE MENS' GIFTS. December 22

The wise men came to worship the newly born Son of God. The child may have been two years old by now. The Bible says that Mary and Joseph lived in a house, so they stayed after everyone else went home. Joseph must have set up shop as a carpenter.

The Bible does not tell us how large the caravan was that came with the wise men, but we can assume it was fairly large because for a trip that far, they would need many provisions.

I can see them being asked where they were going, and they answered "to see the Son of God." "Oh wow, I would like to go; do you have room?"

They brought gifts: gold, frankincense, and myrrh. The first wise man bent down to offer his gift of gold for the king. Gold is the standard in which all other wealth is measured; it is fit for a King. The second wise man bowed down and gave his offering of frankincense, the holy oil for the Son of God. This is the incense used in the temple, a marvelous fragrance for the Holy Child. Then the third wise man bowed down and gave his offering, myrrh, an anointing oil and an oil used for embalming the dead. It was very expensive. Also, Samuel had been anointed David with it to be king of the Jews.

Soon after the wise men left, Joseph's second supernatural dream came. The angel told him to take Mary and Jesus to Egypt. So, Joseph and Mary stayed in Bethlehem after the birth. I am not sure why. Then the wise men brought them money to travel on, which was good timing because the angel told them to leave quickly because King Herod would kill all babies two and under in order to kill Jesus, the real King.

God is surely in control! You cannot read this story and not see God working His plan. Just as the wise men went back home, Jesus would go back home also. He made a gift of Himself to His people and then returned home to His Father.

Jesus gave you and me the gift of everlasting life; will you accept His gift?

God loves you very much!

# WHAT ARE YOU GIVING JESUS ON HIS BIRTHDAY? December 23

What could you give to God who not only has everything but created everything! This question will require much thought; what could the Creator of the universe need from you?

You know there used to be a natural saying during Christmas time; it was either Merry Christmas or Happy Holidays, and you were either a Jew or a Christian. There were some atheists but not very many. Christians have Christmas, Jews have Hanukkah, and the atheists have parties.

When you met someone on the street, you just had to figure out whether they were Jewish or Christian, so you knew whether you would say Merry Christmas or Happy Holidays, and if they were the atheist you would say, "Hey watch out for that light post."

Seriously, what can you give Jesus? Let's think of something.

I would have to say the most important thing, of course, is yourself? He wants your heart. He wants your sinful nature to move out so that the Holy Spirit can move in.

Why would He do what He did? He left heaven's throne room, was born in a stable, worked very hard as a carpenter, lived without a place to lay His head, walked all over Israel, fed and healed sick people, speaking all the way about God's love for man. Then He took an unthinkable beating and death on the cross. If He did not love you and want you to be in heaven with Him for eternity, why would He do all of that? There is only one answer: He loves us! You know they did not kill Him— He offered His life for us. He accepted the mission from God the Father.

If your place in heaven is not already guaranteed, then give Jesus what He wants from you this Christmas; give Him all that you can give Him that He wants from you.

God loves you!

Merry Christmas!

# THE BABY IN A MANGER. December 24

The Creator came to be among His people, and they called Him Emmanuel, (God is with us). He was pure, and the people were stained with their sin. They were two opposites; how could they be united? We were His children, and yet we failed Him. If we could not go to Him because of our sin, maybe He could come to us! He would become flesh and blood and also be God. He would leave the throne of heaven to walk among us. Then we could see Him and experience the perfection that is the Lord and learn how to live and be pleasing to Him. So, He came to us as a baby, not to a castle or a palace, which would be fitting for the King, but a manger in a stable full of animals. He would be sleeping in a feeding trough. The King of kings laying in a manger—how could this be?

This child in the manger was the perfect gift to an undeserving people on the first Christmas Day.

It is important that we understand this truth: all of the Bible points to the message of salvation in Jesus. In fact, the Bible is all about the Lord Jesus Christ, heavens wonder, hell's worry, and humanity's way out from sin and death into the presence of God!

Praise you, Father, for your perfect gift, our Savior Jesus, on Christmas Day!

God loves you.

MERRY CHRISTMAS

# CHRISTMAS DAY. December 25

"I AM" IS HERE TODAY!
Has He touched your heart this year?
Jesus Christ is born on Christmas Day!
He is:
The King of kings!
The Prince of peace!
Son of God!
Son of man!
Emmanuel, God is with us!
Wonderful Counselor!
Almighty God!
Lord and Savior!
Will you unwrap the Christ today on this beautiful Christmas Day and hold him close to your heart this year?
God loves you.
MERRY CHRISTMAS!

# THIS IS THE SEASON FOR PEACE AND HOPE. December 26

Peace and Hope, Romans 5

1-Therefore, since we have been justified through faith, we have peace with God through our Lord Jesus Christ, 2-through whom we have gained access by faith into this grace in which we now stand. And we boast in the hope of the glory of God. 3-Not only so, but we also glory in our sufferings, because we know that suffering produces perseverance; 4-perseverance, character; and character, hope. 5-And hope does not put us to shame, because God's love has been poured out into our hearts through the Holy Spirit, who has been given to us. 6-You see, at just the right time, when we were still powerless, Christ died for the ungodly. 7-Very rarely will anyone die for a righteous person, though for a good person someone might possibly dare to die. 8-But God demonstrates his own love for us in this: While we were still sinners, Christ died for us.

While we were sinners, Jesus died for us, He paid the ultimate price for sinners. Why? Because He loves us much more than we could ever imagine. He died for us so that when we die, we can be with Him forever in a place He is preparing for us.

This is what gives us our hope and peace.

As mere humans, we cannot understand the love that God has for us, but, Lord Jesus, we thank You for it!

God loves you.

# ENCOURAGING WORDS TO ONE ANOTHER.
## December 27

ISAIAH 40,
26-Look up into the heavens. Who created all the stars?

He brings them out like an army, one after another, calling each by its name.

Because of his great power and incomparable strength, not a single one is missing.

27-O Jacob, how can you say the LORD does not see your troubles? O Israel, how can you say God ignores your rights? 28-Have you never heard? Have you never understood?

The LORD is the everlasting God, the Creator of all the earth. He never grows weak or weary.

No one can measure the depths of his understanding. 29-He gives power to the weak and strength to the powerless. 30-Even youths will become weak and tired, and young men will fall in exhaustion. 31-But those who trust in the LORD will find new strength. They will soar high on wings like eagles.

They will run and not grow weary.

They will walk and not faint.

Folks, keep your heads up, do not let your chins drag the ground. God is on His throne and is very much in charge. Spread your wings and fly like eagles!
God loves you.

# HOW COULD GOD LOVE ME? December 28

There is no reason; He just does. His reasons are undefined. It does not make sense to us lowly humans. But I can tell you this; it is not because He just wants your greatness on His team.

It is certainly not about anything we have done, so it must be grace—unmerited grace! Listen to Paul:

> Ephesians 1;
> 3All praise to God, the Father of our Lord Jesus Christ, who has blessed us with every spiritual blessing in the heavenly realms because we are united with Christ. 4Even before he made the world, God loved us and chose us in Christ to be holy and without fault in his eyes. 5God decided in advance to adopt us into his own family by bringing us to himself through Jesus Christ. This is what he wanted to do, and it gave him great pleasure. 6So we praise God for the glorious grace he has poured out on us who belong to his dear Son. 7He is so rich in kindness and grace that he purchased our freedom with the blood of his Son and forgave our sins. 8He has showered his kindness on us, along with all wisdom and understanding.

Be happy today.
God loves you.

# JESUS CAME INTO THE WORLD TO SAVE SINNERS! December 29

This truth is a very surprising thing, a thing to be marveled at, most of all by those who enjoy it. I know that it is to me, even to this day, the greatest wonder that I have ever heard of, that God would ever justify me.

I feel myself to be a lump of unworthiness, a mass of corruption, and a heap of sin apart from His almighty love. I know and am fully assured that I am justified by faith, which is in Christ Jesus (2 Timothy 3:15). I am treated as if I had been perfectly just and made an heir of God and joint-heir with Christ. And yet by nature, I must take my place among the most sinful. Though altogether undeserving, I am treated as if I had been deserving. I am loved with as much love as if I had always been godly, whereas before I was ungodly. Who can help being astonished at this demonstration of grace?

Gratitude for such favor stands dressed in robes of wonder. *

Grace, Grace, God's Grace!
*Charles Spurgeon's, "All of Grace"
God loves you.

# A CLOSER LOOK AT GRACE. December 30

Made Alive in Christ, Ephesians 2,
1-As for you, you were dead in your transgressions and sins, 2-in which you used to live when you followed the ways of this world and of the ruler of the kingdom of the air, the spirit who is now at work in those who are disobedient. 3-All of us also lived among them at one time, gratifying the cravings of our flesh and following its desires and thoughts. Like the rest, we were by nature deserving of wrath. 4-But because of his great love for us, God, who is rich in mercy, 5-made us alive with Christ even when we were dead in transgressions—it is by grace you have been saved. 6-And God raised us up with Christ and seated us with him in the heavenly realms in Christ Jesus, 7-in order that in the coming ages he might show the incomparable riches of his grace, expressed in his kindness to us in Christ Jesus. 8-For it is by grace you have been saved, through faith—and this is not from yourselves, it is the gift of God—9-not by works, so that no one can boast. 10-For we are God's handiwork, created in Christ Jesus to do good works, which God prepared in advance for us to do.

God is gracious; therefore, sinful men are forgiven, converted, and saved, not by anything they did, but by the boundless love, pity, mercy, and grace of the Father to do good works that He has planned for us.

Are you doing what God has planned for you?
Look at Hebrews 4:

16Let us then approach God's throne of grace with confidence, so that we may receive mercy and find grace to help us in our time of need.

Grace is God's perfect gift to us!
God loves you.

*A Father's Love* | 501

# HOW DO WE REPENT? December 31

Acts 5:31

29 Peter and the other apostles replied: "We must obey God rather than human beings! 30 The God of our ancestors raised Jesus from the dead—whom you killed by hanging him on a cross. 31 God exalted him to his own right hand as Prince and Savior that he might bring Israel to repentance and forgive their sins. 32 We are witnesses of these things, and so is the Holy Spirit, whom God has given to those who obey him."

Our Lord Jesus has gone up so that our Holy Spirit may come down. The work that Jesus has done has made repentance possible, available, and acceptable. Jesus is exalted on high so that through the virtue of His intercession for us, repentance may have a place before God.

Without Jesus' sacrifice, our repentance would never be heard. The Holy Spirit convicts us and creates repentance in us by supernaturally renewing our nature and taking the heart of stone out of our flesh (the part of us that resists repentance).

All we have to do is follow His lead. Repentance does not come from an unwilling nature. It comes from free and unmerited grace. Even when you resist repentance, all you have to do is look at the cross, see how Jesus died, and listen to the Spirit. It will take you to your knees. He will convict you, but He won't condemn you if your heart has not completely turned to stone.

Each and every one of us needs to listen to the Holy Spirit. He will tell you when to get on your knees. Please do not put Him off; when you do it once and then twice, it becomes easier and easier to turn your ear from Him, and if you insist He will be quiet.

You will not like the results of such foolishness.

God loves you.

CPSIA information can be obtained
at www.ICGtesting.com
Printed in the USA
FFOW02n1650270618
47261686-50164FF